Praise for
Mozart at the Gateway to His Fortune

"I was so excited to read Christoph Wolff's remarkable new book, which in one fell swoop dispels myths that arose after Mozart's untimely death. Through his meticulous scholarship, Wolff allows us to reimagine the composer at the apex of his artistic powers and with creative and entrepreneurial plans in place to ensure his continuing artistic output as well as his financial stability. A beloved scholar, Professor Wolff proves his point with revelatory insights that take us into the inner workings of this great composer's mind."
—Yo-Yo Ma

"Christoph Wolff's remarkable and splendidly readable book presents a new and welcome picture of Mozart's final years. Without resorting to polemics, it disposes of myths and misconceptions by offering facts and sound judgment. Wolff is a master of minute scholarly research that comprises the circumstances of Mozart's life as well as the music itself. Countering the widespread concept of a decline of Mozart's powers, he perceives his latest works, finished and unfinished, as being the point of a new departure—cruelly curtailed by Mozart's death. I shall listen to the *Magic Flute*, the Requiem, the clarinet quintet, and the E-flat masterpieces—string trio and string quintet—with sharpened ears."   —Alfred Brendel

"In this enthralling tale of Mozart's imperial appointment and his late torrent of compositions, Christoph Wolff argues, with compelling authority, that those musical triumphs—including the Requiem—point not to an autumnal resignation but toward a propulsive future of complex genius."   —Helen Vendler

"Any book by the eminent scholar Christoph Wolff comes with the guarantee of fresh musical insights and a magisterial command of the sources. His latest book on Mozart is no exception. It will help to demystify and transform our understanding of the composer's final years." —Sir John Eliot Gardiner

"For years I've been wondering and the question becomes ever more cogent, what puzzling new language Mozart used for his three symphonies and even the *Magic Flute*. It is a new Mozart, and we cannot simply continue as before. Why? What is it? What does it mean today? To the performer, to the listener? Now I found a helping hand in Christoph Wolff's unexpectedly novel book. We musicians, used to helping ourselves, gratefully embrace his assistance." —Nikolaus Harnoncourt

"A truly different and exciting look at the last years of Mozart's life. I was especially captivated by the last chapter—Mr. Wolff's penetrating comments on Mozart's compositional method are illuminating and also somehow make his genius more personal for us." —Emanuel Ax

Mozart at the Gateway to His Fortune

ALSO BY CHRISTOPH WOLFF

The Organs of Johann Sebastian Bach: A Handbook
(co-author, with Markus Zepf)

Johann Sebastian Bach: Messe in h-Moll

*"Zu gross, zu unerreichbar": Bach-Rezeption im Zeitalter Mendelssohns
und Schumanns* (co-ed.)

Musik, Kunst und Wissenschaft im Zeitalter J. S. Bachs (co-ed.)

"Music of My Future": The Schoenberg Quartets and Trio (co-ed.)

Johann Sebastian Bach: The Learned Musician

*Über Leben, Kunst und Kunstwerke: Aspekte musikalischer Biographie—
Johann Sebastian Bach im Zentrum* (ed.)

*Die Gegenwart der musikalischen Vergangenheit: Meisterwerke
in der Dirigenten-Werkstatt* (ed.)

*Driven into Paradise: The Musical Migration from Nazi Germany
to the United States* (co-ed.)

*The New Bach Reader: A Life of Johann Sebastian Bach in Letters
and Documents* (co-ed.)

The World of the Bach Cantatas (ed.)

*Johann Sebastian Bach und der süddeutsche Raum: Aspekte der
Wirkungsgeschichte Bachs* (co-ed.)

Mozart's Requiem: Historical and Analytical Studies, Documents, Score

Bach: Essays on His Life and Music

A Life for New Music: Selected Papers of Paul Fromm (co-ed.)

*Johann Sebastian Bachs Spätwerk und dessen Umfeld:
Perspektiven und Probleme* (ed.)

Bach, and Handel: The Consummation of the Baroque in Music,
by Archibald T. Davison (ed.)

*Bach Compendium: Analytisch-bibliographisches Repertorium
der Werke Johann Sebastian Bachs*
(co-author, with Hans-Joachim Schulze)

*Bach-Bibliographie: Nachdruck der Verzeichnisse des Schrifttums über
Johann Sebastian Bach* (ed.)

*Orgel, Orgelmusik und Orgelspiel: Festschrift Michael Schneider
zum 75. Geburtstag* (ed.)

The New Grove Bach Family

*The String Quartets of Haydn, Mozart, and Beethoven:
Studies of the Autograph Manuscripts* (ed.)

Bach-Studien: Gesammelte Reden und Aufsätze,
by Friedrich Smend (ed.)

*Der stile antico in der Musik Johann Sebastian Bachs:
Studien zu Bachs Spätwerk*

Mozart
at the Gateway to
His Fortune

———◆◆———

Serving the Emperor,
1788–1791

Christoph Wolff

W · W · *Norton & Company* New York London

For information about permission to reproduce selections from this book,
write to Permissions, W. W. Norton & Company, Inc.,
500 Fifth Avenue, New York, NY 10110

For information about special discounts for bulk purchases, please contact
W. W. Norton Special Sales at specialsales@wwnorton.com or 800-233-4830

Manufacturing by Courier Westford
Book design by Margaret M. Wagner
Production manager: Julia Druskin

Library of Congress Cataloging-in-Publication Data

Wolff, Christoph.
Mozart at the gateway to his fortune : serving the Emperor, 1788-1791 /
Christoph Wolff. — 1st ed.
p. cm.
Includes bibliographical references and index.
ISBN 978-0-393-05070-7 (hardcover)
1. Mozart, Wolfgang Amadeus, 1756–1791. 2. Composers—Austria—Biography.
I. Title.
ML410.M9W632 2012
780.92—dc23
[B]

2012002027

W. W. Norton & Company, Inc.
500 Fifth Avenue, New York, N.Y. 10110
www.wwnorton.com

W. W. Norton & Company Ltd.
Castle House, 75/76 Wells Street, London W1T 3QT

1 2 3 4 5 6 7 8 9 0

for
Wolfgang Rehm and David W. Packard
in friendship

Contents

Website: http://books.wwnorton.com/books/mozart-at-the-
　gateway-to-his-fortune/

Illustrations

———— ◇ ◆ ◇ ————

xi

Preface

———◆ ◆ ◆———

LIKE MANY who have performed, taught, researched, and written about Mozart, I have been drawn from the start to the exploratory and forward-looking drive so characteristic of his music. This feature is apparent everywhere throughout the composer's career, but such final works as the last symphonies, *The Magic Flute*, or the Requiem tend to pose a challenge to the methodological and aesthetic premises long established in Mozart scholarship. In the prevailing view, the endless artistic reservoir of innovative approaches unfolding in Mozart's music is accompanied by a conjectured sense of closure in his art toward the end of his life—a perspective on Mozart's output for which I see neither external evidence nor internal logic. Hence, I realized the need for reassessing the composer's final years from a viewpoint that disregards the usual emphasis on his looming death. Moreover, Mozart's appointment of December 1787 to the imperial court in Vienna, a factor more often underestimated than not, also calls for a reevaluation of its biographical and musical implications. And although some aspects of the discussion in this book have been explored—if perhaps less boldly—in some of my essays listed in the bibliography, all these studies have their own focus and pursue different and independent functions.

In this book, quotations from the letters of the Mozart family are mostly based on the translations by Robert Spaethling (2000) and, if omitted there, by Emily Anderson (1966). Some direct translations from the standard German edition (Bauer-Deutsch) as well as a few silent minor adjustments and modifications in Spaethling and Anderson are my own.

The musical examples in this book have been kept to a minimum. Fortunately, however, the complete works by Mozart are now easily and readily available online and free of charge in the monumental critical edition of the *Neue Mozart-Ausgabe* (NMA): http://dme.mozarteum.at/DME/nma. All references to Mozart's works in this book are made to the NMA.

My discussion in chapter 6 of several chamber music works left unfinished by the composer is supported by a dedicated website hosted by Harvard University, which contains color reproductions of Mozart's autograph manuscripts (ex. 6.6–9). The Harvard website can be found by visiting http://books.wwnorton.com/books/mozart-at-the-gateway-to-his-fortune/. Complementing these visual aids are recordings of these fragments by the Chiara String Quartet, made possible by a grant from the Harvard Department of Music, where the group currently serves as quartet-in-residence under the Blodgett endowment. I am most grateful to the members of the Chiara Quartet for having undertaken this special project and also to my academic department of thirty-five years for having supported it. Readers are encouraged to make use of the recordings on the website in order to be able to hear what is not offered in concert performances or on commercial CDs.

I would like to acknowledge gratefully the assistance of John Z. McKay (Cambridge, MA) in preparing the musical examples as well as the willingness of the following institutions for providing digital scans of the art works or book and manuscript pages in their collections: Stiftung Mozarteum, Salzburg; Österreichische Nationalbibliothek, Vienna; Kunsthistorisches Museum, Vienna; Harvard University's Houghton Library, Cambridge, MA; Biblioteca Donizetti, Bergamo; Beethoven-Haus, Bonn; British Library, London; Fitzwilliam Museum, Cambridge; Sächsische Landes- und Universitätsbibliothek, Dresden; and Stadtgeschichtliches Museum, Leipzig.

My deep thankfulness goes to my good friends and colleagues Ulrich Leisinger (Salzburg) and Robert Levin (Cambridge, MA) for reading and commenting on the entire draft manuscript; also to Dorothea Link (Atlanta, GA) for clarifying a number of issues relating to the first chapter. Their comments clearly helped to make this a better book. I also thank my wife, Barbara, for her sensitive and sharp eye that invariably improves my thinking and writing. Michael Ochs (New York, NY) once again earned my own and my readers' special gratitude for thoughtfully and painstakingly wielding his editorial pen. I greatly appreciate Fred Wiemer's thorough copyediting and, finally, I want to express my thanks to Maribeth Payne of W. W. Norton and her assistant, Ariella Foss, for their interest, patience, and unfailing support.

This book is dedicated to two exceptional individuals who, each in his very own way, have made a great difference not merely in my own Mozart activities but on a much larger scale for Mozart scholarship in general. Wolfgang Rehm (Salzburg), whose veritable leadership actually made the *Neue Mozart-Ausgabe* what it is, guided my first steps into Mozart research and for almost a half century has been a trusted adviser and close friend. For nearly two decades now he has been joined by a true counterpart, David Packard (Los Altos Hills, CA). David combines a deep-rooted love and profound knowledge of Mozart's music with the creative idea of and serious commitment to a *Digital Mozart Edition* for study and performance in order to preserve and advance the legacy of the NMA and to ensure updatable scores in perpetuity. I feel genuinely enriched and privileged in the company of such visionary friends.

—Christoph Wolff
Cambridge, Massachusetts
Summer 2011

Mozart at the Gateway
to His Fortune

Prologue

Mozart, 1788 to 1791: An Inevitable End or a New Beginning?

———◇ ◇ ◆———

Is IT POSSIBLE and does it make sense to deal with the last four years of Wolfgang Amadé Mozart's creative life without being fixated on the catastrophe of the composer's premature end? His death forever changed the course of musical classicism at the turn of the eighteenth century because—to give just one example—it robbed Beethoven of the chance to compose near the idolized role model that originally brought him to Vienna. Indeed, the musical world has never come to terms with the untimely death of one of its greatest heroes. People were shocked when the news broke at the end of 1791, and many were unable to accept that he died from an ordinary illness. Hence, not surprisingly, rumors of unnatural causes sprang up almost immediately and gossip about foul play and murder spread quickly. Notably, persistent tales about Mozart having been poisoned—by Antonio Salieri, the supposedly malicious rival; or Franz Hofdemel, a friend; or Franz Xaver Süssmayr, his pupil and assistant, over two different but equally preposterous love affairs—were endlessly spun out and adventurously embellished. Other stories also arose, such as the killing of Mozart by disgruntled Freemasons. Invariably, the various anecdotes fascinated and entertained generations of Mozart lovers and do not merit further repetition.[1] For a long time scholars have been busy rejecting them, yet by doing so they also kept them alive and brewing. Even now there is virtually no Mozart biography that does not make at least an oblique reference to the possibility that the composer died an unnatural death.

Nevertheless, Mozart biographers and scholars of his music continue to seek plausible clues that might help explain the conditions leading to the composer's final illness and death. According to the prevalent view, his premature end appears as a nearly predictable and almost inescapable eventuality. It is usually attributed to a combination of total exhaustion, desperation over failing musical success, and worry about financial ruin. Mozart's death is often thought of as a personal catastrophe foreshadowed by, and reflected in, some characteristics of his late works—ignoring that a composer in his mid-thirties can hardly write "late" works. Yet, as irrational as it is, the perception of a valedictorian spirit in the music of the final years is still widespread and well accepted. So one can read, for example, poetical statements about "the hauntingly beautiful autumnal world of [Mozart's] music written in 1791, where the sun's rays are slanting sharply and are soon to turn into sunset and twilight."[2] Added to this view is the everlasting image of the composer writing his own Requiem, along with the belief that this idea also influenced the character of its music.[3]

Mounting hardship, disappointment, misery, exasperation, and an increasingly hostile environment have been topoi that invariably tinged the last chapter of Mozart's life from the first anecdotal and personally embellished accounts by Franz Xaver Niemetschek (1798) and Constanze Mozart's second husband Georg Nikolaus Nissen (1828) through the great scholarly biographies by Otto Jahn (1856–59) and Hermann Abert (1919). Still today and in specialized studies, the final years are generally subsumed under the dramatic pretext of "Mozart's decline,"[4] "Mozart's fall,"[5] or similarly calamitous labels. Even a more cautious psychological interpretation of that period under the neutral heading "Endings" has its problems when understood as predominantly overshadowed by the supposedly devastating impact the death of the father, Leopold Mozart, had on the son.[6] Moreover, introducing the year 1791 by indicating that "Mozart somehow managed to stem the drift into silence"[7] essentially returns to the imagery of the autumnal sunset cited earlier—a strangely quixotic view, not exactly auspicious, and far from reflecting a reality that paved the way for, among other things, the successful completion of two innovative major opera projects.

Mozart's final illness in late November and early December 1791, described by his physicians as "acute miliary fever" (*hitziges Friesel Fieber*), was apparently an infection turned fatal because of its grave severity.[8] From the little that is known, including symptoms reported by family witnesses and conclusions about a largely inferred medical history, the most likely immediate cause of death may have been kidney failure.[9] However, even this diagnosis lacks direct evidence. At any rate, the outcome of the illness that confined Mozart to bed for two weeks was by no means inevitable, and it all might just as well have turned out differently.

To be sure, there is no need to whitewash the circumstances that colored Mozart's final years or detract from the image of him as being overworked, worn out and in feeble health, distressed about severe financial debt, and worried about his "honor and credit" (*Ehre und Credit*)[10]—even if these problems were mostly self-imposed. The specific reasons for his monetary troubles remain unresolved, in spite of numerous special studies.[11] However, the content of more than twenty letters to his fellow Mason Michael Puchberg from mid-1788 through mid-1790,[12] a promissory note of October 1, 1790, as well as a suit filed against him by Prince Carl von Lichnowsky in November 1791,[13] reveal that the composer— one of the best-paid musicians in the later eighteenth century—was living well beyond his means by leading an almost aristocratic lifestyle, and that he was handling his financial affairs irresponsibly at best. A year after his death, Mozart's sister Nannerl put it well: "His flaws were that he didn't know how to handle the money."[14]

During what clearly were not altogether happy years following the splendidly successful mid-1780s, Mozart was at times haunted by dark thoughts about his mortality, something he thought of, reflected on, and, being a good Christian, tried to prepare for. The letters of the twenty-two-year-old about the death of his mother in Paris contain particularly moving sentiments in this regard. "When her condition got serious," Mozart wrote, "I prayed to God for only 2 things, namely a peaceful last hour for my mother, and strength and courage for myself—and our gracious Lord heard my prayer and granted me both blessings in rich measure." And a few days later: "Most beloved father! Take care of yourself! dearest sister!— take care of yourself . . . if it's God's will, to be reunited in the hereafter—for which we are destined and created."[15] Curiously, the death of his father in May 1787 was not accompanied by similar emotions when he mentioned to his sister, "You can well imagine how painful the sad news of our dear father's sudden death was for me, after all, our loss is equally great," and then turned rather businesslike to the matter of a public auction of his father's estate.[16]

Mozart was always very much aware of the ups and downs of life. Indeed, without conscious personal experience, open eyes, critical observations, and his own remarkably deep understanding of the human existence, he could not have expressed so admirably the full range—up to the extremes—of individual human situations and their greatly varying direct emotional impact, notably in his seven great operas from *Idomeneo* through *The Magic Flute*. Hence, when he wrote in an undated letter of 1790, "I now stand at the gateway to my fortune,"[17] it does not mean that he naïvely anticipated an easy and carefree future. He realized, however, that he had reached a threshold and entered an eagerly awaited new stage in his career. For at the very end of 1787, Emperor Joseph II took him into his service and named him "composer" to the "imperial-royal chamber music"—a salaried appointment with virtually no obligations but carrying a distinguished title that Mozart immediately attached to his name. Moreover, the emperor's decree was the first step in redefining the top musical hierarchy at the court in Vienna—with Antonio Salieri as court kapellmeister, an assignment involving major administrative responsibilities, and with Mozart as court composer, unburdened by any such chores and entirely free to pursue his own artistic interests. However, what must have counted most for Mozart was the extraordinary public recognition that would soon spread across the entire Old World. It would encourage and stimulate him in his work and enhance his prospects as a musician, allowing him to anticipate a successful, lifelong career.

From the beginning of 1788, Mozart's professional activities promoted by the widely recognized imperial title bear this out in many ways. His musical productivity not only remained in high gear but also took a new turn, whereas, for example, Salieri's compositional engagements decreased, in part by the necessity of his office. Therefore, it seems only reasonable to look at Mozart's last four years without being fixed on the end of a creative life and without speculating about a future that was not to be. It is the composer's extraordinary output from 1788 on, with the three great symphonies K. 543, 550, and 551 of that summer as an early cornerstone that invites a reassessment of that period. Such a new perspective points to an energetic fresh beginning and a promising future for the composer, notwithstanding the economic and cultural impact on Vienna of the Austro-Turkish War of 1788–90.[18] Mozart could now envision ambitious new highs and a period with no proximate end in sight.

This book offers neither a biography of Mozart's last four years nor a general analytical study of his music from this period. The first two chapters, however, have as clear a biographical focus as the last three have a musical one, while chapter 3 serves as a pivotal turning point. The overall aim of this study is to look at Mozart's last creative period, the years in imperial service, in an unaccustomed way. But the Mozart quote paraphrased in the book's title should not be taken to suggest a period of fun and games for the composer. Every life has its ups and downs, but the downside of Mozart's last years has been greatly overstressed at the expense of a more balanced view and need not be reemphasized. Moreover, a reading of the letter, from which this book's title derives, actually also helps to better understand the financial situation. Dating from the end of March or the beginning of April 1790, its purpose is clear: Mozart, in dire need of money, begs his wealthy friend Michael Puchberg once again for a fairly big loan. Possessing a good sense of theatrical drama, he also knows how to construct a rhetorical climax, insinuate his desperate needs, and highlight his state of mind:

. . . my present circumstances are such—that, in spite of these agreeable prospects, I must abandon all hope of future happiness, unless I receive help from a good friend in the meantime.—You may well have noticed some signs of melancholy in me lately—and only the all-too-frequent kindnesses that you have rendered me have kept me silent. But now I call on you once more and for the last time in this most desperate moment, which may determine my entire future happiness, and I call on you with full confidence in your friendship and brotherly love, which you have shown me so often, to help me to the maximum of your own ability. . . . In short!—my future happiness rests in your hands—follow your noble heart—do whatever you can possibly do and keep in mind that you are helping a fair-minded man who will be forever grateful to you and whose problems are all the more painful for him because they involve you and not just himself!—[19]

What does Mozart propose as possible collateral for the loan? In rather glowing terms, and certainly without the intention of misleading his friend, he describes his prospects primarily on the basis of a note received from Baron van Swieten who, next to the emperor, was his most important Viennese patron. He attaches the note to the letter and writes, "You will gather from it, just as I did, that I now have more cause to be hopeful than ever before.—I now stand at the gateway to my fortune."[20] However, the unspecified means to his fortune would be—had to be—founded exclusively and entirely on his composing and performing music, his artistic capital as it were, and the anticipated returns from it. For Mozart, such returns would indeed be a genuine and tangible commodity.

It is particularly noteworthy, however, that the composer opens this very letter by referring to an accompanying gift to his benefactor: "I am sending you herewith, dearest friend, the Life of Handel."[21] The book, which he himself had most likely received from van Swieten,[22] was the German edition of John Mainwaring's Handel biography,[23] the first book-length biography ever of a musician and, at the time Mozart read it, still the only one available. This book was not a meaningless gift. It describes the life of a famous man Mozart would ultimately want to be compared with and judged against—a keyboard virtuoso, composer of operas and oratorios, who worked in the service of the king in a major European capital, an exemplary musician with a full life of seventy-four years, and one who died as a wealthy man. In addition, Mozart also seems to have used Mainwaring's discussion of Handel's excessive love of food as a paradigm for his own situation so that Puchberg, who knew what indulgences and extravagances[24] played such a decisive role in his friend's need for money, might better understand the special needs of a great artist:

> Those who have blamed [Handel] for an excessive indulgence of this lowest of gratifications [his eating habits], ought to have considered, that the peculiarities of his constitution were as great as those of his genius. Luxury and intemperance are relative ideas, and depend on other circumstances besides those of quantity and quality. [. . .] For besides the several circumstances just alleged, there is yet another in his favor; I mean his incessant and intense application to the works of musical art. This rendered constant and large supplies of nourishment the more necessary to recruit his exhausted spirits.[25]

We do not know whether the book (its original exemplar has not survived) contained any specific marginalia or annotations Mozart wanted Puchberg to see. It must, however, have helped Mozart the reader take a look at the big picture for himself by drawing on analogies to Handel, his achievements, and his wealth, all of which were so clearly exposed in the text. The Handel biography, then, could also serve to give his friend and supporter a broad hint at fortune in its ultimate form and explain away his excesses as necessary but negligible. Above all, this eloquent little gift illuminates the composer's strong awareness of his musical net worth, his self-confidence, his forward-looking attitude, and above all, what he generally meant by the kind of fortune he could reasonably count on: fame and wealth. This was not mere wishful thinking on his part, for indeed, both came—the first more quickly than the second. But the sole beneficiary was to be his widow, Constanze, who survived the composer by more than a half-century and upon her death in 1842 still left her two sons a major fortune of some 30,000 florins in cash, bonds, and savings accounts—all based on earnings from Mozart's music.[26]

I

Imperial Appointments: Mozart and Salieri

———◆ ◆ ◆———

Time for Change

NOVEMBER 15, 1787, a crucial date in music history, marks the death of Christoph Willibald Gluck and thus the end of a musical era that had been dominated by this distinguished figure. For

a whole generation, Gluck was Europe's best known and most influential opera composer—indeed its most famous musician. By the 1750s he had premiered works in Venice, Milan, Naples, London, Dresden, Copenhagen, and Prague

1.1. Christoph Willibald Gluck at the keyboard, painting by Joseph-Siffrède Duplessis, 1774–75 (*Vienna, Kunsthistorisches Museum*)

before settling in Vienna. With his *Orfeo ed Euridice*, based on a libretto by Raniero de' Calzabigi and first performed in 1762 by the Italian opera company at the Burgtheater in imperial Vienna, Gluck had opened new perspectives on the ideals of opera by demonstrating how "to restrict music to its true office of serving poetry by means of expression."[1]

Gluck's Viennese activities over more than two decades were crowned in 1774 by an imperial decree granting him the honorary title of "k. k. Hof Kompositor" (royal-imperial court composer) and an annual stipend of 2,000 florins, for which he had to render virtually no services to the court.[2] The appointment was dated October 18, shortly before Gluck's return from his first extended stay in Paris, where the now sixty-year-old composer could celebrate— beginning with *Iphigénie en Aulide*—a number of great triumphs at the Académie Royale de Musique so that he considered accepting a post there and taking up permanent residence in France. As Queen Marie Antoinette in Paris was the sister of Joseph II and news between the Paris and Viennese courts traveled quickly and reliably, the emperor in Vienna was well informed about Gluck's plans. Hence, he reacted efficiently with a counteroffer to prevent losing Vienna's most famous musician permanently to Paris, yet not to preclude further returns there for the 1774–75, 1775–76, 1777–78, and 1778–79 seasons. But he would appear in Paris now adorned with a title from the Viennese court. However, in the late 1770s Gluck increasingly experienced health problems and, after suffering a stroke in 1779 while preparing for his last Paris opera, *Echo et Narcisse*, he returned to Vienna for good and spent his remaining years there in semiretirement.

Mozart encountered Gluck for the first time in 1778 in Paris,[3] but it is unknown whether it ever came to a personal meeting there. However, he did get to know the famous composer in Vienna shortly after he himself moved there. Barely three months into his stay in Vienna, Mozart reported to his father: "Gluck has suffered a stroke, and they say his condition is not very good."[4] The aged composer recovered, however, involved himself in new Viennese productions of three of his older operas—*Iphigénie en Tauride*, *Alceste*, and *Orfeo*—as well as the singspiel *Die Pilger von Mekka* for the 1782–83 season,[5] and attended at least one performance of *Die Entführung aus dem Serail*, which had its premiere on July 16, 1782. Mozart proudly informed his father on August 7: "My opera was given again yesterday—at Gluck's request.—Gluck has given me many compliments about it."[6]

Ten days later Mozart wrote a cryptic note: "My thoughts about Gluck are the same as the one you expressed in your letter, dearest father."[7] Based on Gluck's strong support of *Die Entführung*, Mozart's father apparently harbored some hope that the established master would use his influence in furthering his son's career and operatic ambitions in Vienna. Such wishful thinking shines through in a report on a concert at the Burgtheater, when Mozart wrote his father that "they also played my Sinfonie [K. 297] . . . and my sister-in-law sang the aria *Non só d'onde viene* [K. 294];—Gluck was in a box next to the Langes—my wife was with them;—well, he couldn't find enough words of praise for both the sinfonie and the aria, and he invited all four of us to dine with him next Sunday."[8]

Gluck's vociferous approval of Mozart's work would surely have been noticed in Vienna and especially in court circles. Yet despite his unquestionable backing of Mozart, Gluck was a particularly supportive mentor to someone else. No one in Vienna, least of all Mozart, could fail to observe that he treated Antonio Salieri as his heir apparent. Mozart's senior by six years and music director of the Italian opera in Vienna,[9] Salieri was chosen by the now incapacitated Gluck to take over a new commission for Paris that he himself could not fulfill. The great success of *Les Danaïdes* at the Paris Opera in 1784 resulted in further tragédie lyrique commissions for Salieri, so that he split his responsibilities in the following years between Vienna and Paris, where he also made public reference to his primary commitment to the imperial-royal court.[10]

After one of Salieri's stints in Paris, where his opera *Tarare* (based

1.2. Emperor Joseph II at the keyboard, with his sisters Maria Anna and Maria Elisabeth, painting by Joseph Hauzinger, 1778 (*Vienna, Kunsthistorisches Museum*)

on a libretto by Beaumarchais) was premiered at the Académie Royale in June 1787, he returned to Vienna. The news about the highly successful reception of his new opera had probably preceded him, for Emperor Joseph II demanded that he arrange the work for the Italian opera in Vienna as well. Moreover, a decree dated October 24 and signed by the court's theater administrator, Franz Count Orsini-Rosenberg, appointed him "Kapellmeister of the i[mperial].-r[oyal]. national theater" in recognition of "his superior talents in music, his demonstrated good compositions, and justly earned approbation and altogether the industry with which he carries out his duties in the theater."[11] In this post, he was assigned as a substitute to the aging and ailing court kapellmeister, Giuseppe Bonno.

Three weeks later, when Gluck died on November 15 after having suffered another stroke the previous day, it naturally fell to his protégé Salieri, who had spent time with his mentor during the final days, to take on the responsibility for directing the funeral music. On November 17, the funeral took place, and on April 8, 1788, a memorial service was held, at which Salieri conducted Gluck's last composition, the psalm motet "De profundis clamavi" for four-part chorus and orchestra.[12] Presumably, many of the three hundred professional musicians living in Vienna attended the service.

Mozart, too, would surely have wanted to pay his last respects to Gluck. While his presence cannot be established, he and Constanze had returned from Prague a day or two before the funeral. They had been away from Vienna for more than six weeks so that the composer could put the finishing touches on the score of *Don Giovanni*, oversee the production, and conduct the premiere on October 29. The new opera met with overwhelming success, and the leading Prague newspaper reported that upon entering the orchestra pit, Mozart "had to bow three times before the applause stopped, and the same thing happened when he left the pit."[13] Moreover, the impresario and leader of the opera troupe, Pasquale Bondini (who in December 1786 had brought *Le nozze di Figaro* to Prague, resulting in the *Don Giovanni* commission) turned over to the composer the receipts from the fourth performance of the opera, in addition to the agreed-upon fee.[14]

News of Mozart's great triumph in Prague—much like that of Salieri's in Paris a few months earlier—preceded him to Vienna. Emperor Joseph II learned of it and expressed his desire to see the new opera in Vienna as soon as possible,[15] a wish, however, that could not be fulfilled quickly because of Joseph's escalating entanglement since the summer of 1787 in a war with the Ottoman Empire that would eventually affect everything in Vienna and beyond. Nevertheless, the emperor, far away from the capital in an army camp near Belgrade, had his administrator, Count Rosenberg, issue a written decree on December 7, 1787, that appointed Mozart to the position of "chamber musician" (*Kammer Musicus*) at a salary of 800 florins.[16] As shown by the official court directory for 1789 (fig. 1.3), Mozart now held the elevated position of composer (*Kompositor*) at the top of the *k.k. Kammermusik*, the emperor's private band of twelve court musicians, which included the clarinetist Anton Stadler, Mozart's close friend.

The court appointment did not make Mozart the successor to Gluck, but after Salieri's reassignment as head of the Italian court opera, Gluck's death triggered the process of administrative changes that thoroughly affected the entire imperial court music scene. Joseph II would hardly have been interested in merely seeking a

Hofmusik- und Theatralrechnungs-Revisor.
Hr. Joh. Baptist Thorwart, k. k. Oberstkämmerer-amtssekretär, am Hof 213.

Kais. Kön. Musici bey der Hofkapelle.

Hofkapellmeister.
Hr. Anton Salieri, wohn. in der Spieglgasse 1115.

Hofkapellmeister-Substitutus.
Hr. Ignaz Umlauf, wohn. in der Kingerstrasse 1029, und 8. Singerknaben.

Sopranist.
Hr. Georg Michael Schlemmer, wohn. in der Wiepfingerstrasse 420.

Altist.
Hr. Anton Pacher, wohn. in der Annagassen 1112.

Tenoristen.
Hr. Leopold Panschab, woh. auf dem Spittalberg 135.
Hr. Adalbert Breichta, woh. in der Josephstadt 202.
Hr. Jos. Krottendorfer, wohn. in der Singerstrassen auf der kleinen Chur.
Hr. Valentin Adamberger, wohn. in der Kärntnerstrasse bey dem grossen Pfau.
Hr. Martin Rupert, wohn. im Komediengässel im Eßlischen Haus.

Bassisten.
Hr. Tobias Gsur, woh. auf der hohen Brücke 410.
Hr. Anton Ignaz Ulbrich, woh. in der Josephstadt 107.
Hr. Etrilius Haberla, woh. auf der Posten 120.
Hr. Jakob Bravezi, woh. auf der Pasten 78.
Hr. Joseph Hofmann, wohn. auf dem Salzgries 348.

Organisten.
Hr. Ferdinand Arbesser, wohn. im Ballgässchen 1354.
Hr. Joh. Georg Albrechtsberger, woh. im H. Kreuzerhof 768.

Violinisten.
Hr. Franz Kreybich, woh. auf der Kischerstiege 458.
Hr. Anton Hofmann, woh. in der Theinfaltstrasse 68.
Hr. Johann Kleinp, woh. im Burgerspittal.
Hr.

Hr. Joseph Scheidl, woh. im Ballgässchen 1354.
Hr. Franz Hofer, woh. auf dem Graben 587.
Hr. Wenzl Müller, woh. auf dem Bauernmarkt 519.
Hr. Karl Maratshek, woh. in der Leopoldstadt 160.
Hr. Thaddäus Huber, woh. in der Wollnerstrasse 152.
Hr. Heinrich Baubeimer, woh. in der Leopoldst. 269.
Hr. Joseph Hofmann, woh. in der Tainfaltstrasse 68.
Hr. Zeno Franz Mengel, woh. auf der Pasten 1200.
Hr. Peter Fuchs, woh. in der Naglergasse 185.
Hr. Johann Baptist Hofmann, woh. auf der hohen Brücke 357.
Hr. Joseph Pirllnger, auf dem Salzgries 342.

Violoncellisten.
Hr. Johann Hofmann, woh. im H. Kreuzerhof 768.
Hr. Jos. Oeßler, woh. auf der Schottenbasten 1278.

Violonisten.
Hr. Joseph Cammermayr, woh. im Färbergässchen 297.
Hr. Leopold Krebner, woh. in der untern Böckerstrasse 765.

Tromponist.
Hr. Ignaz Karl Ulbrich, woh. zu Mariahilf 20.

Oboisten.
Hr. Georg Tribenset, woh. in der Josephstadt 3.
Hr. Johann Went, woh. in der Annagasse 1001.

Fagottisten.
Hr. Wenzl Kauzner, im Jakobergässchen 904.
Hr. Ignaz Drobnay, in der Josephstadt 3.

Instrumentdiener.
Joseph Federl, auf der Schottenpasten 1284.

K. K. Hofkammermusici.

Kompositor.
Hr. Wolfgang Mozart, woh. in der Währingergasse 135.

Violinisten.
Hr. Franz Kreibich, woh. auf der Kischerstiegen 453.
Hr. Heinrich Bonheimer, woh. in der Leopoldstadt 269.
Hr.

Hr. Thomas Woborzill woh. auf dem Peter 551.
Hr. Johann Baptist Hofmann, woh. auf der hohen Brücke 357.

Oboisten.
Hr. Georg Triebenset, woh. in der Josephstadt 3.
Hr. Johann Went, in der Annagasse 1001.

Klarinetisten.
Hr. Anton Stadler woh. in der Leimgrube 107.
Hr. Johann Stadler, woh. auf der Leimgrube 4.

Fagottisten.
Hr. Wenzl Kauzner woh. im Jakobergässchen 904.
Hr. Ignaz Drobnay, in der Josephstadt 3.

Waldhornisten.
Hr. Martin Rupp, woh. in der Josephstadt 30.
Hr. Jakob Eisen, woh. in der Leopoldstadt 243.

Obersthofmarschallstab.

Obersthofmarschall.
Se. Excellenz, der Hoch und Wohlgebohrne Herr, Herr Eugen, des Heil. Röm. Reichs Graf Wrbna und Freudenthal, Herr der Herrschaften Hořowitz, Kamarow, Waldeck, und groß Heerlitz, Ritter des goldenen Vliesses etc. Ihrer Röm. K. K. ap. Maj. wirklich geheimer Rath und Kämmerer, woh. in der Dorotheagasse 1122.
Die Amts-Direktion wird von dem Vice Präsidenten des Ni. und Vorderöst. r. Appellationsgericht, Herrn Michael Franz Freyherrn von Kienmayer versehen.

Obristhofmarschallamts-Personal.

Registrator.
Hr. Joseph von Kienmayer k. k. Sekretär, woh. auf der Landstrasse 301.

Amtskabant.
Hr. Joseph Schmid. woh. in der Josephstadt 52.

Kanzleydiener und Amtsboth.
Hr. Joseph Pichler, woh. an der Wieden 263.

Oberst-Hofmarschalstaabspersonale.
Hr. Joh. von Schuppe, Seiner K. K. ap. Maj. wirkl. Rath und geweiter Hofquartiermeister.
C c   B. K.

1.3a–c. Mozart among the musicians in the court directory, *K.K. Hof- und Staats-Schematismus,* for 1789: pages 399–401 (*Vienna, Österreichische Nationalbibliothek*) successor to Gluck since honorary posts required no succession.[17] He rather seems to have been guided primarily by his intention to preserve excellence in the Viennese court music scene and to protect its reputation. The phrasing of the imperial decree on behalf of Mozart (". . . in recognition of his knowledge and ability in music, and the acclaim he earned thereby") resembled the one issued for Salieri two months earlier and the salary amounted to about the same as well, at least initially. This clearly indicated that the emperor and Count Rosenberg intended to create a balanced situation for the two most outstanding Viennese musicans of the younger generation. Moreover, the appointments were remarkably well tailored to the relative strengths of the two individuals. Salieri was entrusted with overseeing and leading the fifty-piece court kapelle as well as running the Italian court opera, a major administrative assignment that recognized what he had been doing informally before and that acknowledged his proven organizational experience. Nevertheless, his responsibilities were later outlined in a set of specific instructions regarding the reorganized court kapelle.[18] Mozart, by contrast, was not assigned any duties whatsoever beyond what the title "composer" implied. Unlike Gluck, who was never a court employee in the formal sense, Mozart as a composer of the emperor's private band of chamber musicians that played music for and with the emperor, would have been required to attend him, too, but on a fairly relaxed if unpredictable schedule.[19] For the time being, however, Joseph II was far away from Vienna, totally occupied by the war efforts, and courtly chamber music was altogether suspended. Like Gluck, therefore, Mozart was entirely free to pursue his creative and performing activities, but he would now conduct his affairs under imperial auspices. His name would be permanently bound up with the court in Vienna, which in effect represented a mutual commitment. The emperor clearly knew very well what suited Mozart best.

What was apparently expected of him—perhaps on an interim basis and communicated to him orally, but not specified by any written contract, and definitely not part of his official functions in the *Kammermusik*—amounted solely to supplying musical entertainment, primarily dances, for the annual carnival festivities held in the Redoutensaal (Redouten Hall) of the imperial residence in the Hofburg between January 7, the day after Epiphany, and Ash Wednesday. Only a few weeks after the appointment in January 1788, Mozart indeed delivered a first set of such works, six German Dances, K. 536. However, his salary essentially embodied a generous annual stipend supporting his activities as a composer and performer without restriction and with the added distinction of being a composer serving the emperor. For the rest of his life, no other musician in the vast Hapsburg Empire held the same title.

The full circumstances of Mozart's court appointment are not entirely clear. It might have been triggered by the spectacular success of *Don Giovanni*, the recent news about Mozart's invitation to London[20] with the threat of losing an asset like him, the death of Gluck, but most likely by a combination of the above. A retrospective account in a court memorandum of December 30, 1791, sheds additional light on the decision, for it mentioned that the late "Kammer Kompositor" had received his title and salary only to prevent that "such a rare musical genius be obliged to seek his earnings and subsistence abroad."[21] This arrangement was exactly parallel to Gluck's, whose appointment in Vienna represented a counteroffer to a promised appointment in Paris. Apart from this, however, it seems that external conditions in 1787 encouraged the emperor and his aides to make some basic and bold organizational changes in the Viennese court music establishment, especially regarding the expensive enterprise of the court opera with its Italian and German branches. Giuseppe Bonno, the seventy-six-year old first court kapellmeister and director of the Italian opera troupe, was ill and disabled; Joseph Starzer, composer of the ballet music had died at age sixty-seven on April 22, 1787. Pertinent decisions were probably postponed for some time because Joseph II became distracted by politics and, in August, was drawn by Catherine II ("the Great") of Russia into the Turkish war. Finally, however, with the death of Gluck, the time had come to begin a major reshuffling of the principal posts.

In doing so, the emperor pursued two unambiguous goals despite their being at odds with one another: on the one hand, economizing and saving money; on the other, ensuring the services and the continuing presence of the best musical talents. Regarding the latter, the emperor's focus was definitely on both Salieri and Mozart. He had known Salieri for a very long time and held him in high esteem.[22] In many ways, Salieri had been a personal protégé of the emperor ever since turning down an offer from Stockholm in 1773 in favor of remaining in Vienna. Mozart, by comparison, was a newcomer to Vienna in 1782, but the music-loving emperor had been fascinated by him for some time. He probably met the six-year-old child prodigy first on October 13, 1762, when the Mozarts had an audience with Emperor Franz I and Empress Maria Theresa, but definitely in 1768, when the young Mozart, during an extended stay in Vienna, composed *La finta semplice*, K. 51, at the request of Joseph II (see below, p. 34). After the adult virtuoso musician relocated to Vienna, the emperor attended many of his performances. In 1783, Mozart wrote to his father about his Burgtheater academy with the performance of, among other pieces, the "Haffner" Symphony, K. 385: ". . . what pleased me most was that His Majesty, the Emperor, was there as well; and how vociferously he applauded me."[23] Just a week later, when the piano concerto K. 415 was on the program at another Burgtheater academy, Joseph II came again and, according to Mozart, "stayed and listened until I had finished playing—and when I left the clavier, he left his loge.—He stayed just to hear me."[24]

Almost simultaneously with Mozart's appointment, a deliberate austerity move by the court on December 5, 1787, dissolved the German singspiel troupe at the Burgtheater.[25] Joseph thereby ended, after more than ten years, his ambitious project of instituting a German national theater that also included singspiel performances,

Table 1.1. **Reorganization of the** *k.k. Hofkapelle,* **1787–88:**
Senior Personnel and Salaries

OFFICES	SITUATION BEFORE NOVEMBER 1787	CHANGES MADE BY MARCH 1788
First court kapellmeister	G. Bonno (1,200 fl.)	A. Salieri (1,200 fl.)
Second kapellmeister (Italian opera)	A. Salieri (853 fl. 12 x), from Oct. 24, 1787	I. Umlauf (850 fl.)
Kapellmeister (German singspiel)	I. Umlauf (850 fl.)	position discontinued
Court composers	J. Starzer (2,000 fl.), † Apr. 22, 1787, for the ballet	W. A. Mozart (800 fl.), for the *Kammermusik,* from Dec. 7, 1787
	C. W. Gluck (2,000 fl.), † Nov. 15, 1787	
	A. Salieri (426 fl. 40 x), for the *Kammermusik,* until Oct. 1787	

to which Mozart in 1782 had contributed *Die Entführung aus dem Serail.* Some members of the German troupe, including Mozart's sister-in-law Aloysia Lange, were absorbed into the Italian company, which no longer had a German counterpart and thus gained new strength. The reorganization of the court opera was finally completed three months later with Salieri's promotion to court kapellmeister upon Bonno's retirement on March 1, 1788.[26] He now earned a base salary of 1,200 florins in the new post, but the major reshuffle resulted in dramatic savings for the court (table 1.1).[27]

The balance achieved in December 1787 by placing Salieri and Mozart in posts earning 853 and 800 florins, respectively, tipped by March 1788 in favor of Salieri, in terms of both finances and status. However, it was apparently not a matter of preferring one over the other when Joseph II appointed the more senior Salieri to the court kapellmeister post. The emperor, not merely an observer but a hands-on shaper of Viennese musical life, knew very well how to judge the different strengths and merits of the two men. Hence, in consideration of his overall musical and managerial experience,

Salieri was the natural choice for running the opera theater and overseeing the entire court music scene. Moreover, Salieri had in 1776 joined and later led the Tonkünstler-Sozietät. Membership in this society, founded in 1771 by Salieri's teacher and former first court kapellmeister Florian Gassmann for raising money to benefit widows and orphans of musicians, constituted an essential step toward integration into Viennese musical life. Virtually all court musicians were members, but Mozart, though participating in, and contributing fairly regularly to their benefit concerts, failed to join the organization.[28]

Mozart would and could hardly have expected an appointment to the top music post in Vienna. His occupying that post would not only have violated the seniority code and other principles, but more important, it would have confined Mozart to a much narrower range of activities. Joseph II knew firsthand how Mozart excelled in operatic composition, but he also realized that unlike Gluck, Salieri, and most other opera and church music composers, Mozart was also a dazzling keyboard virtuoso and a composer equally comfortable with writing instrumental works in all categories—sonatas, quartets, concertos, symphonies, and the like. Emperor Joseph surely held Salieri in the highest esteem and rewarded him accordingly, but no other musician in Vienna received more imperial patronage during the final years of Joseph's life than Mozart.[29] The emperor clearly recognized the peerless musicianship of the multitalented Mozart and, as far as is known, never displayed to anyone—not even Salieri—the kind of spontaneous and ecstatic ovation he showed him. The 1785 incident reported by Leopold Mozart to his daughter from Vienna was not the only one of its kind: "When your brother left the stage, the emperor waved his hat to him and shouted *bravo Mozart*."[30]

The emperor's decision a few years later to provide Mozart with substantial monetary support and to bind him to his court without adding any burdening obligations appears to be extremely considerate and farsighted. In the cases of both Mozart and Gluck, the appointments as court composer were meant to publicly recognize their distinction and to tie them as special assets to the imperial court. The different compensation levels do not reflect differences in estimation but rather a pragmatic weighing of facts. Gluck's salary of 2,000 florins was a competitive matter and set as a counteroffer to the French court, whereas the 800 florins for Mozart can only be properly understood as a permanent promotional stipend enabling its recipient to engage in a totally unrestricted range of performing and compositional activities, with virtually limitless possibilities for additional earnings. Moreover, it was almost twice the 426 florins Salieri had earned in the same post (with many more obligations) between 1785 and his reassignment to the opera in 1787 as Bonno's substitute.[31] The difference in pay between Gluck and Mozart also makes sense when comparing their ages at the time of their appointments—sixty versus thirty-one.

After five years of successful freelance work in Vienna, Mozart was finally holding a court post, which he had long sought, and receiving a permanent regular salary. Leopold Mozart, whose death just six months earlier was certainly still fresh on the son's mind, would have been extremely pleased. Thus, the composer proudly reported the news to his sister Nannerl on December 19, 1787: "You probably know by now that I composed 'Don Juan' in Prague and enjoyed the greatest possible applause—but you probably don't know that His Majesty, the Emperor, has taken me into his services."[32] Upon Nannerl's request for more information, he elaborated after considerable delay: "To answer your question about my service: the Emperor has appointed me into his chamber, in other words, he has given me an official title; *right now* I receive a salary of only 800 florins—but no one else in the chamber earns *as much*."[33] The words "right now" and "as much" underscored by Mozart himself suggest that he may have been led to expect a pay increase at some point.

The times were not at all conducive to increasing expenditures in the music budget of the Viennese imperial court. The burden of the

Turkish War, openly declared on February 9, 1788, affected everything throughout the remaining years of Joseph II's reign, which was marked also by the emperor's rapidly declining health. He died on February 19, 1790, and his brother and successor, Leopold II, quickly brought the war to an end. Nevertheless, the changes made by the previous administration in 1787 and 1788 regarding the court music organization do not merely reflect actions undertaken under financial pressure. They indicate just as much how the music-loving emperor sure-footedly grabbed the opportunity to secure the services of the two most eminent musicians who would bring luster to his imperial Vienna, even in times of austerity. Mozart's *Così fan tutte*, premiered in January 1790, would be one of those wartime products—ascetically staged, requiring a cast of only six solo singers, and playing with the theme of war, but philosophically and entertainingly focused on the subtle and emotional issues of human fidelity.

Prolific under Discouraging Conditions

THERE is no way of knowing whether Mozart had a realistic feeling for, let alone understanding of, the overall political atmosphere and concrete situation of late Josephinian Austria. The extant family correspondence provides a vivid testimony for the general alertness of the Mozarts in domestic and external affairs. But with father Leopold gone, the family correspondence virtually came to a halt, and the most significant source of information about Mozart's everyday life, his observations and perceptions, dried up. Since he and Constanze were at home together most of the time, they had no reason for exchanging letters, except for the very few periods when one of them was away from Vienna. Fewer than a third of the extant letters after Leopold Mozart's death consist of mail for Constanze with narrative content. However, none of them suggest that Mozart paid any attention to the general collapse of the manifold and bold domestic and institutional reforms instigated by Emperor Joseph II; to the disintegration of the intellectual, social, and political ideas by what had been a stalwart representative of an enlightened absolutism; to the widespread criticism of the emperor's internal and external politics; and particularly, to the catastrophic economic consequences brought about by waging war against the Ottoman empire. Nevertheless, the Turkish War was not entirely unpopular with the Viennese, at least not at the beginning. Mozart, too, paid his patriotic tribute when he wrote the orchestral contredanse *La bataille*, K. 535, a piece of martial music on the siege of Belgrade for the entertainment of the Redoutensaal society; the war song "Ich möchte wohl der Kaiser sein" (I wish I were the emperor), K. 539, for bass and a Turkish-style military band; and the song "Beim Auszug in das Feld" (While marching to the battlefied), K. 552, which begins "Dem hohen Kaiser-Worte treu" (Faithful to the emperor's noble word).

Hardly anyone could have anticipated the full extent of the emperor's failed domestic and foreign politics, but Mozart would not have missed their serious impact on virtually all levels of musical life in Vienna. The three-year war against the Ottoman Empire, engaging almost 300,000 Austrian troupes, resulted not only in numerous casualties but also cost the Hapsburg state some 220 million florins.[34] The economic impact was huge and the Emperor and his large aristocratic corps of generals and officers were largely distracted from anything but the war. In 1788, for example, Joseph II spent more than nine months as military commander with his troops away from the capital, only to return in December exhausted and very sick. The emperor had personally ordered the Viennese production of *Don Giovanni*, which was premiered at the Burgtheater on May 7 and received a total of fifteen performances. Yet, in spite of his deep-rooted interest in musical theater in general and his love for Mozart's operas in particular, he was unable to attend a single one, including the last in his (and the composer's) lifetime on December 15.[35] Moreover, all chamber concerts at court were stopped in the fall of 1787 and not resumed until well after the emperor's death, and then only sluggishly. What happened at the court was basically replicated elsewhere, notably among the nobility who had to adjust their lifestyles in view of a war with an uncertain outcome. Moreover, particularly heavy taxes were levied on them, although war taxes had to be borne by the general population as well.

Mozart had the great misfortune of experiencing a period in Austrian history that was marked by considerable economic depression combined with great political instability and uncertainty. In 1789, Joseph II increasingly lost the ability to govern. Leopold II took the reigns immediately after his brother's death at the age of forty-eight in early 1790, but his reactionary administration lasted barely two years. He was not even forty-five when he died on March 1, 1792, exactly three months after Mozart. Only the subsequent government of Leopold's son, Emperor Franz II, could, at least initially, during the short pre-Napoleonic period of his administration, bring about some political stability and relative calm. These would, despite a continuing climate of authoritarian repression, benefit the young Ludwig van Beethoven, who arrived in Vienna in November 1792. Emperor Franz, like his uncle Joseph II, was a declared music enthusiast and in marrying Empress Maria Theresa, had brought to his court one of the most important musical patrons in the Vienna of late Haydn and Beethoven.[36]

Seen in this light, it is all the more astonishing how steadily and productively Mozart went about his business for what turned out to be the last four years of his life. To look only at the major musical events: the year 1788 saw the Viennese production of *Don Giovanni*, with some newly composed material. Thereafter, he wrote three new operas: *Così fan tutte*, premiered at the Burgtheater in January 1790; *La clemenza di Tito*, presented in Prague at the coronation of Leopold II as king of Bohemia in early September 1791; and finally *Die Zauberflöte*, performed for the first time at the end of the same month in the suburban Theater auf der Wieden.

In comparison, the new court kapellmeister Antonio Salieri produced three operas during the same span of time, that is, after his appointment in March 1788. However, two of them—*Il talismano* of September 1788 and *La cifra* of December 1789, both on librettos revised by Lorenzo Da Ponte—were substantially based on earlier works. Only *Il pastor fido,* on a Da Ponte text, was newly composed, and its overture had been taken from an earlier opera.[37] Moreover, it was performed only six times at the Burgtheater in 1789, whereas in the following year, Mozart's *Così fan tutte*, on Da Ponte's libretto *La scuola degli amanti*, received ten performances, with significantly higher box-office receipts. That Salieri originally was supposed to write the music for *La scuola* but, after some preliminary drafts, turned the work over to Mozart, indicates the heavy administrative load that severely curtailed the court kapellmeister's creative drive.[38]

Considering all new and repeated opera productions at the Burgtheater during the four-year period 1788–91, the court kapellmeister clearly took the lead, with 97 performances of six different operas. Naturally, he was also more visible as a conductor and no less as the person organizationally responsible for the entire theater program, which over the four years included operas by Anfossi, Cimadoro, Cimarosa, Dutillieu, Guglielmi, Martín y Soler, Nasolini, Paisiello, Seydelmann, Storace, Sarti, Tritto, and Weigl—with Martín (97) registering the largest number of shows and Paisiello (73) and Guglielmi (72) following.[39] Nevertheless, Mozart made an impressive showing as well, with a performance record of 54 for just three operas, *Figaro, Don Giovanni,* and *Così*. To these must be added three insertion arias, K. 578, 582, and 583, provided for operas by others, rounding out the strong presence of his music at the court theater. Moreover, he also contributed to Schikaneder's suburban theater in the collaborative singspiel *Der Stein der Weisen*[40] of 1790 and with *Die Zauberflöte* and its seemingly endless string of performances after the premiere on September 30, 1791.

Mozart's compositional program, as it were, and also his related performing engagements, were strikingly different from the activi-

Table 1.2. Mozart's Completed Nonoperatic Works, 1788–91

Arias and Songs: Scenes and arias (K. 538, 540a–c, 541, 577–580, 582–584, 612, 625, Anh. 245), 1788–91; canzonetta (K. 549); songs (K. 552), 1788; 3 songs for Archduke Franz and Princess Theresa (K. 596–598), 1791.

Other Vocal Music: Canons (K. 55–559, 561–562), 1788; motet "Ave verum corpus" (K. 618); cantatas "Die ihr des unermeßlichen Weltalls Schöpfer ehrt" (K. 619) and "Laut verkünde unsre Freude" (K. 623), 1791.

Symphonies: E-flat major, G minor, and C major (K. 543, 550, 551), 1788.

Concertos: For piano in D and B-flat major (K. 537, 595), 1788 and 1791; for clarinet in A major (K. 622), 1791.

Orchestral Dances: K. 534–536, 567–568, 1788; K. 571, 585–586, 1789; K. 599–606, 1791.

Chamber Music: Clarinet quintet (K. 581), 1789. String quintets in D and E-flat major (K. 593, 614), 1790–91. String quartets in D, B-flat, and F major (K. 575, 589, 590), 1789–90. Divertimento (string trio) in E-flat major (K. 563), 1788. Piano trios in E, C, and G major (K. 542, 548, 564), 1788. Sonata for piano and violin in F (K. 547), 1788.

Piano Music: Sonatas for piano in F, B-flat, and D major (K. 533/494, 570, 576), 1788–89. Variations in D major (K. 573) and F major (K. 613), 1789 and 1791. Adagio in B minor (K. 540), 1788; Gigue in G (K. 574), 1789. For beginners: sonata for piano in C (K. 545), 1788.

Other Works: Adagio and Allegro in F minor (K. 594), 1790; Fantasia in F minor (K. 608), 1791; Andante in F (K. 616), 1791—all for mechanical organ. Adagio and Rondo in C minor/C major for glass armonica, flute, oboe, viola, and cello (K. 617), 1791; Adagio in C for glass armonica (K. 356), 1791.

---

ties of Salieri and the other Viennese opera composers, most of them his seniors. These focused almost exclusively on music for the theater, and if they wrote instrumental works at all, they invariably added up to a few largely inconsequential compositions. Mozart, on the other hand, always maintained a broad range of creative activities and sustained, even stepped up, his multidirectional approach after his imperial appointment. A survey of his productivity outside the realm of opera generates an impressive list of works in nearly all genres and categories (table 1.2), a repertory unmatched by the rather meager output of the court kapellmeister, Salieri.[41]

Mozart's thematic catalog, a kind of musical diary begun in

Table 1.3. Entries of Completed Works in Mozart's Thematic Catalog, by Year

YEAR	NO. OF WORKS	KEY WORKS
1784	11	6 piano concertos, 1 piano quintet, 2 string quartets
1785	20	3 piano concertos, 1 piano quartet, 1 piano-violin sonata, 2 cantatas
1786	19	*Le nozze di Figaro, Der Schauspieldirektor,* 1 symphony, 3 piano concertos, 1 horn concerto, 5 chamber works
1787	21	*Don Giovanni,* 2 string quintets, 3 other chamber works
1788	30	3 symphonies, 1 piano concerto, 3 piano trios, 1 string trio
1789	16	7 arias with orchestra, 1 clarinet quintet, 1 string quartet
1790	6	*Così fan tutte* (composed in 1789), 2 string quartets, 1 string quintet
1791	23	*La clemenza di Tito, Die Zauberflöte,* 1 piano concerto, 1 clarinet concerto, 1 string quintet

February 1784 that lists with dates all completed works,[42] does not truly indicate the composer's overall productivity, in that works of a greatly different scale and pieces of varying complexity—operas, songs, symphonies, short keyboard pieces—each receive a single individual entry. Nevertheless, it provides a gauge that permits some general conclusions, and the entries of the new major compositions for each of its eight years presents an instructive picture (table 1.3).

The years 1788 and 1790 stand out from the preceding years by presenting sharply contrasting figures. Indeed, the rich instrumental yield of 1788 in particular, headed by a set of three grand symphonies, bears out the suggestion that Mozart increased his compositional efforts because, as imperial court composer, he felt motivated—perhaps even obliged—to deliver substantially more to the music world at large. The year 1790, on the other hand, clearly marks a creative low, even though it began in January with the highly successful premiere of *Così fan tutte*. Work on this opera, however, was essentially completed during the previous year, in which Mozart was also absent from Vienna for two months on a trip to Prague, Dresden, Leipzig, and Berlin. Thus, the productivity in 1789, complete with a major opera, represents more of a normal output by Mozart's standards.

The precipitous drop in 1790 to a mere six entries in Mozart's thematic catalog occurred in the year in which Joseph II died. There is no reason to mistrust the low number which, nevertheless, includes with the two "Prussian" Quartets, K. 589 and 590, and the D-major Quintet, K. 593, three stellar works of chamber music. At the same time, 1790 was a year in which Mozart drafted a particularly large number of compositions that he left in a fragmentary state, intending to complete them at a later point (see chap. 6). Later that year, Mozart also left Vienna for three months from September through November, borrowed money in order to travel in style to Frankfurt am Main for the coronation of Leopold II as Holy Roman emperor, to perform there, and to visit other places for the sake of making connections on the way to and from the Rhine-Main area in Germany. This was the very year when the political winds changed in Vienna, when waiting to see what would happen was prudent, and when Mozart found himself particularly strapped financially, plagued by doubts that Vienna was the right place for him, and at times beset by a depressed mood. A few words about the disappointments he felt and the indifferent environment he encountered on his three-month exploratory trip in Germany characterize his gloom: "If people could see into my heart I should almost feel ashamed. Everything is cold to me—ice-cold."[43]

At the same time, these two sentences from the letter of September 30, 1790, from Frankfurt to Constanze must not be isolated and, thereby, blown out of proportion. On the whole, it is a sweet and tender letter that opens with "Dearest little wife of my heart!," explains in general terms attempts at making "some business deal" in order to please "my little wife," and expresses his frustrations: "It's true, I am known and respected here; but well—No—let's just see what happens." As a letter writer, Mozart is particularly good at pacing the sequence of informative and emotional passages, often dramatically punctuated. Therefore, it is impossible to seek in his correspondence a barometer of his true state of mind. Did he not see himself earlier in the same year "at the gateway to his fortune"? In Mozart's fast-paced life, things always changed quickly, and the external conditions from 1790 to 1791, with the termination of the Turkish War, also changed for the better. Hence, it hardly surprises when matters in 1791 looked quite different for Mozart as well. Virtually from the beginning of the year, he returned to a truly exceptional rate of productivity.

Despite his overall flight of creativity and impressive average musical output from 1788 to 1791, Mozart's financial affairs were in considerable disarray, beginning, curiously, when for the first time he started drawing a regular salary as an immediate benefit of the court appointment. With 800 florins annually, he was better off than ever before. By comparison, the court organist Johann Georg Albrechtsberger earned 300 florins. Mozart's new salary would take care of the basic family living expenses, including housing costs and food. For example, the rental fee for the most expensive apartment the Mozarts ever occupied in Vienna, at 8 Schulerstrasse (inner city, no. 846) and where they lived from 1784 to 1787, amounted to 450 florins. Their apartment in 1790–91 at 8 Rauhensteingasse, where Mozart would die, rented for 330 florins.[44] Nevertheless, just before Mozart moved there and in spite of taking out a loan, he still had to pawn his furniture in order to help finance his trip to Frankfurt for the coronation.

That Mozart, at the point of his greatest financial misery, decided to move into a spacious, attractive, and well-located apartment may seem puzzling, but it suggests that with the Turkish War ended and a new imperial regime in place, he expected higher earnings, and not unreasonably so. Anticipated extra income that failed to materialize had haunted him since 1787. The first indication of a rising habit of overspending and borrowing became evident in the fall of that year, when Mozart the downright debtor ordered that proceeds from the auction of his father's estate be transferred to Michael

Puchberg, the faithful creditor, businessman, music lover, fellow Mason, and good friend. Mozart apparently owed him 1,000 florins at the time. In the following years, until April 1791, he borrowed varying sums of money from him. Mozart apparently paid much of it back during his lifetime, but Constanze after her husband's death still faced a debt mountain of about 3,000 florins, even if that sum may then have been inflated.[45]

In the absence of the kind of lively correspondence Mozart had conducted with his father over many years, the letters and notes to Puchberg requesting financial help and asking for sums varying between 100 and 500 florins take on disproportionate prominence. Moreover, the total sum Mozart borrowed from Puchberg, although he asked for much more, really doesn't add up to much.[46] In this context it is noteworthy that in June 1788 he proposed to his supportive friend: "If you would have the kindness and friendship to support me for 1 or 2 years with 1 or 2 thousand florins at a suitable rate of interest, you would help me keep my field and plow!"[47]—the latter being a metaphor for the basics, not luxuries or extravagances. Mozart estimated that he needed a bridge loan for about two years of no more than 2,000 florins, an estimate that in retrospect looks quite accurate. Puchberg did not accept the proposal, perhaps because he viewed Mozart's ongoing cash-flow problems less optimistically than the composer himself, and he may well have been right.[48] But "in the 18th century private debts were at least as common as personal loans and overdrawn bank accounts are today,"[49] and Mozart's reputation and public visibility certainly made him creditworthy.

A primary reason for the financial crunch was the lack of performing opportunities in Vienna during the years of the Turkish War, cutting into Mozart's public appearances as a virtuoso pianist. This development coincided with increased household expenses as the result of a growing family[50] as well as fairly regular and extraordinary medical costs primarily for Constanze's ailments and for the cures in Baden near Vienna (prescribed by her doctors and taken

July–August 1789 and June–July 1791.[51] Moreover, Mozart aimed at a style and standard of living deemed proper for an imperial court composer.[52] Finally, to all these justifiable expenditures must be added the incalculable and unverifiable cost related to the composer's cavalier indulgences like his passion for various kinds of gambling,[53] which he frankly admitted but never specified, and which were well known to friends like Puchberg[54] but may well have alienated him from some others.

Mozart's average annual earnings in the mid-1780s had been very high—conservatively estimated around 4,000 florins[55]—and even during the last four years they were well above the average for musicians. The figures for 1788 to 1791, verifiable from letters and documents and exclusive of the court salary, amount to 1,025, 2,535, 1,865, and 3,725 florins, respectively, but do not include possible other income from unknown sources.[56] Nevertheless, the documented figures show a significant decline during the war years. It is no wonder that under those conditions, a frequently frustrated Mozart became depressed, suffered from melancholy, or, as he himself put it, was "beset so frequently by black thoughts (which I have to chase away forcibly)."[57]

At the same time, the rate at which Mozart prepared works for printing and distributing by Viennese and other publishers had no precedent in the years before 1788. It indicates the composer's interest in promoting his music and also reflects his growing success and renown amid a wider European public (table 1.4).[58] Even though the publications would not immediately generate much profit and some works were simply "given away" to printers, Mozart seems to have calculated that his business with publishers would gradually turn into a reliable and steady source of additional income.

Many of the publications that appeared soon after Mozart's death had been initiated and planned by the composer. This pertains, for example, to the piano Gigue K. 574, the String Quintet K. 406, the string Divertimento K. 563, and the violin-viola duos K. 423–424 (Artaria, 1792); the piano concerto K. 451 (Bossler, Speyer), and the

Table 1.4. Publications, 1788–91

YEAR	PUBLISHER	WORKS
1788	Artaria (Vienna)	Piano Trio ("Kegelstatt"), K. 498; three piano trios, K. 502, 542, 548
	Hoffmeister (Vienna)	Piano Sonata, K. 533/494; Fugue for 2 Pianos, K. 426; Adagio and Fugue for Strings, K. 546
	Bossler (Speyer)	Flute quartet K. 285b
	Sieber (Paris)	Symphony K. 297
1789	Artaria (Vienna)	String quintet K. 515; six contredanses K. 535a; twelve German dances K. 536–537; twelve minuets K. 568
	Storace (London)	Piano Trio K. 564—publ. prior to Artaria edition of 1790
1790	Artaria (Vienna)	Piano Trio K. 564; string quintet K. 516; six German dances
1791	Artaria (Vienna)	Three string quartets K. 575, 589, 590; piano concerto K. 595; piano variations K. 613; Andante for mechanical organ K. 616, version for piano; six minuets K. 599; twelve German dances K. 600; twelve minuets K. 585; twelve German dances K. 586; first fascicles of 38 numbers of piano-vocal scores in single issues for Die Zauberflöte K. 620 in two nearly simultaneous editions—Artaria competing with Kozeluch (Musikalisches Magazin)
	Schott (Mainz)	Piano-vocal score of *Don Giovanni*, K. 527
	Hummel (Berlin and Amsterdam)	Piano variations K. 573—publ. prior to Artaria edition of 1792

two piano concertos K. 271 and 449 (André, in Offenbach). These constitute only a selection of the works published in 1792, but along with the publications of 1793 and the subsequent years, they confirm a steady upswing.[59]

Seen in the light of his borrowing pattern, Mozart seems to have anticipated both an increasing demand for his works and, eventually, substantial monetary returns, not just from publishing but from all his musical activities. His letter to Puchberg of June 1788, in which he requests a bridge loan for one or two years in order to offset "irregular income," suggests that he was not afraid of bolstering his credit rating by using his music as equivalent value. Puchberg may have thought of his musical friend's talkative manner and homemade philosophy of economics as amusing, but Mozart clearly felt he could afford mortgaging his musical future:

> You probably know yourself as a matter of *experience* and *truth* how dreadfully hard, indeed, how impossible it is if you have to depend on your livelihood from one irregular income to the next; without a certain *minimum capital*, it is impossible to keep one's affairs in order.— with nothing you can create nothing;—if you will do this service of friendship for me, I would be able, *primo*, to pay my bills at the *proper time*, in other words, with a certain ease, whereas at present I have to *postpone* my payments and then spend my *entire income* all at once, often at a *most inconvenient time.—Secondo*: I would be able to work with a *freer mind* and *lighter heart* and consequently *earn* more.—As to securities, I don't imagine that you would have any doubts!—you know my situation quite well—and you know my *sincerity!*[60]

Haydn died a rich man at age seventy-seven in 1809, though primarily as a result of his two extended tours to England, 1790–92 and 1794–95. From the outlook of 1788 and the years following, Mozart in his early thirties had even better prospects of wealth much sooner in life. He could actually take note of concrete signs indicating that things were about to turn around when, only a few days before his death, a group of Hungarian aristocrats offered him an annual honorarium of 1,000 florins; and an even higher offer arrived around the same time from Amsterdam.[61]

Toward Spirited Partnership

MOZART the court composer was not formally subordinate to the highest-ranking court musician, Salieri the court kapellmeister.

Hence, not bound by regularly scheduled duties throughout the year, Mozart could go about his business quite independently. Nevertheless, he certainly crossed paths with Salieri frequently, even outside his specific duties of providing musical entertainment in the Redoutensaal for the carnival balls that were patronized by the imperial family and were attended primarily by the Viennese noble families and a wide range of aristocrats. Although Mozart's official function and title was "composer" (*Kompositor*) for the court chamber music, he usually referred to himself in letters and other documents as "kapellmeister in actual i.-r. services" (*in wirklichen k.k. Diensten*),[62] employing the title kapellmeister in the generic sense frequently used for a composer-conductor. The Burgtheater poster for the Viennese *Don Giovanni* premiere in May 1788 specifically calls him "*Kapellmeister in wirkl. Kayserl. Diensten*," thereby sanctioning the legitimacy of that title.

Mozart's official courtly home then was the court chamber ensemble. However, because of the war-related absence of Joseph II from Vienna and in the aftermath of his death in early 1790, the generally highly active chamber music scene of former times had come to a standstill. As a result, the functions of the chamber composer largely evaporated and the Redoutensaal carnival festivities embodied virtually all that remained. The minuets, contredanses, and German dances written for this purpose in four carnival seasons must therefore be considered much like an unintentional resi-

1.4. Antonio Salieri, engraving by Johann Gottfried Scheffner, c. 1790 (*Vienna, Österreichische Nationalbibliothek*)

due—though a repertoire without equal in elegance, instrumental coloration, rhythmic variety, and overall musical refinement. The emperor's original and primary goal must have been quite different. By appointing the most accomplished and versatile composer of chamber music in the first place, he must have meant to enhance rather than diminish the court's chamber music. However, the political circumstances dictated otherwise, and the fallout affected Mozart directly. Astonishingly, however, his creative involvement seems to have been almost immune to those circumstances, for he devoted himself to writing all kinds of chamber music in various trio, quartet, and quintet configurations as never before, and he surely did so with the ultimate goal of presenting the repertoire in the emperor's chambers (see table 1.2).

Salieri had been a fixture in the Viennese court music establishment since 1766. As such, he most likely met and heard the child prodigy when the entire Mozart family established temporary residence in Vienna from September 1767 to January 1769. The young Mozart composed and presented there, among other works, sonatas, symphonies, and sacred music for the dedication of the *Waisenhaus* (orphanage) Church. On January 19, 1768, the Mozarts were invited to an audience with Empress Maria Theresa and her son, the young emperor Joseph II who, according to Leopold Mozart, "asked the boy twice whether he would like to compose an opera and conduct it himself. Wolfgang said yes."[63] He subsequently wrote the opera buffa *La finta semplice*, K. 51 (on a libretto by Carlo Goldoni) in Vienna from April to July 1768, but the piece never came to be staged in the imperial city. Leopold Mozart attributed this lack to jealousy and all kinds of intrigues that, despite a formal complaint filed with the emperor, prevented the opera from being performed.[64] "What sort of an uproar," Leopold reported to a friend in Salzburg, "do you suppose has secretly arisen among the composers—what?—today it is a Gluck and tomorrow a boy of twelve who is sitting at a keyboard and conducting his opera—yes, in spite of all their grudging envy!"[65] In 1768, Salieri was not yet a force in the Viennese theater scene, but the experience surrounding *La finta semplice*[66] lastingly colored Mozart's, and especially Leopold's, perception of Viennese opera culture.

The Mozarts paid their third extended visit to Vienna in the summer of 1773, July to September, by which time the twenty-three-year-old Salieri had already made a name for himself as an opera composer. His opera *La fiera di Venezia* was performed there in 1772–73, and Mozart must have liked the music because he picked a passage from its second finale as a theme for his keyboard variations K. 180, composed, apparently, in 1773. Salieri, however, remains unmentioned in the Mozart family correspondence of that time; his name first appears in an entry made by Mozart in his sister's diary on March 17, 1780, with a reference to a terzetto by Salieri,[67] and thereafter in a letter to his father of December 19, 1780. Mozart, then at work on *Idomeneo* in Munich, brings up an unidentified aria "with oboe solo" by Salieri, suggesting that he liked the piece.[68] But it is only after Mozart's settling in Vienna several months later that Salieri as a person enters his life. In one of the first letters from Vienna to his father,[69] he tries to assess his chances for a future in the capital city and debates whether he "would be better off here than at home" and find a post with "a better salary." After observing the Viennese musical landscape for barely a month, he clearly got a good feel for the circulating rumors and predicted with remarkable accuracy: "When [the court kapellmeister Giuseppe] Bonno dies, Salieri will become Kapellmeister—then [court composer for the Nationaltheater Joseph] Starzer will get Salieri's position and Starzer's position?—well, no one has been mentioned yet." He could not, of course, anticipate that Joseph Starzer would die in 1787; but, with some sense of frustration, he got a good feel for forthcoming developments and his own uphill struggle.

Apparently from the very beginning, Mozart somehow saw in Salieri an impediment to his success in the imperial city, blaming him indirectly for blocking a Viennese performance of *Idomeneo*: "The emperor killed it for me, for the only one who counts in his eyes is

Salieri."[70] However, in making such an exaggerated statement, he apparently did not know of the emperor's declared indifference to opera seria[71] and Joseph's deliberate pursuit of establishing a German national opera. Both of these sentiments eventually benefited the commission in 1782 of Mozart's singspiel *Die Entführung aus dem Serail*, which met far greater success than Salieri's *Der Rauchfangkehrer*, whose 1781 premiere Mozart attended.[72]

Mozart related to his father[73] what was supposedly "a trick by Salieri," linked to repercussions from a performance of Pasquale Anfossi's opera *Il curioso indiscreto,* to which he had contributed the insertion arias K. 416 and 418 for his sister-in-law, the singer Aloysia Lange. Lowering himself to the same level as his presumed adversaries and striking a feisty tone that Leopold Mozart was likely to appreciate, he wrote about "how we could outshine our enemies." The story as such involves modest degrees of slander and intrigue typical of the everyday theater world. Feeling surrounded by enemies in Vienna was an attitude developed by Leopold Mozart and instilled in his son ever since the 1768 debacle of *La finta semplice*. "Mozart may have suffered from cabals in which Salieri played a role, but evidence of such activities and of Salieri's role in them is of course slim."[74]

A crucial and probably decisive event regarding a developing partnership between the two musicians occurred during the carnival of 1786. Joseph II commissioned two one-act operas to feature, in deliberate juxtaposition, the German opera company and the Italian opera buffa troupe. The two composers were also juxtaposed, again a deliberate choice by the emperor: Mozart with *Der Schauspieldirektor* and Salieri with *Prima la musica e poi le parole* were both to present satirical musical plays on the creation and production of an opera.[75] A great success for both composers, the event seems to have helped put the relationship between the two on a professional level. It primarily aided Mozart at the height of his fame in Vienna as a greatly admired virtuoso pianist and instrumental composer to secure a foothold in the complex Viennese opera scene. As it happens, he was now intensely at work on *Le nozze di Figaro*, his first collaboration with Lorenzo Da Ponte, to be premiered on May 1 of the same year. Salieri, on the other hand, thanks to the illness of Gluck, had his principal operatic venue in Paris between early 1784 and the fall of 1787 and returned to Vienna only sporadically.

Mozart's imperial appointment in late 1787 would, as such, hardly have any further effect on the relationship between the two musicians, since it appears to have been coordinated with Salieri's kapellmeister appointment. Be that as it may, Mozart and Salieri operated independently of one another, conscious that they were the two most eminent musical personalities in Vienna. Whether Mozart was occasionally plagued by a sense of asymmetry in their unequal ranks, let alone by jealousy, remains a matter of speculation. There is no question, however, that ambitions and financial concerns made him keep looking for further advancement. Curious in this connection is a letter drafted by Mozart in April or May 1790 after the death of Joseph II and addressed to Archduke Franz, who as the oldest son of the incoming emperor Leopold II—and the future Franz II—was closely involved in governmental affairs:

> I make so bold as to beg your Royal Highness very respectfully to use your most gracious influence with His Majesty the King with regard to my most humble petition to His Majesty. Prompted by a desire for fame, by a love of work and by a conviction of my wide knowledge, I venture to apply for the post of a second kapellmeister, particularly as Salieri, that very gifted kapellmeister, has never devoted himself to church music, whereas from my youth up I have made myself completely familiar with this style.[76]

Three points are worth noting: (1) the post of second kapellmeister did not officially exist on the court's roster; (2) Mozart shows his respect for Salieri, suggesting that he did not want to compete with him; and (3) by comparing Salieri's lack of interest in sacred music[77] with his own accomplishments in this realm, Mozart suggested that the new kapellmeistership be defined primarily in terms of responsibility for sacred music (see chap. 5, p. 135). The last point is of particular importance because this petition has usually been interpreted as an attempt to gain a theater post in direct competition with Salieri, even stab him in the back in the realm of opera. However, the wording makes it quite clear that Mozart is aiming at a post unmistakably distinct from Salieri's responsibilities. Furthermore, Mozart would hardly have been so naïve as to dream up the proposal independently, and it is also unlikely that Mozart would have submitted the letter without first consulting certain authorities, perhaps even Salieri himself. Even though the post of second kapellmeister as such was never established, the formal approach in whatever form to Archduke Franz, who played a major role in his father's administration, may nevertheless have had its desired effect. For a year later, the magistrate of the City of Vienna responded positively to Mozart's application for the post of adjunct to the ailing kapellmeister Leopold Hofmann at St. Stephen's Cathedral, with the assurance that he would receive the primary appointment with the full salary of 2,000 florins when the post should fall vacant. It is likely that Archduke Franz had a hand in this matter. At any rate, it would complete the reorganization of the music scene in the imperial residential city and Austrian capital begun under Joseph II with the appointment of a top cast to the principal posts, now including a cathedral kapellmeister.

The relationship between Mozart and Salieri was marked, so it seems, by mutual respect, which extended also to Italian opera, the one major area where their musical interests and professional ambitions overlapped directly. In all other musical activities and notably as a virtuoso pianist, Mozart had no equal in Vienna, something Salieri himself would have readily admitted. As for the Italian court opera, there was another name that played a decisive role at the imperial court: Lorenzo Da Ponte. He had come to Vienna in 1781 at the recommendation of his mentor Caterino Mazzolà, court poet in Dresden, whom he had assisted there. Da Ponte, thirty-two years old at the time, was not hired to replace the then eighty-one-year-old Viennese court poet Pietro Metastasio. It more or less came to this, however, when the grand old man of opera seria, who had retired from the stage long ago, died in 1782. In the following year, Joseph II appointed Da Ponte court poet to the Italian theater. There and in collaboration with, among others, Gluck, Martín y Soler, Salieri, and Mozart, the emperor put his distinct stamp on Viennese-style Italian opera buffa.

On May 7, 1788, barely three months after Salieri's appointment as first court kapellmeister, the Burgtheater—home of Italian opera at the Viennese court—mounted a production of *Don Giovanni,* Mozart's latest opera, which had been premiered in Prague. On August 29 of the following year, a new production of *Le nozze di Figaro* also opened at the Burgtheater and was kept in repertory until February 9, 1791. During that run, *Così fan tutte* was premiered on January 26, 1790, and ran until August 7, 1790.[78] This opera was Mozart's third collaboration with Da Ponte, but one with a curious prehistory. Its libretto was written with the title *La scuola degli amanti* (The school for lovers) and differs from the preceding operas, based on well-known literary subjects and characters created by Beaumarchais and Cervantes, respectively. The new comedy, however, tells a timeless story about true love in a contemporary setting, involving two officers being called to war duty and making a bet about the faithfulness of their sweethearts. The story's place of action, Naples, might well be imagined as contemporary wartime Vienna.

Mozart changed the opera's title to *Così fan tutte* (So do all [women]) and kept the original heading merely as a subtitle. This change may be seen in conjunction with the current-affairs background of the story because it sends a message to the theater audience even before the opera's plot unfolds. The message projected by the new title "So do all"—imagine that it's you!—differs fundamentally from the neutral lesson in moral philosophy in *La scuola degli amanti*. But the composer also had a musical reason for his significant encroachment on the librettist's literary choice. He picked the single most meaningful line in Da Ponte's libretto, "così fan tutte"[79] (act 2, scene 14, immediately preceding the finale) as a phrase or indeed a motto to capture the moral quintessence of the opera. Deviating from the libretto, however, he has the line "così fan tutte" sung twice, and not just by the old philosopher Don Alfonso, as Da Ponte wanted it. In Mozart's version, the first statement is presented by Don Alfonso somewhat hesitatingly, its deceptive cadence making it sound more like a question. However, the emphatic repeat of the melodic phrase, assigned to all three male singers—that is, including the officers Guglielmo and Ferrando—turns its meaning into a strong statement of fact:

1.1. *Così fan tutte*, act II, no. 30 (mm. 20–26): Musical motto.

Moreover, Mozart includes the same C-major double phase in the overture as a wordless instrumental surprise statement toward the end of the movement (mm. 228–41), but it had occurred less dramatically earlier, at the conclusion of the slow introduction (mm. 8–15). The composer here counts on the audience's ability to recall this musical moment when the same melody, now with words, magically reappears just before the finale sets in. The opera's title and musical motto blend into one.

While the title change points to the imaginative design of Mozart's musical dramaturgy, the libretto was not originally written for him but for none other than Antonio Salieri.[80] In fact, Salieri composed the first two of the three terzetti that form the opening scene of act 1, "La mia Dorabella" (Ferrando, Don Alfonso, Guglielmo) and "È la fede delle femmine" (Ferrando, Don Alfonso, Guglielmo). Yet, he composed these pieces not before fall 1789.[81] Why did he not finish *La scuola degli amanti*? He must have fancied the libretto or he would hardly have started work on it. Most likely, administrative tasks and time pressure prevented him from completing the opera for the 1789–90 season because he had to make revisions for the resumption of his ill-fated *Il pastor fido* in October 1789 and also compose and prepare the premiere performance of *La cifra* (Da Ponte) for December 11, 1789.[82] By then Mozart was hard at work on *Così fan tutte*, which was premiered on January 26, 1790.

It may well have been Lorenzo Da Ponte who approached Mozart after learning that Salieri had given up on *La scuola degli amanti*. Yet Salieri surely knew that Mozart had taken over "his" opera and, according to Mozart, was not too happy with the turn of events. In late December 1789, in a letter to Puchberg, Mozart refers to a forthcoming private rehearsal of his new opera and writes: "I am inviting only you and Haydn—I will tell you in person about some of Salieri's cabals, all of which, however, have already come to nothing."[83] At the time, Salieri also had a falling out with Da Ponte over *Il pastor fido*. The court poet was dismissed at the end of the 1790 theater season and held Salieri primarily responsible, but the ouster was actually part of a theater reoganization by Leopold II to which Salieri himself also fell victim: he was released from his managerial responsibilities at the Burgtheater in the same year.[84] At any rate, the problems surrounding *Così fan tutte*, whose revised title Da Ponte never approved and later continually referred to as *La scuola degli amanti*, may not have amounted to much more than a different view about an effective opera title, a minor controversy in everyday theater business.

Whatever the case, the renaming of the opera could hardly have had a lasting effect on Mozart's relationship with Salieri. However, assessing this professional and personal relationship in greater detail is made difficult by the scarcity in Mozart's letters of references to Salieri, all of which are favorable except for the unspecified "cabals" in the 1789 letter just cited. Most telling, however, is Mozart's very last letter, written on October 14, 1791, to his wife in Baden, containing a report on the previous day's performance of *Die Zauberflöte*:

. . . at 6 o'clock I fetched Salieri and [the singer] Mad.^me [Caterina] Cavalieri with a carriage and took them to my box. . . . You can't believe how sweet they both were—and how much they enjoyed not only my music but the libretto and everything.—Both of them told me it was an *opera* fit to be played at the grandest festivity, before the greatest monarch—and they would certainly go and see it more often because they had never seen a more beautiful and more pleasant spectacle.— Salieri listened and watched with great attention, and from the overture all the way through to the final chorus there was not a single number that did not elicit from him a "bravo" or "bello." He and Cavalieri went on and on thanking me for doing them such a great favor.[85]

Less than two months later, Mozart was dead and on December 6 buried at the suburban St. Marx Cemetery—in a common grave with no mourners in attendance, in accordance with the custom in Josephinian Vienna. However, prior to the burial in the early afternoon, a funeral procession moved from the Mozart apartment in Rauhensteingasse to St. Stephen's Cathedral. Following the casket were the widow, Constanze; her sisters and other members of the Weber family; Baron van Swieten; Mozart's students Franz Jacob Freystädtler, Franz Xaver Süssmayr, and Otto Hatwig; then Mozart's colleagues and friends Johann Georg Albrechtsberger, Anselm Hüttenbrenner—and Antonio Salieri, who had visited the sick composer at his bedside two days before his death.[86] At three o'clock, they all attended the private ceremony of blessing the body in the Chapel of the Holy Cross in St. Stephen's Cathedral, after which the hearse took off with the coffin.[87]

A few days later, on December 10, 1791, exequies for Mozart were held at St. Michael's,[88] the parish church of the court and home of the Tonkünstler-Sozietät, the association of court musicians. The service had been organized by Emanuel Schikaneder—impresario, librettist, and the original Papageno in *Die Zauberflöte*—and his colleague Joseph von Bauernfeld, on behalf of Vienna's court and theater musicians.[89] Moreover, a Viennese newspaper reported that "the Requiem, which he composed in his last illness, was performed."[90] This performance within less than a week of Mozart's death could have been confined only to the finished part of the Requiem, that is, basically the Introit and Kyrie movements.[91] Since most of the musicians must have come from the court, it is likely that the court kapellmeister conducted them in paying their tribute to the deceased imperial-royal court composer. If that was indeed the case, Salieri would have paid two court composers their final honors—first his mentor Gluck and then, only four years later, his junior colleague Mozart.

2

Explorations Outside
of Vienna

Traveling Again

MOZART'S IMPERIAL APPOINTMENT carried with it no residential obligations. Just as Gluck spent extended periods away from
Vienna, Mozart could contemplate the same. But in his case, there
was an understanding that he would at least be available for the
annual Redoutensaal festivities during the carnival season, a responsibility he carried out faithfully. Throughout the rest of the year—
that is, for at least ten months—he would be able to move around
freely, a privilege he must have appreciated from the outset, even
though he made no use of it in the first year.

After establishing residence in Vienna in 1781, Mozart did not
leave the city for nearly six years, with the sole exception of a 1783
family visit to Salzburg. In contrast, during the first two-and-a-half
decades of his life, he had traveled extensively, mostly in the company of his father. More often than not, these trips crisscrossing
western Europe involved long periods away from his Salzburg home.
Principal destinations between 1762 and 1781 included Munich,
Vienna, Mannheim, Brussels and Amsterdam, Paris, London, and
Italy (Verona, Venice, Milan, Florence, Bologna, Rome, and other

cities). The situation changed drastically in 1781 when, without a firm, salaried position in Vienna, he had to become self-reliant and expand his income-producing activities, which he did by means of a busy schedule of composing, performing, and teaching. As his opportunities for work steadily increased, however, he also needed to defend his hard-won territory against competing musicians. So for a long time, largely professional circumstances and economic considerations prevented him from undertaking the kind of travel he had been accustomed to from his childhood days. Yet he always understood its importance, as he expressed in an early letter to his father from Paris: "Without traveling one remains a poor creature; that goes especially for people in the arts and sciences!"[1]

By 1787, Mozart had built a solid foothold in the Hapsburg capital as well as an ever-growing reputation beyond the city's walls. Instead of going on strenuous performance tours, he now gained his renown through published works, the distribution of compositions in manuscript, and especially through the increasing popularity across the German-speaking lands of his 1782 singspiel *Die Entführung aus dem Serail*. The work was produced in well over forty cities—right away during the 1782–83 season in Prague, Bonn, Frankfurt, and Leipzig, but soon also reaching Weimar, Dresden, Hamburg, Lübeck, Rostock, Berlin, and Königsberg, as well as more distant places like Amsterdam and Riga.[2] Mozart became well aware of this development outside Vienna, where the National singspiel at the Burgtheater was closed down in 1783.[3] Therefore, he must have been especially pleased when "a society of great connoisseurs and amateurs" in Prague invited him for a new production of *Le nozze di Figaro* (premiered 1786 in Vienna) in January 1787. This made him undertake his very first concert trip in many years, and the spectacular success of *Figaro* then led to the commission of *Don Giovanni*, premiered some nine months later in the same year, which brought the composer back to Prague for a second time.

In 1786, Mozart received an invitation to London for the spring of 1787—actually three years before the much older Haydn was officially asked—but he declined primarily on the advice of his father.[4] When this invitation was renewed a year later, it apparently helped him finally obtain the much-desired court appointment, but it conflicted with family obligations because the Mozarts were expecting their fourth child in December 1787. Yet, the newly awarded imperial title combined with the Prague experience and the postponed London invitation must have reawakened in Mozart the kind of cosmopolitan ambitions to which he had grown so accustomed since childhood days.

But times were now different in many ways, as the married Mozart was responsible for a growing family. Nevertheless, he undertook both Prague journeys in 1787 together with his wife, Constanze, who was pregnant during the second trip. Prague could be reached from Vienna in two days, and both trips were concluded within four to six weeks. For the time being, however, Mozart could not consider the kind of extended stay abroad that Haydn—who from 1790 to 1792 spent a year and a half in London—could easily afford, although he surely envisioned it for the future. Thus, he had to curb the Berlin and Frankfurt trips of 1789 and 1790, lasting fifty-seven and forty-three days, respectively, and carry them out without Constanze. Moreover, these two extended concert tours were largely exploratory, not arranged by prior invitations, and thus more costly. So they would hardly have been feasible, let alone rewarding, as a joint husband-and-wife venture.

There is no question that the Mozart of 1787–88 saw a genuine need to reconnect directly and personally with the wider European scene. On October 8, 1790, he wrote to Constanze: "Sometimes the thought comes to me that I should perhaps travel *farther afield* [suggesting England]—but . . . I would deeply regret it if I had stayed away from my dear wife for such an indefinite and perhaps even *fruitless* period."[5] At this point, he did not have to dispel the widespread reputation he had once won as a child prodigy when he was presented throughout Europe by a determined and ambitious father. From the mid- to late 1770s, he had been able to demonstrate in Mannheim, Paris, Munich, and elsewhere his mature and increasing prowess as a virtuoso performer and unusually gifted composer. But like Gluck and other major figures of the contemporaneous musical world, and especially now in the service of the emperor, Mozart clearly wanted to demonstrate a strong presence in his own right. Branching out of Vienna on his own terms, even with the limitations imposed on him by financial constraints and his young family, remained an ever-increasing and important goal.

Frankfurt, 1790: The Self-Styled Ambassador

DESPITE being at the seemingly lowest point in his financial situation, Mozart the imperial kapellmeister departed in grand style on September 23, 1790, for the imperial coronation ceremonies of Leopold II in Frankfurt. He was accompanied not only by his brother-in-law Franz Hofer but also by a servant driver. The small party rode in comfort in Mozart's own recently acquired carriage; the rented horses would be changed from one mail station to another.[6] Just before his departure, he made arrangements to move into a new apartment in the Rauhensteingasse in the center of the city near the cathedral—the largest city dwelling ever occupied by the Mozarts,[7]—where the family would remain until well after the composer's end. But the move itself on September 30 had to be managed in his absence by Constanze alone.

At the time, Mozart faced serious debts. While apartment and living expenses were covered by the court salary, he still needed to borrow 1,000 florins against a promissory note[8] in order to be able to afford the deluxe trip in his own coach, which the status-conscious composer must have deemed absolutely necessary. Unlike Salieri and his group of fifteen court musicians, he was not part of the imperial entourage[9] and undertook the trip at his own risk, yet largely without an impresario or other aide to plan the concert tour and organize everything else in advance. Curiously, a third invitation to England for December 1790 to July 1791 arrived while Mozart was traveling. It was extended by the manager of the Italian opera in London, Robert May O'Reilly and included a commission of 300 pounds sterling for two new operas. Unfortunately, the letter, dated October 26, reached Mozart only after his return to Vienna on or near November 10,[10] when it had become too unrealistic a proposal to be followed up on short notice. On the other hand, it indicated to the composer what lay in store for the long term.

Although Mozart had no official function at the imperial coronation, held in the Frankfurt cathedral on October 9, he was not a silent bystander to the festivities. A number of events had been prearranged by or for him, if not very efficiently. On October 12, a performance of *Die Entführung* was presented by the electoral theater troupe of Trier led by Johann Böhm, with whom Mozart lodged in Frankfurt and who probably had alerted Mozart in advance of the planned opera production. A *Don Giovanni* production, planned in the composer's honor for October 5, regrettably had to be called off. It was replaced by a work by Carl Ditters von Dittersdorf that was less challenging for the performers, the opera troupe from the electoral court of Mainz.[11] Ten days later, on October 15, Mozart gave a concert at the Frankfurt theater. The program began with a "new grand symphony," that is, one from the group of three symphonies K. 543, 550, and 551. He then played two piano concertos, K. 459 in F major of 1784 and K. 537 in D major of 1788, and improvised a fantasy.[12] The concert "was a splendid success from the point of view of acclaim," he told his wife in a letter written on the same day, and added, "but rather meager in terms of money."[13]

The next day, Mozart left for Mainz where, on October 20, perhaps as a consolation prize for the canceled *Don Giovanni*, he was asked to perform for Prince-Elector and Archbishop Friedrich Karl von Erthal and his guests at a private event, for which he received 165 florins. He then paid a surprise visit to his familiar Mannheim, where he assisted with the dress rehearsal for *Figaro* on October 23 and attended the performance on the next day, before leaving for

Munich. He arrived there on October 29 and participated in concerts given on November 4 and 5 by Prince-Elector Carl Theodor. The latter knew Mozart well from his Mannheim stint in 1777–78 and thereafter commissioned him to write *Idomeneo*, which premiered in Munich in 1781. The concerts, presented in the Kaisersaal of the palace, were arranged in honor of King Ferdinand IV of Naples and his wife, who made a stopover in Munich on their return from Frankfurt. Mozart's comment in a letter to Constanze—"what an honor it is for the court of Vienna that the King of Naples has to hear me in a foreign country"[14]—is quite telling because it indicates how genuinely ambassadorial he understood his imperial title and function to be. And it goes without saying that he could perform this self-styled role only by arriving and departing in his own coach and with his own driver.

Although the whole trip had been poorly cobbled together, it was a well-calculated undertaking. The principal reason for Mozart's attending the Frankfurt ceremonies consisted of the unique opportunity, by way of running his own sideshow, to renew old acquaintances and make new connections among the many members of the assembled European royalty, princes, and high aristocracy, in the hope that those with musical interests might hear about his presence and would want to approach him. The invitations to Mainz and Munich most likely materialized on the basis of previously established contacts, but who else actually attended his Frankfurt opera performance and concert and whether he received promises for later invitations remains unknown. Functioning as his own manager, Mozart met with a number of old acquaintances on the way to and from Frankfurt and, in general, intended to further his business prospects, perhaps also with an eye toward impressing the new imperial administration of Leopold II in Vienna.

Mozart's en-route letters to Constanze, who kept worrying about her husband's big loan of September 1790, oscillate between wishful thinking, guarded optimism, and deep frustration. One day he writes, "I'm determined to do as well here as I possibly can."[15] Then, in conjunction with "the wish to bring home a lot of money," he states: "To be sure, I am famous, admired, and popular, but people here are even greater skinflints than the Viennese."[16] In the final analysis, the journey was not taken altogether in vain, for Mozart was apparently able to repay his loan of 1,000 florins quite soon and, although his financial troubles were by no means over, the available records demonstrate that in 1791 he needed to borrow a mere fraction of what he asked for in the three preceding years. Things were definitely looking up, in part because his expectations were not too ambitious to begin with: in his first letter from Frankfurt, he expressed the hope, "This way everything could be paid off and there would even be a little left over so that after I get back I would be able to completely concentrate on my *work*."[17]

Leipzig and Berlin, 1789

IN ALL likelihood, Mozart would not have made the journey to Frankfurt and the Rhine-Main region if the previous and slightly more extended concert tour to Leipzig and Berlin via Prague and Dresden had not been a promising beginning. The itinerary in table 2.1 underscores that Leipzig and especially the Prussian residences Potsdam and Berlin were the primary destinations, while Prague and Dresden served more as way stations.[18] Notwithstanding abiding speculation, there is not a shred of evidence that Mozart traveled north in order to seek a new position at either the Dresden or Berlin courts. The purpose of this trip, the very first taken by Mozart after his court appointment, was to find ways to widen his base of operations through institutional and personal contacts. Especially since his imperial appointment, Mozart may have been waiting for an opportunity to visit some of the major northern musical centers where his music had been performed for years.

Traveling to Dresden, Leipzig, and Berlin was intended, in contrast to the Frankfurt trip, not only to establish new relations and

Table 2.1. Mozart's Itinerary, April–June 1789

DATES	STATIONS
April 8 (Wed.)–April 12 (Sun.)	Departs Vienna via Prague,[a] arrives Dresden on Easter Sunday: stays 5 full days[b]
April 18 (Sat.)–April 20 (Mon.)	Departs Dresden, arrives Leipzig: stays 3 full days
April 24 (Fri.)–April 26 (Sun.)	Departs Leipzig, arrives Potsdam: stays 5 full days
May 2 (Sat.)	Departs Potsdam, arrives Berlin: stays 2 full days
May 5 (Tue.)–May 8 (Fri.)	Departs Berlin via Potsdam,[c] arrives Leipzig:[d] stays 8 full days
May 17 (Sun.)–May 19 (Tue.)	Departs Leipzig, arrives Berlin: stays 8 full days
May 28 (Thu.)–June 4 (Thu.)	Departs Berlin via Prague,[c] arrives Vienna

a. Half-day stopover. b. Full days exclusive of travel. c. One-day stopover. d. Spring trade fair (*Ostermesse*), May 3–12.

earn money but also to become acquainted for the first time with an area that was of considerable musical significance in Protestant Germany yet completely unfamiliar to Mozart. When his father Leopold ambitiously mapped out his European tours in the early 1760s to show his musical children around, the Seven Years' War between Austria and Prussia (1756–63), which resulted in Empress Maria Theresa's losing traditionally Austrian Silesia, was still dragging on. Hence he limited the itineraries from Salzburg to the east, west, northwest, and south in such a way that they avoided all territories either allied with Prussia or affected by a war that now, in 1789, had long become history. It does not surprise us, therefore, that Mozart cast an eye on, and felt drawn to, this part of the world, which boasted some of the most attractive musical centers in Europe.

Mozart did not wait for a formal invitation but took advantage of a business trip to Berlin made by his Masonic brother, admirer, and piano student Carl von Lichnowsky (fig. 2.1), who thanks to his privileged status might open doors to the royal courts in Dresden and Berlin otherwise closed to commoners. The prince's family owned estates in Silesia, which lay in Prussian territory since the end of the Seven Years' War, and so they had to divide their loy-

2.1. Prince Carl von Lichnowsky, miniature by an unknown artist (*Bonn, Beethoven-Haus*)

alty and balance it between Vienna and Berlin.[19] The journey was not planned much in advance, nor was it prepared in any detail. On the contrary, the erratic itinerary and the sequence of events demonstrate that almost everything happened ad hoc. Also, it remains unclear where the initiatives originated—whether the composer asked Lichnowsky for the favor of letting him accompany him on the upcoming trip or if the invitation came from the prince. At any rate, the two-month tour took place in the aftermath of the carnival season, when earning possibilities in wartime Vienna were especially bleak.

Mozart had high hopes for success, as the first two lines of the little poem he wrote for Constanze shortly before his departure indicates: "When I shall travel to Berlin / I truly hope for much honor and glory . . ."[20] In the end, however, Mozart's total cash receipts from the trip were on the meager side. To this must be added the bizarre story that the prince, claiming serious cash-flow problems, borrowed 100 florins from his companion.[21] It happened around May 15, when the two travelers parted, since Mozart extended the journey in order to return to Berlin. All in all, he brought home some 700 florins. On the other hand, had he stayed home instead, he would hardly have earned a fraction of the sum he collected on the trip and, furthermore, would have let pass the many musically relevant connections he was able to make.

Mozart's letters to his wife Constanze during this important journey, which began on April 8, 1789, and ended on June 4, provide the available information on the various stops and events. However, since a number of the letters were lost in the mail and never reached Vienna,[22] very little of what happened in Potsdam (5 days), Berlin (10 days), and Leipzig (11 days) can actually be accounted for. The few principal income-producing performances included an April 14 concert at the Dresden palace of King Friedrich August III that featured the Piano Concerto in D major, K. 537. It was followed by a public competition on April 15 with Johann Wilhelm Hässler on both organ and fortepiano. In Leipzig the main event consisted of a concert on May 12 in the Gewandhaus with a particularly rich program. For Berlin, only a single recital is recorded, on May 26 in the royal palace and in the presence of Queen Friederike Luise. The elaborate Leipzig program (fig. 2.2; see also below, p. 67), presented by the Gewandhaus Orchestra in a public concert hall to a predominantly bourgeois audience and lasting more than three hours, clearly stands out in every respect, for Mozart was able to introduce himself in an all-inclusive way as conductor, pianist, and composer of instrumental and vocal works. All the more disappointing for Mozart was the apparent disparity between artistic effort and financial reward in the face of an appallingly small audience. He reported to Constanze: "The concert was a splendid success as far as applause and honors go, but it was all the more disappointing in terms of income."[23]

This unsatisfactory outcome is symptomatic and relates first and foremost to the ad hoc arrangements that had to be made throughout the

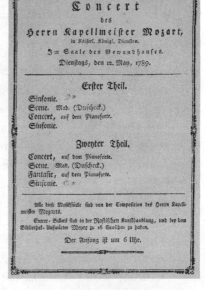

2.2. Playbill of Mozart's Leipzig Gewandhaus concert of May 12, 1789 (*Leipzig, Stadtgeschichtliches Museum*)

entire tour. In the absence of sufficient advance planning, which at least to some extent was customary at the time, the various private and public appearances all had to be arranged on short notice. The ambitious Gewandhaus concert, too, apparently was hastily arranged only after Mozart reached Leipzig on April 18. The date was set for May 12, even though he would have to return from Berlin in order to take advantage of the Leipzig spring trade fair, which traditionally brought some 30,000 guests from all over Europe to the city. The composer was by no means unknown in Leipzig, which boasted a flourishing musical culture, the oldest bourgeois orchestra in Germany, and a rising music trade and publishing business. His instrumental works had been performed by Johann Adam Hiller in Gewandhaus programs since 1781; *Die Entführung aus dem Serail* saw its first Leipzig performances in 1783 and *Don Giovanni* in 1788, the latter running parallel with the Vienna production.[24] Yet, despite the proper advertising of the "Concert given by Herr Kapellmeister Mozart, in imperial-royal service," the house was papered because the arrangements for bringing together a large paying audience toward the end of the spring trade fair proved to be insufficient.[25] At the same time, Mozart realized that the "splendid success" of his visit left a lasting impression on the audience and especially on the various musical institutions in Leipzig, so the concert tour could only further his career.

Long-term benefits were surely on Mozart's mind when he met some leading figures in the various music centers. Therefore, he would hardly have underestimated the wide-ranging influence of certain key musicians such as the Saxon Oberkapellmeister Johann Gottlieb Naumann, one of whose masses he heard at the Dresden Hofkirche; the director of chamber music at the Prussian court, Jean-Pierre Duport; the Leipzig Thomaskantor Johann Friedrich Doles; his substitute, successor, and former Gewandhaus kapellmeister Johann Adam Hiller; and the current Gewandhaus kapellmeister, director, and later Thomaskantor, Johann Gottfried Schicht.

An unplanned result of the visit to Dresden was a silverpoint

2.3. Wolfgang Amadé Mozart, silverpoint drawing by Doris Stock, Dresden, 1789 (*Salzburg, Stiftung Mozarteum*)

portrait of Mozart, drawn from life on ivory paper by the artist Doris Stock. Created on April 16 or 17, 1789,[26] it is the last of several extant portraits of the composer that originated during his lifetime. The particular hairstyle he is shown wearing here, as on other portraits, may well have been cultivated specifically to cover his ears, which were both notably deformed.

An anonymous drawing from around 1820 purports to compare one of Mozart's deformed ears with a common ear. The drawing, which is reproduced as a plate in Georg Nikolaus von Nissen's 1828 biography, bears the annotations "Mein Ohr" (my ear) and "ein gewöhnliches Ohr" (a common ear), written by Mozart's youngest son, Franz Xaver Wolfgang (1791–1844), whose ear it actually represents. The word "Mein" was crossed out and "Mozarts" was written in by Nissen, Franz Xaver's stepfather,[27] who in his biography (p. 586) refers to the ears the son had inherited from his father.

Mozart's unusually shaped external ear (missing earlobe, tragus/ antitragus, and conch) was early on considered evidence of the composer's unusual musical gifts. Beginning in the late nineteenth century, however, anatomical and pathological studies interpreted the

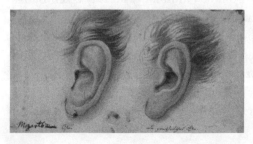

2.4. Mozart's ear vs. common ear, anonymous watercolor (*Cambridge, Mass., Harvard University, Houghton Library*)

congenital malformation in conjunction with the otorenal complex as evidence of chronic kidney problems and the likelihood that kidney failure caused the composer's death.[28]

Mozart spent time twice in the secondary residence of the Prussian kings in Potsdam, eighteen miles southwest of Berlin, but apparently waited in vain for public or private engagements. King Friedrich Wilhelm II was present in Potsdam at the time and did receive notification of Mozart's arrival and his wish "to worship His Royal Majesty with his talents."[29] But the king did not make himself available and referred him to Duport, his cellist and director of chamber music. On April 29 in Potsdam, Mozart composed the K. 573 piano variations based on a minuet by Duport. For the next stop in nearby Berlin, nothing is documented either, except for a brief newspaper report announcing the arrival of Prince Carl von Lichnowsky on May 2 in his coach-and-four and his departure three days later; Mozart is not even mentioned.[30] The composer's later stay in Berlin without Lichnowky was planned for eight full days, as he indicated from Leipzig in a letter to Constanze ("It appears I will *have* to stay at least a week in Berlin"),[31] but without giving any reason for the prolonged stay. The phrase as such suggests, however, that he had received engagements which required him to stay that long. Yet, only three are documentable.

On the evening of May 19, the day of his second arrival in Berlin, Mozart attended a performance of *Die Entführung,* which had been in the repertoire of the Nationaltheater in Berlin since October 1788. Four days later, he was present at the concert of the gifted nine-year-old Johann Nepomuk Hummel, who was taken by his father on an extended European concert tour, 1788 to 1792. Hummel had been Mozart's pupil since 1786 and, in recognition of the little boy's talents, he taught him without fee. On May 26, Mozart finally was able to perform before the Prussian queen in the royal palace. Nothing further is documented, not even when, where, and through whom he received the royal commission for a set of six string quartets and the 100 Friedrichs d'or (700 florins)[32] he brought home to Vienna. All the other income went into his hotel, transportation, and other travel expenses. With the prince gone, he no longer enjoyed a free ride, but one may safely assume that the imperial kapellmeister would continue to travel in style.

What else could have made Mozart stay a full eight days? Berlin in the 1780s and '90s saw a remarkable rise in bourgeois musical culture, so Mozart most likely got involved in some of the flourishing concert venues and salons of the city. The most active concert series was run by Johann Friedrich Carl Rellstab, who owned the oldest music store, lending library, and publishing business in Berlin.[33] Himself a fine keyboard player, he had been a pupil of Johann Friedrich Agricola, a student of Johann Sebastian Bach's, but he later abandoned plans to study with Carl Philipp Emanuel Bach in Hamburg and instead took over his father's printing firm. In 1787, Rellstab established a subscription series of "Concerts for Connoisseurs and Amateurs." They took place biweekly, either at members' homes or, fairly regularly, at the Hotel Zur Stadt Paris. Curiously, the Hotel Paris is where Mozart is known to have stayed during his second Berlin sojourn.[34] Therefore, it seems likely that Rellstab not only had a hand in making lodging arrangements for Mozart but also let him play in his series. Indeed, on May 9 (that is, shortly after Mozart's first Berlin sojourn), Rellstab ran an ad in the newspaper *Berlinische Nachrichten von Staats- und gelehrten Sachen* where he announced the availability in his store of "the complete compositions by Mozart."[35] Clearly an exaggerated notice, it likely refers only to Mozart's keyboard works, more specifically to various editions by different publishers and probably including commercial manuscript copies of unpublished keyboard works. It may well be that Mozart traveled with a representative collection of his keyboard music to sell to dealers or give copies to interested private individuals. In July 1789, merely a month or so after Mozart's second visit, Rellstab began publishing Mozart pieces, first four popular arias from *Die Entführung* and in the following years many more works in various genres—certainly one tangible result of the concert tour.[36]

For business leaders and the intelligentsia (though not for the general public), Sara Levy's musical salon represented another important gathering place in late eighteenth-century Berlin.[37] Madame Levy was the daughter of Daniel Itzig, banker of Kings Friedrich II and Friedrich Wilhelm II and, as such, the most prominent and powerful Jew in all of Prussia. Along with Moses Mendelssohn, Itzig became a key figure in developing a climate of emancipation, both civil and intellectual, that served as a model for Europe's largely ghettoized Jewish communities. A highly cultured man, Itzig made sure that his fourteen children all received a musical education; the sisters Bella (Felix Mendelssohn Bartholdy's maternal grandmother), Zippora, Fanny, and Sara were pianists. Sara, the most talented of them and a performer of professional stature, became a truly pivotal figure in the emerging bourgeois musical culture of the Prussian capital.

Sara Itzig studied in the early 1780s with Wilhelm Friedemann Bach, whom she supported financially in his old age. After her marriage in 1784 to the banker Samuel Salomon Levy, who was also musically trained, she conducted a weekly musical salon in their spacious mansion in the heart of the city, on what is now the Museum Island. Her music room featured a harpsichord and a fortepiano and could easily accommodate a small orchestra. It is evident from her extensive library that while her music programs focused on keyboard and chamber music, they also included orchestral works, primarily keyboard concertos. For example, she commissioned Carl Philipp Emanuel Bach's last work, the Double Concerto in E-flat major, Wq 47, for harpsichord, fortepiano, and orchestra of 1788. Her salon attracted musical connoisseurs from among Berlin's financial and intellectual elite, including the brothers Alexander and Wilhelm von Humboldt, the theologian Friedrich Schleiermacher, and the philosopher Johann Gottlieb Fichte. She herself also performed in public as keyboard soloist—notably at the concerts of the Berlin Sing-Akademie founded in 1791—until around 1810, when she retired and gradually gave away much of her considerable music collection to the Sing-Akademie and to individual musicians of the younger generation.

Mozart likely came into contact with Madame Levy during his Berlin trip and may have performed in her salon, since he had a close connection with her family. Sara's older sister Fanny happened to have moved to Vienna in 1776 after marrying the banker Nathan Adam Arnstein,[38] and was Mozart's landlady for eleven months beginning in August 1781. He took "a very prettily furnished room"[39] in the large house "Auf dem Graben" (inner city, no. 1175) primarily occupied by the Arnstein family.[40] Though he lived there on the third floor among the family's coachmen, valets, and maids, he must have communicated with the musically well-educated lady of the house.[41] The name Arnstein appears among the subscribers to Mozart's private concert series given in 1784 at the Trattnerhof. Thus, she belonged to Mozart's patrons, along with Maria Christine von Lichnowsky, wife of Mozart's travel companion of 1789, whose name is also found on the same subscription list.[42]

Although Fanny Arnstein does not turn up in Mozart documents after 1784, she belonged to van Swieten's circle and played an influential role after 1800 in setting up the Gesellschaft der Musikfreunde in Vienna. At any rate, the Arnstein connection provided a personal link to Sara Levy that Mozart could hardly have missed. As Madame Levy, Mozart's junior by five years, often visited with her sister Fanny, an earlier encounter with Mozart in Vienna lies in the realm of possibility, too. And finally, Sara's husband Salomon Levy, also an active musician, was a Freemason. Hence, the Masonic travelers from Vienna had fellow Masons at the Tolerance Lodge, the Berlin lodge that accepted Jews by special permission of King Friedrich Wilhelm II.[43] This connection could have proven even more useful to Mozart when, staying in Berlin for the second time, he no longer had his princely escort.

Bach Circles at Home and Abroad

CARL VON LICHNOWSKY, Mozart's travel companion of 1789, came to be known best as Ludwig van Beethoven's earliest and strongest patron. Between 1795 and 1804, Beethoven dedicated to him, among other works, such momentous compositions as the Piano Trios, op. 1, the *Sonate pathétique*, op. 13, the Piano Sonata in A-flat major, op. 26, and the Second Symphony. A dedicated and experienced musician, Lichnowsky had studied law in Leipzig and Göttingen for six years before returning to his native Vienna in 1782. His legal studies apparently left him enough room to nourish his musical interests and improve his keyboard skills.[44]

Lichnowsky must have gotten to know Mozart fairly soon after returning to Vienna, for he, too, became a regular guest at concerts sponsored by Baron Gottfried van Swieten, a friend of Carl Philipp Emanuel Bach's and a passionate promoter of Handel and Bach's music. Mozart had participated in his various concert venues from early 1782 and later, as imperial kapellmeister, took on a major role by conducting Handel oratorios and other large-scale works, beginning in March 1788 with C. P. E. Bach's oratorio *Die Auferstehung und Himmelfahrt Jesu*, Wq 240. The prince's younger brother Moritz studied piano with Mozart for some time, and Carl himself later took lessons with him as well. Initial contacts between the prince and Mozart may have gone through Mozart's early Viennese patroness Maria Wilhelmine Countess Thun-Hohenstein, whose daughter, Maria Christine, would marry Carl von Lichnowsky in 1788. Beyond this, both Mozart and Lichnowsky joined the Freemasons at the Viennese lodge Zur Wohltätigkeit

2.5. Baron Gottfried van Swieten, engraving by Johann Georg Mansfeld, 1790 (*Vienna, Österreichische Nationalbibliothek*)

in the same year—1784—perhaps also the time when the prince started to study with the composer.[45]

Mozart in all likelihood went to the prince's mansion to give the lessons, saw Lichnowsky's music collection, and noticed that his shelves held more works by Johann Sebastian Bach than he had previously had access to. Today the collection is no longer intact, but still extant from it are manuscripts of Bach's Inventions and Sinfonias, BWV 772–801; the English Suites, BWV 806–811; the French Suite, BWV 814; the Suite in E-flat major, BWV 819; the Fantasy in C minor, BWV 906; and the Six Preludes, BWV 933–938.[46]

During his Leipzig student days, from 1776 to 1780, Lichnowsky probably received music instruction from the Thomaskantor and former Bach student Johann Friedrich Doles. In Göttingen, from October 1780, he established a close connection with—and likely became a student of—Johann Nikolaus Forkel, who would eventually write the first Bach biography, *Ueber Johann Sebastian Bachs Leben, Kunst und Kunstwerke* (Leipzig, 1802). Forkel's extensive manuscript collection of Bach's keyboard works formed the basis for the copies in Lichnowsky's own collection, most of them dating from 1782, the year of his departure from Göttingen. Mozart, of course, needed no introduction to Bach's music, but the possibility to converse with someone who, unlike other Bach enthusiasts, was familiar with the original Bach sites in Leipzig as well as the exposure to more Bach music would certainly have interested him and perhaps given Lichnowsky's lessons a special flavor.

Lichnowsky represented the younger generation, but Mozart had at least one admirer among the older Viennese noblemen who had been a direct keyboard student of Bach's, Count Wrbna-Freudenthal, a subscriber to his private academies in 1784.[47]

A Leipzig connection also pertained to another academy subscriber, Reichshofrat Carl Adolph von Braun,[48] the highest-ranking Lutheran justice in the imperial court. One of the first noblemen Mozart came in closer contact with in Vienna, he referred to him as "the greatest connoisseur of piano music."[49] A law student in Leipzig during the 1730s, Braun apparently played a part in the Bach circle and later in Vienna maintained close ties with C. P. E. Bach. The older generation of Leipzigers finally included the most powerful man in Vienna after the emperor, the imperial chancellor Wenzel Anton von Kaunitz-Rietberg, who had received his law degree from the University of Leipzig in 1731. Kaunitz had serious musical interests and likely encountered Bach's music, if not the composer himself, at some of the festive academic events held in conjunction with the regular visits to Leipzig of Dresden royal family members. A report of 1774 that Gottfried von Swieten, then the imperial ambassador at the Prussian court, wrote to his superior Kaunitz speaks to the prince's familiarity with Bach. Here the baron departs from politics, discusses an organ recital given by Wilhelm Friedemann Bach, and tells about a conversation he had with Friedrich II ("the Great") in which the king recalled Johann Sebastian Bach's 1747 visit to Potsdam.[50] The imperial chancellor's musical interests came across, too, when he invited Mozart to his office in 1782 after Mozart established his residence in Vienna. The composer wrote to his father about it: "At the end of my visit he said to me: I am much obliged to you, my dear Mozart, for taking the trouble of coming to see me."[51] Hence, Kaunitz must also be counted as a strong supporting force behind the scenes in obtaining a court position for Mozart.[52] Anticipating enticing offers from London, Paris, and other places abroad, he reportedly said about Mozart early on, that "such people come into this world only once in a 100 years, and they should not be driven out of Germany—especially when one is fortunate enough to have them right here in the capital,"[53] a statement that gives further credence to the rationale for the appointment in the court memorandum of December 30, 1791 (cited in chap. 1, p. 16).

Curiously, in musical Vienna, Mozart then found himself in, as it were, a Bach neighborhood, consisting of influential patrons who had either seen the phenomenal keyboard virtuoso Johann Sebastian Bach in action personally (Kaunitz and Wrbna) or maintained connections with his sons (van Swieten, von Braun, and the Itzig sisters) or with his students (Lichnowsky). They now came to admire the dazzling genius Mozart and could draw a connection between the two musicians from different eras who were without peers. Mozart himself was, of course, familiar with the Bach name since his childhood days. After all, he sat on the lap of Bach's son, Johann Christian, in London in 1764; explored as a fourteen-year-old how to write piano concertos (K. 107) by adapting Johann Christian's sonatas op. 5; and began in the early 1770s studying fugues by Johann Sebastian.[54] Still, in Vienna the young composer experienced Bach in a different context, especially when he became involved with the circle of musical connoisseurs around Baron van Swieten.

When Mozart wrote to his father on April 10, 1782,[55] "Every Sunday at 12 noon I go to visit Baron van Suiten [*sic*]—and there we play nothing but Händl [*sic*] and Bach.—I am just putting together a collection of Bach fugues—that is Sebastian as well as Emanuel and Friedemann Bach," he actually wrote the letter in his third-floor room in the Arnstein house.[56] Mozart's manuscript collection has not survived, but some manuscripts from Fanny Arnstein's rich collection of Bachiana, most of which she brought from Berlin, still exist, among them a copy of six fugues by C. P. E. Bach, Wq 119, and her copy of a two-piano arrangement of J. S. Bach's trio sonatas for organ, BWV 525–530, three movements of which Mozart arranged for string trio (K. 404a).[57] Wilhelm Friedemann Bach's "Eight Fugues," Fk. 31, might well have been there, too, for they were particularly popular with the Itzig family and were mostly kept together with fugues from J. S. Bach's *Well-Tempered Clavier*. Therefore, the major sources for Mozart's study collection of fugues by the three Bachs were conveniently located on his landlady's music shelves.

For both Lichnowsky and Mozart, the joint trip of 1789 must have been a meaningful experience, though in different ways. Traveling in the company of a world-famous musician could only bring luster to the prince and make him socially more attractive. For Mozart, Lichnowsky's noble rank would play a role at court visits, but in particular, the prince could serve as a competent guide in the Bach city. Though not located on the direct route from Dresden to Berlin, Lichnowsky's business destination, Leipzig must have been on the itinerary from the outset. Mozart knew that his work was not unknown there, for he had learned six years earlier of the success of the Leipzig performance of his singspiel: "My German opera *Die Entführung aus dem Serail* has been performed both in Prague and Leipzig excellently and with the greatest applause," he informed his father at the time.[58] For Lichnowsky, on the other hand, it meant a return to a familiar place where he had lived and studied for four years and where he could now introduce his music teacher to the Bach sites in a city that prided itself on its musical traditions and continuing musical activities. It is reasonable to assume that the encounter with Bach's historic neighborhood in Leipzig represented a strong interest of both travelers, in light of the general Bach focus of the journey, the connection with the Bach circle in Vienna, and the expected contacts with Berlin's Bach circle and the Itzig family's "Bach cult." Mozart certainly was neither a naïve Bach worshiper nor a retrospectively oriented composer, but in his own search for musical innovation, particularly at this more public stage of his career, he was continually fascinated by the surprises and challenges he found in Bach's music.

The task of making the various individual and institutional contacts in Leipzig fell to Carl Immanuel Engel, organist of the Catholic court chapel in the Pleissenburg, at the time the only Catholic house of worship in the Lutheran city. Engel was also impresario of a public concert series in the Apel House at Market Square, conductor of the Italian opera productions in the Leipzig theater, and organizer of the musical presentations at the Freemasons' Lodge, adjacent to the Pleissenburg.[59] He was not yet organist at the Pleissenburg when Lichnowsky had attended Mass there, so the two of them would not have met before. On the other hand, Mozart might have learned that Engel had conducted the first Leipzig performance of *Don Giovanni* in 1788, less than a year before his visit. It was staged there by the Guardasoni troupe, the same company that had premiered the work under the composer's direction in Prague.[60]

Two private concerts were held at houses of prominent Leipzig music patrons.[61] The first one took place shortly after Mozart's arrival on April 21 or 22 at the home of Ernst Platner, professor of medicine and a former rector of the university, and the second three weeks later at the home of Christian Friedrich Ludwig, another medical professor, dated by an entry Mozart made on May 13 in the friendship album of Ludwig's wife.

Platner, an influential board member of the Gewandhaus concerts, expressed delight over Mozart's playing at his house[62] and may have played a decisive role in making the last-minute arrangements for Mozart's appearance in the city on May 12 during the time of the trade fair. A former student of the St. Thomas School and a pupil of Thomaskantor Doles, Platner taught physiology, though he would later switch to philosophy. Already in the late 1770s, when Lichnowsky studied in Leipzig, he offered lectures in aesthetics that specifically touched on Johann Sebastian Bach's art of composing fugues. In characterizing the phenomenon of the sublime, he used "the Bachian fugue as an example of the basic aesthetic gestalt (*ästhetische Grundgestalt*) of the great or strong. . . . It is like a drop of fortifying spirit."[63] Platner's conversation with Mozart may well have gone in such a direction and given Mozart an opportunity to react, perhaps by referring to his concept for the finale of his "Jupiter" Symphony. The idea of the sublime played a major role in the aesthetic theory of the symphony in the late eighteenth century, and it was a subject of genuine interest to Mozart.[64]

By 1789 the cultivation of Bach's music was firmly established at Leipzig and Berlin, the two main centers of uninterrupted Bach tradition, and it was established almost as well in Vienna. In addition, a growing number of literary references helped launch Bach's legendary reputation. In a typical example, the Berlin kapellmeister

Johann Friedrich Reichardt extollingly announced, in 1781, the first complete edition of Bach's four-part chorales, published by Breitkopf (1784–87), and coined the phrase "the greatest harmonist of all times and nations." Although familiar with a good range of Bach's works and well aware of the composer's significance, Mozart could hardly have been prepared for the degree of Bach veneration found among music connoisseurs in Leipzig and Berlin. At the same time, he himself defined this atmosphere of veneration in his own way by playing, without preparation, a free public organ recital in the St. Thomas Church on April 22. Although performing on a substantially rebuilt organ that had very little in common with the instrument of Bach's time, Mozart improvised so admirably for an hour that no less an expert than Thomaskantor Doles felt as if "old Seb. Bach (his teacher) had risen from the dead."[65] According to an eyewitness report, Mozart "applied all artful harmonic procedures in very good taste and with the greatest facility and developed the themes extempore magnificently, among them the Lutheran chorale "Jesus, meine Zuversicht."

Mozart also visited the St. Thomas School, next to the church. If he was received in Cantor Doles's office there, he would have set foot in what was once Bach's composing room (*Componirstube*). Later, Mozart "expressed fervent reverence upon listening to one of his [Bach's] motets and looking at his works." The choir apparently sang for him its showpiece, Bach's vocally demanding motet "Singet dem Herrn ein neues Lied," BWV 225, a piece of polyphony that clearly stunned the Viennese composer. And in order to satisfy his curiosity, he ordered a manuscript copy of the motet for eight voices.[66]

Three weeks later, after Mozart's return from Berlin, the Gewandhaus concert on May 12 gave him the opportunity to amaze his audience and confront them with works they could not have heard before, because almost all were of recent origin and none of them published or available in manuscript circulation. Mozart must have brought his personal performing parts with him from Vienna. The extended and difficult program (fig. 2.2, above) required much preparation even for a professional ensemble like the Gewandhaus Orchestra, so Mozart probably used much of the time since his arrival on May 8 for rehearsals. The concert had two parts:

    I. Symphony in D Major, K. 504, "Prague," movement 1; Scena *Ch'io mi scordi di te*, K. 505, with soprano Josepha Dušek; Piano concerto in B-flat Major, K. 456; "Prague" Symphony, movements 2–3).

    II. Piano Concerto in C Major, K. 503; Scena *Bella mia fiamma*, K. 528, with Mme. Dušek; Fantasie (improvised piano solo); Symphony in C Major, K. 551, "Jupiter."[67]

The program, not only of extraordinary length (almost three hours) but probably the most ambitious one Mozart ever undertook, demonstrated to players and listeners an exceptional degree of innovation at all levels. Even the only older work on the program, the B-flat-major piano concerto of 1784, was something special: its heavenly, expressive Andante in G minor has no parallel as a set of variations—with its crossing-over modulation to B minor and polymetrical juxtapositions of $\frac{2}{4}$ with $\frac{6}{8}$ time. The two symphonies embodied the symphonic genre on a scale unheard of, and both concertos featured extraordinary instrumental interplay between soloist, strings, and winds. The virtuoso concert arias with obbligato piano were included to evince the vocal art of Josepha Dušek of Prague, one of Mozart's favorite singers, as well as the sophisticated yet moving musical language of the opera composer and his pianistic prowess. Moreover, the orchestral scores of all the pieces show an unusual variety of instrumental textures and colors, culminating in a wind complement of 1 or 2 flutes, 2 oboes, 2 bassoons, 2 horns, 2 trumpets, and timpani in the symphonies and the concerto, while the aria K. 505 calls for 2 clarinets, 2 bassoons, 2 horns, solo piano, and strings.

The concert concluded with the "Jupiter" Symphony. The Leipzig

2.6a–b. Gigue in G major, K. 574, Leipzig 1789 (Vienna: Artaria, 1792)
(*Dresden, Sächsische Landes- und Universitätsbibliothek*)

performance of this work in the context of the other compositions reflected well-calculated and imaginative programming on Mozart's part. The grand program that featured him as composer-conductor-soloist was crowned by a complex contrapuntal finale, a movement showing a new orchestral polyphonic vision. Though certainly not conceived as an homage to Bach, the master of fugal polyphony, the Leipzig performance of the finale would surely have evoked such thoughts among the connoisseurs. Then, wrapping up his visit in the Bach city a few days later, he paid another, more private tribute to the spirit of the local genius. On May 16, his last day in Leipzig, he wrote "a little Gigue" into the friendship album of Carl Immanuel Engel and entered this musical miniature of intricate polyphony in his own thematic catalog on the following day. Engel had apparently done a lot of legwork in order to accommodate his Viennese guests and, especially, to facilitate venues for the musical star, so Mozart wanted to thank and honor his young colleague with an appropriate gesture.

Engel would not have misread what Mozart intended to communicate: the Gigue in G Major, K. 574 (fig. 2.6), was certainly meant to be a token of gratitude—"true friendship and brotherly love," according to the dedication—but at the same time it acknowledged the composer's debt to two of his musical idols, Bach *and* Handel. The short piece of 38 measures picks up on the gigue of Handel's Suite no. 8 in F minor, HWV 433/5, from the *Suites de pieces pour le clavecin* (London, 1720). The Handel movement serves as a model for the basic rhythmic-melodic, textural, and formal layout of the gigue. Bach-style elements enter via the chromaticized shape of the theme, the application of thematic inversion at the beginning of the second part, and the harmonically enriching chords in both right and left hands. Mozart ingeniously synthesizes the various components and peppers the setting by applying differentiated and intricate articulation marks, by constantly oscillating between major and minor modes, and by emphasizing an asymmetric and syncopated rhythmic drive that hammers out, in measure 22, the accented notes *B-flat* and *A* in the left hand, followed by *c″* and *b′* in the right—spelling out in German nomenclature B-A-C-H. The piece, in a nutshell, represents Mozart's aesthetic goal of imaginative compositional innovation on the basis of the best available traditional craftsmanship. He calls it "a little gigue" but it does not fit the nature of an old-fashioned suite movement; rather, it anticipates the type of fanciful character piece that would later emerge in the Mendelssohn-Schumann generation.

Judging from the calligraphy of the entry, Mozart did not compose the work directly into Engel's album but copied it from a draft or composing score. He may first have improvised the piece at one or more of the house concerts in Leipzig and Berlin and then written it down on paper, from which he copied it into the album.[68] Mozart took the composing manuscript, which is now lost, back to Vienna and gave the piece to his publisher Artaria, who surely recognized its unique character. Artaria printed the gigue as a freestanding little piece on a small bifolio and issued it in 1792, only a few months after the composer's death.[69]

Mozart's 1789 visit left particularly lasting impressions in Leipzig, where he established close connections that could have developed into more fruitful relationships. But as time took its course, only his widow Constanze Mozart would benefit from the excitement over her husband's musical visit. Five years after Mozart's death and three years after the performances of his Requiem in Süssmayr's completion in Vienna and Wiener Neustadt, the first presentation of the Requiem beyond the original performing sites was mounted 1796 in Leipzig at the Gewandhaus under the direction of Johann Gottfried Schicht. The composer's widow had provided the score and attended the performance.[70] During her stay in Leipzig, the music publisher Breitkopf opened discussions with her about future Mozart editions.[71]

On a different stage, Mozart's relations with Prince Lichnowsky soured some time after their joint trip though not likely because of it. The context and reasons lie completely in the dark, for Lichnowsky's name does not appear in connection with Mozart documents until about a month before the composer's death. On November 9, 1791, the prince filed a lawsuit against Mozart seeking payment for an "unrecoverable debt" amounting to 1,435 florins and 32 kreuzer, either by way of seizure or by withholding the sum from his court salary.[72] It is not known whether Mozart ever learned of this suit before falling ill, but Lichnowsky apparently dropped it after learning of the composer's death and maintained silence about the matter. Maybe the somewhat eccentric man later realized that he had misjudged Mozart's situation and, therefore, wanted to make up for it by being particularly generous to the young Beethoven, whom he invited to live in his house after the composer's arrival in Vienna and, curiously, took him too in 1796 on a trip to Dresden, Leipzig, and Berlin. That relationship, however, also cooled off later when in 1806, in an ironic turn of events, the prince fell into disfavor with Beethoven.[73]

Personal characters and human relations aside, the impact of Vienna's Bach circle on Mozart, and by extension on the history of musical composition, can hardly be overestimated.[74] Its loosely linked members represented an eminent nucleus of Mozart's musically well-educated and critical audience, listeners who could admire spectacular instrumental virtuosity just as much as complex and demanding compositional designs and, therefore, had high expectations for both the quality and depth of a piece of music. This nucleus can be identified from the list of subscribers to Mozart's private academies of 1784,[75] the only list that helps determine his principal audience in Vienna, his students, and the hosts of his house concerts. It reveals a group of listeners knowing, collecting, studying, and performing music by Johann Sebastian Bach and his sons. They included two constituencies: (1) the older generation of Wrbna, Braun, and Kaunitz, to which the prefect of the imperial library, Gottfried van Swieten—later Mozart's main sponsor—was a newcomer; and (2) a more contemporary company with Fanny Arnstein, Prince Lichnowsky, Franz Joseph Prince Dietrichstein, whose father Franz Ludwig had at one time also taken lessons with Bach in Leipzig, and the imperial knight Franz Joseph von Hess, about whose music library a contemporary remarked, "what Handel and the three Bachs have written can be found there."[76] To these must be added Ferdinand Philipp Prince Lobkowicz, who around 1750 in Berlin composed a symphony, alternating for the fun of it measure by measure with Carl Philipp Emanuel Bach,[77] and Mozart's senior colleague and friend, the court organist Johann Georg Albrechtsberger with his rich holdings of Bach materials, who was also in touch with the Viennese Bach enthusiasts.

Mozart could not have wished for a better environment of musically discriminating listeners who could appreciate his unique and innovative way of responding to the challenges of Bach's art of free and strict composition, daring harmonies, modern polyphony and, in short, his "musical wisdom," as Haydn once put it.[78] They also must have realized how, at the same time, Mozart was able to lift what he internalized onto a refined new plateau as, for example, in the six string quartets originating between 1782 and 1784, a set later published and dedicated to Haydn. Mozart could communicate in particular with these very listeners who did not make him shy away from complex textures and contrapuntal devices even in opera, where it was least expected. In this regard the composer could engage in a dialogue with at least a select part of his listeners yet without neglecting the audience at large. Without recourse to the retrospective style that was favored in the more conservative, theoretically and philosophically minded Bach circles in Leipzig and Berlin, Mozart—keenly aware of the emperor's love of fugues though in a taste prevailingly shaped by Italian conventions[79]— turned the lively, largely aristocratic, and hence powerful Viennese Bach tradition very much in a creative direction with a remarkable demonstration of innovative compositional procedures based on Bach's technical models. This all happened before Haydn took up residence in Vienna and Beethoven arrived there. The latter had studied Bach's *Well-Tempered Clavier* under his teacher Christian

Gottlob Neefe in Bonn, and Haydn, who in 1799 referred to Bach as "the man from whom all true musical wisdom proceeded,"[80] acquired for himself a score of the B-minor Mass, possibly only in 1804 from the van Swieten estate.[81] But neither of them experienced the kind of interaction Mozart lived through in Vienna. By way of this dynamic communication with his cultured and encouraging musical audience, he established an excitingly novel foundation for a synthesis of solid compositional craft and imaginative musical discourse that differs substantially from the mere utilization of polyphonic techniques and devices well known in Vienna and that will be discussed in greater detail in the following chapter. Yet, for this nonretrospective breaking of new musical ground, the little Gigue K. 574 makes as exemplary a case as the overture to *The Magic Flute* on a much grander scale. His original manner of connecting with Bachian principles created one of the decisive factors in what gave the new Viennese style its classic basis.

3

Grand Ambitions: Expanding Compositional Horizons

◆ ◆ ◆

A Musical Announcement

THE IMPERIAL DECREE about Mozart's appointment, signed by Franz Xaver Wolfgang Count Orsini-Rosenberg, General Theater Director (*Generalspektakeldirektor*), reads:

From His Apostolic Majesty, Emperor of the Holy Roman Empire, King of Hungary and Bohemia, Archduke of Austria, etc. Our most gracious sovereign, concerning Wolfgang Mozart, graciously appended: that it has been H[is]. I[mperial]. & R[oyal]. Apost[olic]. Maj[esty].'s pleasure to do him the most signal honor of appointing him H[is]. M[ajesty's]. Kammermusikus, in view of his knowledge and ability in music and the approbation he has earned thereby, and to graciously command the I. & R. Treasury to assign him a salary of eight hundred florins per annum from 1 December of this year.

In pursuance of which the Imperial resolution is herewith imparted to the said Wolfgang Mozart and the present decree of the High Chamberlain's Office drawn up at Imperial command at his guarantee.

Rosenberg.

Pres. I. & R. High Chamberlain's Office.

Vienna, 7 December 1787.[1]

This appointment to imperial service was without question the single most important external event to befall Mozart since moving from Salzburg to Vienna. For him, Vienna was clearly the place to be, as he indicated on April 4, 1781, in a letter to his father shortly after his arrival there: "I can assure you that this here is a magnificent place—and for *my Métier* the best place in the world."[2] A year later, he moderated his view somewhat, but presented himself in a demonstratively self-assured manner: "These Viennese gentlemen, by whom I mean mainly the emperor, had better not think that I am on this earth alone for the sake of Vienna.—There is no monarch in the world I'd rather serve than the emperor—but I shall not go begging for a post here."[3] And so he apparently never did, but when he was finally offered an appointment, he hastened to spread the word, publicizing it as quickly and widely as possible. No newspaper or official bulletin, however, heralded Mozart's elevation to a court post;[4] even his sister in Salzburg learned about it only from a letter she received from her brother on December 19.[5] Troubled or not by the lack of official court broadcast, Mozart took this public relations matter into his own hands and did so by making use of the medium he was able to control—music.

On January 3, 1788, he entered in his thematic catalog "An Allegro and Andante for piano solo."[6] The two sonata movements in F major and B-flat major, K. 533, were the first compositional efforts undertaken after the imperial appointment and were intended for a three-movement sonata cycle. For the final movement, however, Mozart turned to an extant composition, the Rondo in F, K. 494. He then rushed the sonata to the printer's so that the new work, the

3.1. Piano Sonata in F major, K. 533, title page (Vienna: Hoffmeister, 1788) (*Cambridge, Mass., Harvard University, Houghton Library*)

Sonata in F major, K. 533,[7] was available on the market by late January or early February 1788.[8] Its title page now featured the important news: the line below the author's name read in prominent lettering "au Service de sa Majesté I[mperial]. et R[oyal]" (fig. 3.1).

At about the same time or a little later, the C-minor Fugue for Two Pianos, K. 426, appeared on the market and repeated on its title page the announcement, not in French but in Italian: "all attuale Servizio di Sua Maesta J: ë R:" (fig. 3.2).[9] The concurrent issuance of these two keyboard works by one and the same publisher, Hoffmeister of Vienna, was no coincidence. Their title pages demonstrate Mozart's eagerness to let the musical world know about his elevated rank. Pressed for time, he chose two earlier keyboard works—K. 426 from 1783 and K. 494 from 1786, respectively. As keyboard publications had by far the widest circulation in music, the self-advertisement in French and Italian would not only reach the right kind of audience but also, unlike notifications in local newspapers, be more broadly disseminated across Europe.

Throughout the spring of 1788, title pages and concert announcements, subscription advertisements and opera posters, contained

3.2. Fugue for Two Pianos in C minor, K. 426, title page (Vienna: Hoffmeister, 1788) (*Cambridge, Mass., Harvard University, Houghton Library*)

references to Mozart's appointment, most often in the form of "Kapellmeister Mozart in wirkl. Diensten Sr. Majestät" (in actual service of His Majesty),[10] the title Mozart himself preferred and routinely used for the rest of his life. As late as August 1788, Mozart could not help but report such detail to his sister:

> On the advertisement that was posted for the premiere of my Prague opera "Don Giovanni" . . . and on which there are certainly not *too many* particulars about me, for the management of the Imperial Theatre were responsible for it, it is stated: *The Musick is by Herr Mozart, Kapellmeister in actual service of His Majesty, the Emperor.*[11]

The appointment clearly meant much to him, as it definitely increased his prestige beyond Vienna and beyond the Hapsburg Empire. It would also not have been lost on Mozart that a composer as eminent as Franz Joseph Haydn—twenty-four years his senior, much closer in age to Gluck, and active within the Austro-Hungarian heartlands—lacked a similar imperial attribute. Moreover, and perhaps most critical, the title defined Mozart's status among the court musicians and decisively elevated and buttressed his standing within the Viennese musical community at large. How vitally important the title must have felt to him may be seen in the fact that other Viennese composers equally "in actual service of His Majesty" did not advertise their status similarly. Analogous title pages of publications by, for instance, Gluck, Salieri, Umlauff, or the court organist Johann Georg Albrechtsberger are not known.

Returning to the two keyboard publications of January 1788, the exceptionality and size of both editions were impressive and not meaningless since the two-piano fugue K. 426, extending over 119 measures on 10 pages (5 each for cembalo I and cembalo II), had no equivalent on the contemporaneous music market, and the piano sonata, K. 533, reached a lengthy 20 pages. Indeed, its unparalleled opening movement set a record for a Mozart piano sonata and most likely for all such sonatas of the time. Its 239 measures exceeded the length of its closest contender, the C-minor antecedent K. 457, by some 30 percent. Mozart also revised the Rondo K. 494 of 1786 so that the galant single piece would serve as an authoritative sonata finale and match the aspirations of the newly composed movements. He also extended the rondo by inserting an elaborate cadenzalike passage of 27 measures. Hence, the much enlarged scale of the three-movement sonata easily warranted publication as a single issue and justified the departure from the established norm of sonata prints.[12]

Beyond this, the two printed editions of K. 533 and K. 426 carried an inherent musical message as well. The composer knew well that Joseph II was especially fond of the strict polyphonic style, not only in church music but also in instrumental works. The prominent reference to "imperial service" on the title pages of both publications even raises the possibility of a surrogate dedication to the emperor.[13] The emperor himself had received a thorough musical education, could play the piano reasonably well, and liked to study scores (see fig. 1.2).[14] In one of his first letters from Vienna, Mozart reported to his father, "My main goal right now is to meet the emperor in some agreeable fashion . . . I would be so happy if I could whip through my opera [*Idomeneo*] for him and then play a fugue or two, for that's what he likes."[15] Therefore, the decision to publish the C-minor Fugue K. 426 at this juncture must be seen as an effective and public means of paying respect and expressing his gratitude to the emperor. Only a few months later, this gesture of devotion was further enhanced by the publication of a new string arrangement of the very same fugue, amended by the newly composed slow introduction, K. 546.[16] Moreover, even though the Sonata K. 533 did not include a fugue, its opening movement represented Mozart's first and only piano sonata that featured imitative polyphony from the very start; its second movement is polyphonically conceived as well. The emperor and everyone else would have immediately noticed such an unusual approach to sonata style.

Moreover, since both the Sonata K. 533 and the Fugue K. 426 embody highly polished examples of strict composition, Mozart took the high ground by presenting himself to the musical world that remembered the "wunderkind" not merely as a keyboard virtuoso but, in particular, as a master of complex musical designs. The two publications made a deliberately nonpopulist aesthetic statement by paying homage to time-honored traditional polyphony and, at the same time, by putting the latter to work in fashioning novel effects.

The extraordinarily sophisticated compositional makeups of the two sonata movements K. 533 and the substantive revision of the earlier Rondo K. 494 correspond well with one another. The fact, however, that the F-major Sonata is based on two components of different origin provoked serious and sustained criticism in Mozart scholarship, going all the way back to the work of Otto Jahn and Ludwig von Köchel in the midnineteenth century. The addition of the rondo finale was perceived as musically incoherent and culminates in an emphatic declaration like "the addition of the Rondo K. 494 to bring about a complete sonata was not by Mozart."[17] Such harsh criticism, compounded by the assignment of two numbers in the Köchel catalog (1862) and in all editions of the sonata resulted in the work's largely unfavorable reception and sporadic performances right down to the present. However, in the context in which this special sonata originated, the piece reveals its true character and signals the open and unmitigated claim of the composer to his elevated status. In fact, the ambitious sonata—whose large-scale format, intricate compositional design, and technical demands are without parallel in Mozart's keyboard music—encapsulates the composer's affirmation of the imperial distinction he received. This prompted him to challenge the musical community at large—professional colleagues, musical connoisseurs, and dilettantes alike.

The sonata as a whole represents a unique and exemplary case in more than one way.[18] First, its opening movement, like no other late-eighteenth-century piece, shows a systematic exploration of a sonata form structure with three distinct subjects and a closing idea (ex. 3.1, table 3.1).[19] Themes 1 to 3 are based on scale patterns of different rhythmic shapes and each also possesses the triadic melodic quality that is openly exposed in the chordal device of the closing idea, x. Second, the movement features thematic material designed for nonfugal yet strictly contrapuntal treatment that actually begins even before the second theme is introduced. Texturally, the sonata manifests truly equal treatment of the two hands on the keyboard. For example, themes 1 and 2 feature, in their symmetric right- and left-hand entries, elements that make them suitable for double counterpoint and imitation in close succession (ex. 3.2). They also allow for contrapuntally combining the principal ideas, as Mozart does using themes 1 and x at the very beginning of the development

Table 3.1: Overall Design of the Allegro, K. 533

SECTIONS	EXPOSITION				DEVELOPMENT				RECAPITULATION				
Sequence of ideas:	1	2	3	x	1	x	2	x	1	2	x	3+1	x
Harmonic plan:	F	C	v/v	C	c	A	d	v⁷	F	F	C	F	F
Measures:	1	42	66	89	103	116	125	140	146	169	190	193	226

3.1. Piano Sonata K. 533/I: Themes 1–3 and transition motif x.

3.2. K. 533/I: Contrapuntal imitation (mm. 33–37).

3.3. K. 533/I: Beginning of development section (mm. 103–5).

3.4. K. 533/I: Reprise, combination of themes 1 and 3 (mm. 202–8).

section (ex. 3.3) and themes 1 and 3 in leading strikingly to the culmination point of the recapitulation (ex. 3.3–4).

Thus, the complementary design of all four musical ideas—three themes and a closing group—pursues the goal of achieving formal unity by multiple means. Mozart's concept here strongly reflects the musical criteria of aesthetic coherence, which played a decisive role in molding the musical discourse of a sonata.

The issue of structural coherence was in the air. Heinrich Christoph Koch's *Musikalisches Lexikon* (Frankfurt, 1802) discusses "unity" (*Einheit*), which took on a key role in new artistic objectives.[20] Indeed, this term quickly established itself and assumed such fundamental and axiomatic importance in the philosophy of art that it soon disappeared from musical lexicography.[21] Yet, for late-eighteenth-century composers the definition and function of unity as a novel aesthetic concept was by no means self-evident. Koch, whose music dictionary was already in prepration during Mozart's lifetime, wrote what may well serve as a commentary perfectly fitting the first movement of K. 533:[22]

> If the single parts or sections of a musical piece aim by all their means at the purpose of the whole, if they are designed to serve this end and not to lead to incidental and irrelevant ideas, then one can say the total piece has unity. According to Sulzer's explanation,[23] unity is what helps us understand how many things can form parts of one and the same thing. All aestheticians agree that unity is an indispensable requirement of all products of the fine arts. This quality is a necessity inasmuch as a work of art, if we are to take pleasure in it, makes only a single total impression. However, this is not possible if the material and its elaboration lack unity.

The aesthetic question of musical unity also affects Mozart's revision of K. 494, for it is the new version of the F-major Rondo that made it suitable as a sonata finale that corresponds to the first movement. The very nature of the changes made to the slightly older piece indicates a meaningful adjustment because the inserted new section, mm. 143–69, provides a fresh and original accent (ex. 3.5a). It also features the fortepiano's low bass register, with the lower octaves no longer off-limits for the right hand—nor indeed for both hands—and Mozart thereby pays attention to a more flexible and colorful use of the instrument. (The preceding Andante movement, too, displays at the end a move into the bass register.) More important, however, is the opening and core portion of the musical insert that introduces a densely constructed and powerfully

3.5. K. 533/II: (a) Rondo, head motif; (b) contrapuntal expansion (mm. 152–57).

cascading imitative elaboration of the uncomplicated rondo theme (ex. 3.5b).

The expansion of the Rondo reflects a clear sense of polyphonic upgrading and thereby serves the purpose of unity in the sonata structure. Additionally, the insert creates a motivic analogy to the principal theme of the opening movement: Mozart stretches the ascending interval of the third in the rondo theme to a fourth and a fifth, thereby connecting the finale to the sonata's opening. It closes the cycle by providing balance to the character of the first movement, the most sophisticated polyphonic sonata movement Mozart ever wrote.

The remarkably discursive Sonata K. 533 of 1788 has no parallel among Mozart's keyboard sonatas. His last two, and again more compact, piano sonatas of 1789 in B-flat and D major, K. 570 and K. 576 (both published posthumously), continue the openly polyphonic trend but do not challenge the unique position of the F-major work. Whereas true pathos and grand expressive gestures are the composer's central concern in the earlier C-minor work K. 475, the F-major work K. 533, with its unique scale and complexity, demonstrates a primary interest in constructive thinking and transparent design as well as in intellectual and material penetration of the chosen musical substance. This is also reflected in the extreme tensions and cascading dissonances of the Andante middle movement. This grand sonata, in which Mozart presented himself to the wider European public as the new imperial court composer, was to underscore both his prestige as keyboard virtuoso and his stature as a cultured composer. At the same time, it typifies a novel, more expansive, audacious, and sophisticated approach to instrumental composition in general. After all, it stands at the very beginning of an impressive series of large-scale instrumental works that was to include the three grand symphonies of 1788 as the most stunning affirmation of what might cautiously but appropriately be referred to as Mozart's "imperial style."

The court appointment provided, apart from basic financial security, the prestige of the imperial kapellmeister title and secured for Mozart a permanent base of operation in the capital of the Hapsburg Empire. Ever since settling in Vienna, he had hoped for a court appointment. Having now been taken into "the service of his Majesty" with an annual stipend and only minimal obligations, he was able to forge and plan ahead as never before. Moreover, the new title motivated and perhaps even propelled him to demonstrate not only that he had earned and deserved it but also that he perceived the honor as a musical commitment. Mozart's subsequent creative output, and notably that of 1788, definitely supports this assumption, but the unaccustomed guaranteed income apparently also had a harmful impact in that it encouraged the composer to take greater financial risks and to live beyond his means. Based on past experience, but failing to take into account the economic repercussions of the Turkish War waging from 1788 to 1790, Mozart overestimated the possibilities for supplementary earnings, misjudged and prematurely counted on an accelerated accumulation of wealth that he had every reason to expect eventually.

A Garden Apartment for a Bold Start

MUCH different from the steady living conditions back home in Salzburg, Mozart moved around quite a bit in Vienna—a habit

Table 3.2: Mozart's Homes in Vienna, 1787–91*

DATE	AREA: HOUSE NO.	ANNUAL RENT
Sept. 1784–May 1787	City: Grosse Schulerstrasse, no. 846 "Carmesinahaus"	450 fl.
May 1787–Dec. 1787	Suburban: Landstrasse, no. 224	200 fl.
Dec. 1787–June 1788	City: No. 281 "Zum Mohren"	230 fl.
June 1788–Jan. 1789	Suburban: Alsergrund, no. 135 "Zu den drei Sternen"	250 fl.
Jan. 1789–Sept. 1790	City: No. 245 "Zum St. Nikolaus"	300 fl.
Sept. 1790–Dec. 1791	City: Rauhensteingasse, no. 970 "Kleines Kaiserhaus"	330 fl.

*Lorenz 2010.

typical at the time among younger professionals in a metropolitan city. The various homes, altogether eleven for the entire Viennese decade,[24] included two places in the Viennese suburbs that Mozart rented beginning in two subsequent summers, 1787 and 1788 (table 3.2). Life was generally quieter there and more favorable space could usually be obtained for a smaller rental fee.[25] Apart from this, moving for part of the year to summer places was quite fashionable among the aristocracy and affluent families, and after all, Mozart was not immune to living beyond his means. However, the motivation for his decision in 1787 may have included the idea of spending part of the time—more than six weeks, in fact—in Prague for the production of *Don Giovanni*. One year later, however, the situation was very different. First of all, as the recipient of an annual stipend of 800 florins from the court, he had a fixed base salary and saw himself in an economic situation considerably better than ever before. Second, and from a creative perspective more important, the imperial appointment obviously sparked some particularly ambitious composing plans for which he needed and wanted a different environment.

The suburban apartment Mozart chose in 1788 was notably different from all the places he had lived in before. It not only offered much more space—its seven rooms provided about 198 square meters (2,130 square feet)—but as a ground-floor dwelling, it also included a garden. Mozart specifically mentioned the latter when he described the place as "*more pleasant* in spring, summer, and fall—because I also have a garden."[26] This garden apartment, the only such residence Mozart ever occupied in Vienna, rented for 250 florins and was by far the largest and most attractive, but also the most expensive, apartment in the three-story house. The other eighteen apartments in the building, which included a two-story back section, were much smaller, most renting for 28 to 80 florins annually.[27]

On June 17, 1788, the day he moved into the Alsergrund house, no. 135, Mozart wrote one of his first begging letters to his Masonic brother Michael Puchberg and mentioned at the end of it:

> We'll be sleeping tonight for the first time in our new lodgings where we are going to be this coming *summer* and *winter*;—basically, it's all the same to me, if anything it's an improvement. I don't have much business in town anyway and, because I'm not interrupted as much by visitors, I shall have more time and leisure for work.[28]

The phrase "more time and leisure for work" is no hollow expression. It relates not only directly to the request "for a loan of 1 or 2 thousand florins at a suitable rate of interest" made at the outset of the same letter so that he "would be able to work with a *freer mind* and *lighter heart* and consequently *earn* more," but indeed also to an unbelievably productive season in the composer's creative life. This becomes immediately clear from the extremely packed schedule revealed by Mozart's thematic catalog for the summer of 1788 (table 3.3).

At the same time, the life of the young Mozart family had anything but a happy beginning in their new quarters. When they moved, their baby daughter Theresia, born December 27, 1787, was gravely ill with an intestinal disorder and died on June 29, 1788,

Table 3.3: Excerpt from Mozart's Thematic Catalog, June–September 1788

DATES	COMPOSITIONS (major works boldfaced)
Sunday, June 22	**Piano Trio in E, K. 542**
Thursday, June 26	**Symphony in E-flat, K. 543**
June (no specific date)	March in D, K. 544; Piano Sonata ("Sonata facile") in C, K. 545; Adagio (added to the Fugue) in C minor, K. 546
Thursday, July 10	**Sonata in F for Piano and Violin, K. 547**
Monday, July 14	**Piano Trio in C, K. 548**
Wednesday, July 16	Canzonetta "Più non si trovano," K. 549
Friday, July 25	**Symphony in G minor, K. 550**
Sunday, August 10	**Symphony in C, K. 551 ("Jupiter")**
Monday, August 11	War song "Beim Auszug in das Feld" K. 552
Tuesday, September 2	Eight Canons K. 553–558, K. 560b, and K. 561
September (no specific date)	Two Canons K. 559 and K. 562
Saturday, September 27	**Divertimento in E-flat for Violin, Viola, and Violoncello, K. 563**

only two weeks after they took up residence in the new garden apartment. Even though child mortality was one of the facts of eighteenth-century life and the family had experienced it twice before, it is all the more remarkable that Mozart managed to remain immersed in a virtually nonstop composing spree as reflected by the entries of major works he completed on June 22 and 26 as well as on July 10 and 14.

In a period of a little more than three months, Mozart completed seven major multimovement chamber and orchestral works. The repertoire, adding up to more than four hours of music, comprised a violin and piano sonata, a string trio, two piano trios, and three symphonies—all of them exemplifying distinctly different concepts and formats than previous works of the same categories. The Trio K. 563, the only composition in the group without a precedent in Mozart's oeuvre, implies by its heading "Divertimento . . . a sei Pezzi" a conscious recognition of its out-of-scale design in six movements. Besides, as none of these big works are known to have been commissioned for specific performance occasions, the decision of undertaking such an extraordinarily ambitious compositional program appears to have rested solely with Mozart himself.

The question of what might have motivated such a bold and varied instrumental summer program has never been posed. Even a narrower version of this question, focused solely on the purpose of the three grand symphonies, proved troublesome. No specific performance dates for the 1788–89 season or later are documented, leading even to the Romantic assumption that these works were never heard during the composer's lifetime—a view still widespread even though it has long been rejected, for good reasons.[29] Yet, with the exception of the carnival-season events in the Redoutensaal, the opera productions, and a few other publicized performances, there is little documentation available on Mozart's concert-giving in Vienna, notably on those under private sponsorship after 1787, the year in which Leopold Mozart died. As Wolfgang's letters to his father in Salzburg were the primary source of information about the various music-making activities, for most of which no public records exist, the end of this extensive correspondence brought also an end to the regular reports about these kinds of proceedings in Vienna.

Mozart's clear expression of the need for "more time and leisure to work," together with his move to a comfortable and quiet place, implies that there were concrete plans he intended to realize. At least one of them can be surmised, because the two piano trios K. 542 and 548 of June–July 1788 were apparently written not for scheduled performing occasions but more likely under a deadline set by the Viennese music publisher Artaria. Immediately after they were completed, they were rushed into production. A newspaper announcement of November 12, 1788, indicates that they were put on the market before the end of the year as a set of three piano trios, including K. 502, which was already finished in 1787.[30] A specific reason also exists for the origin of the elaborate Divertimento K. 563. According to a letter from Mozart to Constanze,[31] he wrote it for Michael Puchberg, who may have commissioned it, received it as a special favor in return for financial support, or most likely provided only a private venue for this most unusual trio's first performance.

A plan for the three symphonies is more difficult to substantiate. Nevertheless, it is highly unlikely that Mozart would undertake such a major task without a clear idea about the presentation of these works. Besides, evidence pertaining to the G-minor Symphony K. 550 points to performances during the 1788–89 season, and by extension may well apply to the other two symphonies.[32] As for K. 550, the autograph score shows traces of a revision that can only relate to a performance of the work, namely Mozart's addition of a pair of clarinets to the woodwind complement (see below, p. 98). This alternative version with clarinets is corroborated by an extant set of original performing parts,[33] even if no places or dates are recorded. In addition, a recent documentary discovery shows that the G-minor Symphony was performed at a concert under the patronage of Baron Gottfried van Swieten.[34] Although no date is given nor any information provided on the other two symphonies, it makes sense to assume that all three symphonies were intended for presentation in the concert series organized by van Swieten.

The baron's regular concerts and programs generally remain undocumented because of their private nature, but it is known that in the 1788–89 season they included the presentation of two Handel oratorios arranged and conducted by Mozart: *Acis und Galathea* (K. 566, November 1788) and *Der Messias* (K. 572, March 1789), in German translations. As the oratorio performances require a substantial orchestra, there would be no obstacles to the use of symphonies as a frame for oratorio performances or to provide entr'actes within them. Additionally, van Swieten had a particular interest in the symphonic genre as proven, for example, by C. P. E. Bach's dedication of his "Sei Sinfonie" Wq 182 of 1773 to his Viennese friend and patron. Bach would later also send the autograph score of his new set of symphonies for large orchestra Wq 183 (Leipzig, 1780) to Vienna,[35] so their performance there may be assumed as well. Van Swieten had been a strong promoter of Bach's music,[36] and the latter's large-scale cantata *Auferstehung und Himmelfahrt Jesu*, Wq 240, with the aria arrangement K. 537d, was conducted by Mozart on February 26 and March 4, 1788, at the mansion of Count Esterházy, one of the aristocrats in van Swieten's circle, and repeated for the general public on March 7.[37] The Bach symphonic connection in particular makes it even more plausible that van Swieten played a role in the origin and first performances of the three Mozart symphonies, too. After all, the baron was Mozart's most faithful supporter from the mid-1780s on as well as the one major patron who not only attended Mozart's exequies (the memorial service on December 10, 1791) but also provided financial assistance for the education of the two sons the composer left behind.

The Notion of "Imperial Style"

ESTABLISHING and differentiating between distinct chronological style periods in the creative life of artists usually raises more questions than it answers. In this respect Mozart's case proves more difficult than most, not just because of his premature death but also because of his creative lifespan of nearly thirty years. However, the momentous dividing line drawn in 1781 between the composer's Salzburg and Vienna years has always been recognized. Fundamental changes in his musical language indeed occurred after the move to Vienna and were already foreshadowed by the remarkable achievement of his first great opera, *Idomeneo*, composed and premiered January 1781 in Munich, an absolute peak in Mozart's music up to that point. The subsequent further evolution of Mozart's musical language, however, was caused not only by his emancipation from a domineering father and the narrower confines of the Salzburg scene but also, and probably predominantly, by both the challenges of making a living as a musician in the competitive environment of a true metropolis and the exposure to the many facets of musical culture in the capital of the Hapsburg Empire.

To subdivide the Viennese decade into distinct stylistic units proves additionally difficult because of Mozart's productive output, his steadily increasing experience, and the unusual range of his compositional activities in the various instrumental and vocal genres from piano music to opera. Characteristic phases, however, can be observed in his increased use of contrapuntal polyphony as exemplified by the six string quartets of 1782–84, later dedicated to Haydn; his embedding of a virtuosic keyboard part in a colorful instrumentation with a multifaceted complement of winds in the piano concertos of 1784–86 and the Quintet for Piano and Winds K. 452; and his portraying individualized musical characters and conceiving grippingly dramatic ensemble scenes in the operas of 1786–87, *Le nozze di Figaro* and *Don Giovanni*. Nevertheless, these specific qualitative turns in Mozart's music that became of lasting importance in the development of his musical language do not as such define or delineate separate periods of style.

The absence of any sharp internal demarcations in the music of Mozart's Viennese decade—above and beyond the watershed situation of 1783–84 represented by the "Haydn" Quartets, the piano concertos K. 449 and 450, or the Sonata for Violin and Piano K. 454—has invited an approach to a stylistic periodization based on emotional and psychological explanations, with a particular focus on either the death of Leopold Mozart in 1787 and its hypothetical musical compensation in *Don Giovanni* or on the fallout from the composer's alleged estrangement from patrons and audiences, financial troubles, and bleak, desperate outlook. Since such parameters, especially when only assumed, lack any evidence for periodization, Mozart's court appointment, an unambiguous biographical fact with a direct professional link, provides a safer ground for drawing such boundaries. It offers a turning point with immediate and long-term implications for the composer's artistic standing and future. Although not as fundamental and definitive as his departure from Salzburg in 1781, his imperial appointment represented a truly decisive moment within his Viennese decade inasmuch as he, from the very beginning, had eagerly awaited a tangible sign of public recognition by the emperor. Thus, the designation of an "imperial period" or an "imperial style" reflects an objective matter of fact and provides a marker for the composer's last four years and his works from that time.[38]

This is definitely not to suggest, however, that Mozart's music written from 1788 to 1791—including the three symphonies, the significant body of chamber music, the operas *Così fan tutte*, *La clemenza di Tito*, and *Die Zauberflöte*, as well as the Requiem—can be subsumed under a uniform style category. In this regard, the label of "late style" occasionally used for Mozart's last years, while certainly inappropriate for someone in his early thirties, also never really comprised a clearly delineated and consistent manner of writing. The final stretch does not appear fundamentally different from the decade's first half in terms of continuing advancement. Yet, what emerged at the turn of 1787 is a remarkably mature steadiness in finding a balance between past musical experiences and a deliberate, often daring exploration of new ways, including those that move in such disparate directions as simplified melodic contours (see below, p. 103), sophisticated chromaticism, dissonant counterpoint, and emotionally charged musical rhetoric that began with the creation of three grand symphonies and their near predecessors, the string quintets K. 515 and 516 and the Sonata K. 533.

How does an intentionally new approach manifest itself in Mozart's output from 1788? The Sonata K. 533 encapsulates and concisely defines the meaning of imperial style in contrast with what came before: innovative, ambitious, expansive, complex, technically sophisticated, conceptually erudite though on the surface simple and elegant, and aesthetically compelling throughout. The unmatched format and substance of the extraordinary group of instrumental works written in the summer of 1788 (table 3.3.) emphatically corroborate and amplify the direction in which Mozart was now moving. But the general trend is reflected even in the works that do not fit the mold of elaborate musical discourse yet also reveal the uplifting consequences from the imperial appointment—just like the modest pieces of musical entertainment for the festive carnival receptions in the Redoutensaal in Vienna, music deriving from the only official responsibilities of the new *Kammer-Kompositor*.

Mozart dutifully delivered a repertoire of remarkably refined contredanses, minuets, and German dances for the four seasons from 1788 through 1791, although he received no separate contract for these. Having earlier supplied orchestral ballroom dances for the Salzburg archiepiscopal court in the 1770s, he could easily have churned out such pieces. Yet, he apparently had an interest in providing the imperial court with superior examples of functional music for courtly entertainment, supplying a great variety of short pieces for an orchestral ensemble with a prominent wind complement. However, as this rich and varied repertoire plays virtually no role in modern concert life, the elegant ancillary pieces are little known.

As early as January 1788, Mozart composed the two contredanses K. 534 and 535 and the set of six German Dances K. 536 to cover the rest of that winter's carnival season. For the next two seasons, he wrote many more such works, altogether well over eighty (K. 567–568, 571, 585–588a, 599–604, 606–607, and 611). Despite their strict adherence to the standard types of simple triple- and duple-meter dance models, regular 4- and 8-measure melodic periodicity, and strict ABA form with contrasting trio sections, they demonstrate an extraordinary degree of rhythmic sophistication, applying syncopations and multilayered patterns of metric values. Moreover, they show great registral and combinatorial variety in their colorful orchestral scoring; harmonic surprises created by unexpected chord progressions, dissonances, and chromaticism; dynamic contrasts and crescendo-decrescendo special effects; jokes and pictorial devices; and sudden mood changes. Only few individuals within the partying and dancing aristocracy would have noticed the innovative and subtle qualities of the musical entertainment provided to them by a resourceful Mozart. More people, however, might have paid attention to the witty musical imagery of the sounds of sleigh bells, thunder, or the hurdy-gurdy in *Die Schlittenfahrt* (The Sleigh Ride), K. 605, no. 3, in *Das Donnerwetter* (The Thunderstorm), K. 534, and in the Minuets and German Dances K. 601 and 602, respectively. Even stronger are the concrete wartime allusions in the contredanse *La Bataille* (The Battle), K. 535, which includes with its *Marcia turca* a direct reference to the ongoing campaign against the Turks, and in *Der Sieg vom Helden Coburg*, K. 587, representing a musical tribute to the victory of General Friedrich Josias von Sachsen-Coburg-Saalfeld over the Ottoman troops on September 22, 1789, near Cluj in what today is Romania.

Virtually the entire dance repertoire composed for courtly entertainment was published in several collections during Mozart's lifetime, beginning in 1789. The editions must have circulated widely, as the publisher Artaria had to provide several reprints for most. The apparent popularity of the pieces shows that the imperial kind of musical entertainment supplied by the imperial capellmeister Mozart for the Redouten Hall could also be reproduced in the lesser residences and, thereby, provide luster for the empire's nobility at-large.[39]

Mozart's close working relationship with the Artaria publishing house gave him ready information about and access to this firm's publishing program. Given his contacts in 1787–88 with Artaria, which was then publishing the F-major Duet Sonata for piano, K. 497, and four piano trios—K. 498 ("Kegelstatt") and the set of K. 502, 542, and 548—Mozart would surely have become aware of the big Haydn project that Artaria just finished in 1787, the publication of the so-called "Paris" Symphonies. The six symphonies nos. 82–87 had been commissioned from Haydn by the Masonic directors of the Concert de la Loge Olympique in Paris and were composed in 1785–86. Artaria published the first set of three, in the keys of C major (no. 82, "L'Ours"), G minor (no. 83, "La Poule"), and E-flat major (no. 84), as *Trois Simphonies à Plusieurs Instruments* (Vienna, 1787). Remarkably, Haydn's works of this set show exactly the same keys as Mozart's final three, only in reverse order.[40] Another striking similarity occurs between the two symphonies in E-flat major, Haydn's no 84 and Mozart's K. 543, in that they are the only ones to feature slow introductions.

These direct if broad parallels can hardly be coincidental. On the contrary, Mozart's symphonic plan looks very much like a conscious and well-considered counterproject that picks up on Haydn's pattern, yet purposefully opens his own symphonic trilogy with an overture-like Adagio in E-flat. Clearly, Mozart admired Haydn as symphonist but responded to the senior colleague's works in his own special way. A direct parallel occurred earlier, when he reacted creatively to Haydn's string quartets op. 33 (Artaria: Vienna, 1781) with a quartet series of his own, composed between December 1782 and January 1785 and then dedicated to Haydn with an admiring preface (Artaria: Vienna, 1785). He composed the six works one by one between December 1782 and January 1785 and then dedicated their publication as a set to Haydn with an elaborate preface (Artaria: Vienna, 1785). As in the case of the quartets, Mozart's symphonies do not resemble their models in terms of thematic, formal, and other respects, let alone concrete allusions. Conceptually, they go in different ways, too. Still, it is particularly noteworthy that Mozart used the same keys, by no means an obvious choice, but concluded with the radiant natural mode of C major. It also suggests that he wanted the pieces to be compared, if only in a general sense as symphonic statements on a loftier scale.

The dissimilarities Mozart would have wanted to be noticed pertain especially to the tonal ground schemes. Only in the C-major Symphony ("Jupiter") does he use the same key for the slow movement that Haydn did, the subdominant F major. In the Andante of his E-flat-major Symphony, Mozart departs from Haydn's B-flat major and chooses the subdominant A-flat major instead. However, the greatest difference shows up in the two G-minor works.

Haydn limits the minor mode to the opening movement only. After the E-flat Andante that the symphonies have in common, Haydn continues in G major, whereas Mozart returns to G minor for both the Minuet and the concluding Allegro. The younger composer, however, not only plans a more sharply focused key scheme for the three cycles of symphonic movements; he also engages in more daring and provocative harmonic details. A brief section from the Andante con moto of K. 543, the first of the three symphonies, presents a particular case in point. Here (mm. 87–108) Mozart modulates chromatically and enharmonically within twenty measures from the movement's home key of A-flat major to A-flat minor, B major, B minor, F major, D-flat major, A-flat minor, A-flat major, and finally to E-flat major—creating the kind of shocking, haunting, and deeply moving effect so germane to the idea of the sublime in the late eighteenth-century concept of the symphony.[41] With compositional master strokes like this, he immediately leapt to the peak in order to shape the emerging new symphonic ideals.

The most immediate distinction between Haydn and Mozart occurs in the thematic design of the defining opening movements (ex. 3.6–7). In the principal themes of the E-flat (after the slow introduction) and G-minor works, Mozart presents both widely spread-out and differentiated musical ideas taking up 12 and 16 measures, respectively, whereas Haydn opts for rather concise statements of 8 measures each. The organization of the themes' period structure also differs significantly when comparing Mozart's AA′ BB′ C (K. 543) and AB A′B′ CC′ D (K. 550) designs with Haydn's A BB CC′ (no. 84) and AB A′B′ (no. 83). Only the C-major openings are similarly spaced, limited to 8 measures, and make use of strong dynamic contrasts. However, Mozart constructs a theme of four symmetric members AB (*forte, piano*) A′B′ (*forte, piano*) whereas Haydn subdivides his theme into two contrasting halves, an explosive fanfare followed by a mellow melodious responding phrase: AB (*fortissimo, piano*). The treatment of fundamental materials clearly illustrates two different compositional approaches

3.6. Mozart: Last three symphonies, opening themes: (a) E♭ major K. 543;
(b) G minor K. 550; (c) C major K. 551.

3.7. Haydn: *Trois Simphonies* (Vienna, 1787), opening themes:
(a) C major H. I/82; (b) G minor H. I/83; (c) E♭ major H. I/84.

and immediately demonstrates how Mozart aims at solutions well
beyond Haydn's model.

Apart from the opening symphonic statements, Mozart generally sought and realized a more complex elaboration of the
thematic-motivic material and along with it a more intricate harmonic treatment, achieved primarily by two means: first, by extending the lengths of the movements and thereby the overall format
of the symphonies in their entirety; and second, by enlarging the
complement of winds and thereby significantly expanding the vertical span of the symphonic scores. Haydn's symphonies nos. 82–84,
like the other three "Paris" symphonies, are uniformly scored for an

orchestra of strings with seven winds (1 flute, 2 oboes, 2 bassoons, and 2 horns). In contrast, Mozart enhances his pinnacled key-modality scheme by differentiated instrumentaion, deploying up to ten winds:

K. 543: E-flat major mode: 1 flute, 2 clarinets, 2 bassoons, 2 horns, 2
    trumpets, and timpani (= 10 winds, percussion)

K. 550: G minor mode: 1 flute, 2 oboes, 2 bassoons, 2 horns (= 7
    winds, percussion: first version);
    1 flute, 2 oboes, 2 clarinets, 2 bassoons, 2 horns (= 9 winds,
    percussion: second version)

K. 551: C natural mode: 1 flute, 2 oboes, 2 bassoons, 2 horns, 2
    trumpets, and timpani (= 10 winds, percussion)

Thereby, the composer sharpens the individual profile and character, increases the overall expressive means for each work, and opens up a multiplicity of registral choices for coloristic instrumental combinations. Orchestral sound as such assumes a new role in Mozart's symphonies. The opening of the second theme in the first movement of the G-minor Symphony presents a case in point. Here the sharing of a single melodic phrase by strings and winds that delicately transforms instrumental colors indicates Mozart's interest in crafting innovative orchestral techniques:

3.8. K. 550/I: instrumentation (alternating strings and winds) of second theme (mm. 44–47); in the second version of K. 550, the oboe part is played by a clarinet.

The external symphonic dimensions, which have a direct impact on the internal musical discourse, are determined by the different sizes of the working scores used by the two composers. For Haydn, 10-staff manuscript paper sufficed whereas Mozart needed paper ruled with 12 staves:

Haydn, symphonies nos. 82–84: 67, 60, and 69 pages, respectively
Mozart, symphonies K. 543, 550, and 551: 75, 85, and 91 pages,
respectively

Rough comparisons like these provide only very approximate proportional values. Nevertheless, along with measure counts and
scorings they show quite clearly that the horizontal and vertical
dimensions of Mozart's scores are 25 to 30 percent larger than
Haydn's and indicate that he pursued a decidedly more spacious
approach. He thereby achieved three goals at once: leaving more
room for internal musical refinement; attaining more differentiated
dynamics, volume, and colors of sound; and providing a more individualized musical character for each symphony.

The first three "Paris" Symphonies by Haydn, in their formal
variety, melodic and rhythmic elegance, instrumental brilliance,
and broad range of expressive devices, proved a genuine challenge
to Mozart. Although no newcomer to the symphonic genre, he had
written symphonies in Vienna only sporadically: two in 1783, K. 385
("Haffner") and K. 425 ("Linz"), and one at the very beginning of
1787, K. 504 ("Prague")—works in their own right without, however, the kind of cyclical coherence and momentous musical logic
of the model Haydn established in his *Trois Simphonies*. At the same
time, Mozart had gained considerable experience in another genre
of orchestral music, the piano concerto, which, besides Haydn's
symphonies, served as an important backdrop for his novel symphonic approach of 1788.

If a prototype for the kind of orchestral trilogy represented by
the three last symphonies[42] can be found, it is the group of three
piano concertos designed for Mozart's subscription academies of
the 1785–86 season: the concertos K. 482 in E-flat, K. 488 in A, and
K. 491 in C minor. As three-movement types, they illustrate perfect
tonal and modal balance, not only by their overall key structure but
also by a systematically planned variety in the scoring of their wind

complements, which in its differentiation is comparable to that of the symphonies K. 543, 550, and 551:

> K. 482: E-flat major / C minor / E-flat major (flat keys, major/minor modes): 1 flute, 2 clarinets, 2 bassoons, 2 horns, 2 trumpets, and timpani (= 10 winds, percussion)
>
> K. 488: A major / F-sharp minor / A major (sharp keys, major/minor modes): 1 flute, 2 clarinets, 2 bassoons, 2 horns (= 7 winds)
>
> K. 491: C minor / E-flat major / C minor–major (minor/major/ natural modes): 1 flute, 2 oboes, 2 clarinets, 2 bassoons, 2 horns, 2 trumpets, and timpani (= 12 winds, percussion)

Neither the three piano concertos nor the three last symphonies were planned as a cycle in the sense of a cyclical performance in one sitting. The two groups of works nevertheless bear in their conceptual relationship—internally among themselves as well as in juxtaposition as groups—all the design features of a complementary set of three. Both sets culminate in an extended, towering finale, a work featuring uncommon length and complexity, shockingly expressive character, and an exceptionally large orchestra: the piano concerto K. 491 with its elaborate variation movement and the symphony K. 551 with its various fugati in sonata guise.

The only orchestral composition immediately preceding the three symphonies is the Piano Concerto in D major, K. 537, of February 1788, a work handled by Mozart with considerable restraint when compared with the C-major Concerto, K. 503, of December 1786 and the earlier concertos from K. 450 through K. 482, 488, and 491. The main difference between K. 537 and the aforementioned concertos consists in the treatment of winds, the hallmark and most distinctive feature of Mozart's piano concertos since the B-flat-major Concerto, K. 450, of 1784. Although the score of K. 537 includes 1 flute, 2 oboes, 2 bassoons, 2 horns, 2 trumpets, and timpani, these parts are expressly marked "ad libitum." In other words, the winds are neither independent nor in any way essential. The work can just as well be performed "à 2 violini, viola e Basso," that is, with strings only. This almost regressive character of K. 537, with its unadventurous scoring, has been thought to indicate a loss of the composer's interest in the piano concerto genre.[43] Such an interpretation is in line with the assumption of a general "fallow period" following the success of *Don Giovanni* and is in step with Mozart's supposed difficulties in mounting public concerts and his problems in holding on to his audience or even finding one, all "proven" by the lack of any documented performance of K. 537 until April 1789.[44]

However, the autograph score tells a different story. Notated on paper of six different types, the score clearly developed in various stages and in all likelihood was begun more than a year before the work's completion and perhaps postponed because of the time-consuming *Don Giovanni* production of 1787 in Prague.[45] Moreover, the deliberate and consistent character of the autograph score of K. 537 suggests that the provision of alternative accompaniments for this concerto was intentional and planned for a specific purpose, rather than signaling any problem in the orchestral design. The advantage of the alternative accompaniment lies in its flexibility, permitting both chamber- or orchestral-style performances as needed for different occasions, and allowing for a choice between a more intimate performance setting and a more formal and public presentation. After K. 503, Mozart did not write a work on the grand scale of the series of eleven concertos beginning with K. 450. The four early Viennese concertos, K. 413–415 and K. 449, offered modest alternatives between strings only and ad libitum winds, whereas in the case of K. 537 the differences were quite dramatic: string ensemble on the one hand and a full orchestra on the other.[46] In other words, the D-major Concerto adopts the achievements of the eleven concertos from 1784 to 1786 and, by adding formal expansion, pianistic virtuosity, compositional refinement, and harmonic and contrapuntal sophistication, Mozart lifts his piano concerto writing onto another plane.

It would be unusual had Mozart composed the concerto K. 537[47] and recorded it in his thematic catalog on February 24, 1788, without a specific performance to follow immediately. To present it in its magnificent orchestral garb would require a representative setting, but wartime Vienna would obviously not accommodate the kind of subscription concerts Mozart had organized in earlier years. Nevertheless, some large private and public concerts took place in the spring of 1788, and, as mentioned above, Mozart conducted the oratorio *Auferstehung und Himmelfahrt Jesu* by C. P. E. Bach three times in late February and March, the first concert only two days after the entry of K. 537 in his diary.[48] Could not Mozart have played his brand-new piano concerto at this same occasion between the two parts of the oratorio-like cantata?[49] As it happens, the Bach work required exactly the same orchestra, including D trumpets, as K. 537. The first documented performance—apparently with strings-only accompaniment—took place at the Dresden court on April 14, 1789, in the chamber of the electress Maria Amalia. Clearly, K. 537 was a perfect piece for traveling, quickly mounting a performance, and making a big impression.[50]

The only piano concerto to follow, the B-major Concerto K. 595, was premiered by Mozart at a public concert in Vienna on March 4, 1791. The gap of almost exactly three years between the two works is misleading, however. With K. 595, too, Mozart appears to have returned in 1791 to an unfinished working score from an earlier time, between December 1787 and February 1789, but most likely 1788.[51] More specific conjectures, that the first 300 measures of the first movement, the entire Larghetto, and the opening 39 measures of the finale were drafted by February 1789,[52] may well be too bold. However, substantial portions of K. 595 definitely predated the completion of the work on January 5, 1791, by at least two years. At any rate, K. 595, like K. 537, indicates that Mozart no longer continued the course of new paths for the genre of piano concerto so vigorously pursued from 1784 through 1786 as evidenced by the series of eleven works from K. 450 to K. 503.

On the other hand, an unusual and defining element of K. 595

is the overt "cantabile" shape of the opening movement's principal theme. None of the earlier concertos, including K. 537, exhibits such a seemingly effortless, simply shaped, and strikingly melodious "signature" theme within an allegro movement, first introduced by the violins but preceded by an "empty" preparatory accompanimental measure (as it occurs also at the very beginning of the Symphony K. 550). It is this elegantly tuneful kind of opening material that also lends its unmistakable character to the opening of the Clarinet Concerto K. 622 from late 1791.[53] Even the draft of a first movement for the D-Major Horn Concerto K. 412, also from late 1791,[54] shows a similar kind of triad-centered melodic profile:[55]

3.9. Opening themes: (a) Piano Concerto K. 595; (b) Clarinet Concerto K. 622; (c) Piano Concerto K. 488.

Mozart hardly ever suffered from a lack of melodic invention. The sheer abundance of lyric melodies, especially in slow but also in fast movements, throughout his instrumental and vocal oeuvre therefore precludes any generalized categorization. However, this sort of forthright melodic-rhythmic simplicity and elegance is largely absent in the first movements of previous concertos, with perhaps one particularly clear exception: the A-major Concerto K. 488 of 1785. There the melodic contour anticipates later stylistic designs that add a new facet to the composer's energetic musical discourse in the multifarious beginnings of fast, sonata-form concerto openings. At the same time, the melodic design of K. 488 (ex. 3.9c) in its much wider compass (G-sharp–F-sharp), more complex rhythm, and varied articulation shows a clear difference to the more serene and mellow shape of the later themes. This development, however, reveals not so much a general stylistic change as an approach toward broadening thematic choices in order to increase clarity of form and to enhance the array of expressive devices. For the signal-like opening gesture of a multimovement instrumental structure invariably determines the unfolding and interplay of all further musical constituents.[56]

The compositional strategies Mozart pursued during the years that turned out to be his final ones are also related, at least to some extent, to a kind of rebalancing act as seen in his deemphasis of the piano concerto. With two-thirds of his entire production in this genre originating from the first half of the Viennese decade, the two samples represented in K. 537 of 1788 and K. 595 of 1791 suggest a retreat from the piano concerto, which to a large extent defined his reputation and had contributed significantly to his standing with the general public. However, he still composed two piano concertos for himself and also one each for horn and clarinet, suggesting that he had not lost interest in this genre altogether. But he clearly wanted to reduce his efforts in this regard. The decision made by the newly appointed court composer to write a single piano concerto vis-à-vis three symphonies in 1788 may indicate a deliberate choice against the type of large-scale solo work—which had enabled self-fulfillment as both keyboard virtuoso and composer—in favor of the symphony as his foremost musical vehicle "for the expression of the grand, the festive, and the sublime."[57]

The immediate musical context for the conceptual and preparatory phases of the three symphonies in spring 1788 included the Vienna performance of *Don Giovanni*,[58] premiered on May 7 and followed by eleven performances in May, June, July, and on August 2. The close time link between the opera performances and the completion of the symphonies on June 26, July 25, and August 10 brings to mind a similar situation in January 1787, when the origin of the Symphony K. 504 coincided with Mozart's Prague performance schedule for *Le nozze di Figaro*. The particular internal connection between opera and symphony as the largest vocal and instrumental genres is not meaningless, notably in that opera and symphonic performances often took place in the same theater. Franz Xaver Niemetschek, eyewitness to the Prague performances of both *Figaro* and the D-major Symphony, characterizes Mozart's symphonies as "masterpieces of instrumental music, full of surprising transitions; they have a fleeting, fiery course so that they instantly attune the soul to the expectation of something sublime."[59]

Thus, it was logical for Mozart, wanting to make a major musical statement in his newly elevated position, to turn to the most elevated of instrumental genres. In symphonies of sweeping size, he could best display his expert talent as a composer of instrumental music and shape the works entirely according to his ideas, especially since he was his own "librettist," as it were, in determining the expressive content of the work. That he had a large audience in mind can be inferred from the well-above-average size of the orchestra's wind complement. Moreover, as suggested by the announcement of the appointment in the publications of K. 533 and K. 426 early in 1788 and in the Artaria print of the three piano trios K. 502, 542, and 548 later in the same year, Mozart probably planned on publishing the symphonies, too. Also, he surely hoped for international distribution, noting that Artaria's 1787 edition of Haydn's *Trois Simphonies à plusieurs Instruments* appeared more or less simultaneously in 1788 from the Viennese firm's international partners: Forster, and Longman & Broderip, both in London; Hummel in Amsterdam; and Imbault in Paris. A similar arrangement would have suited Mozart's ambitions as well.

Indeed, the Artaria firm had published a Mozart symphony once before, in 1785: K. 385 ("Haffner") in a set of 13 instrumental part books, that is, the same format as Haydn's three symphonies nos. 82–84 two years later. Mozart's differently scored three last symphonies, on the other hand, would for practical reasons have required three separate sets of parts and with altogether many more pages than any prior symphonic print. And this indeed is the way they were published, and it must be assumed that none other than Mozart himself had at least initiated the pertinent arrangements with Artaria. The "Jupiter" Symphony (with 13 part books) then appeared as the first in 1793, less than two years after the composer's death, and the G-Minor Symphony (11 part books)[60] several months later in 1794. The E-flat-major Symphony (14 part books) followed in 1797. It can well be imagined that during the Turkish War such a publishing project would have been unrealistically expensive and that the project had to be put on hold for better times. Therefore and understandably, Mozart and Artaria focused during the war years on chamber music. The publication of the piano trios in 1788 was followed by that of the string quintets K. 515 and 516 in 1789 and 1790, respectively. These quintets, as such, representing the most orchestral type of chamber music, may well have served as preliminary substitutes for the symphonies, exhibiting yet another aspect of Mozart's grand ambitions, another face of his imperial style.

4

"Vera Opera"
and *The Magic Flute*

———◇ ◇ ◇———

What's in a Name?

WHENEVER MOZART turned to a new genre of composition, or returned after a lapse of time to a familiar genre, he usually made conceptual changes that resulted in a new outlook for the pertinent works. This is particularly true of the three last symphonies, dating from 1788, in comparison with their irregularly spaced forerunners "Haffner," K. 385, from 1782; "Linz," K. 425, from 1783; and "Prague," K. 504, from 1786. The habit of engaging in new compositional approaches applies to both instrumental and vocal works, but it affects, perhaps most markedly, the areas of musical theater and church music.

The two opera projects from Mozart's last year provide exemplary cases in this regard, especially since they are so deeply intertwined chronologically. *Die Zauberflöte* had, for the most part, been completed before the score of *La clemenza di Tito* was begun. Accordingly, Mozart's entries for the two works in his thematic catalog are found under "Jm Jullius" (in July) and "den 5:ᵗ September" (on September 5), respectively. Their premieres, however, took place in reverse order: *Tito* on September 6 in Prague and *The Magic Flute* on September 30 in Vienna, after Mozart had put the finishing touches on the latter by adding two missing instrumental numbers, the "March of the Priests" and the overture, entered under the date "den 28:ᵗ September."[1]

When Mozart actually began working on either opera is much less clear, though *Tito* definitely came second. There is neither a contract nor other documentation available that would give any concrete starting date for *The Magic Flute*. Yet even if there were one, it would have been preceded by preparatory discussions with Emanuel Schikaneder, the impresario of the Theater auf der Wieden in Vienna. A reasonable assumption is, however, that Mozart embarked on the opera in the late spring of 1791, probably soon after completing the String Quintet in E-flat, K. 614, on April 12—the largest and most demanding of the six compositions written between April and July, the time he mainly worked on *The Magic Flute*. As for *Tito,* there is at least the contract signed on July 8 by the Prague theater director Domenico Guardasoni with the Bohemian Estates. The first—and politically correct—choice for composing a work to be presented at the coronation of Emperor Leopold II as king of Bohemia would have been Antonio Salieri, the court kapellmeister. But he declined, making way for Mozart, as he had done earlier in the case of *Così fan tutte* (see chap. 1, p. 24). However, Mozart most likely did not enter the picture for the coronation opera until mid-July 1791, that is, around the time he was intensely involved with the music for *The Magic Flute*.

The two works represented diametrically opposed operatic genres, opera seria and singspiel, as determined by their subject matter and the design of their librettos. Mozart's entry for *Tito* in his thematic catalog expressly refers to the work as an "opera seria," but he specifically qualifies it by adding "ridotta à vera opera" (reduced to a true/genuine opera). Primary credit for the arrangement goes to the librettist, the Dresden court poet Caterino Mazzolà, who thoroughly rewrote the original opera text by Pietro Metastasio. The historical subject matter as well as the moral and political message of the opera—a dramatic representation of the Roman emperor Titus countering with clemency the evil actions of his enemies— was an appropriate choice for celebrating the enthronement of a new ruler. Metastasio's famous libretto of 1734 had been used for many comparable court ceremonies and had already been set by dozens of composers. Time pressure alone would have made it impossible for Mozart or anyone else to write the music for a traditional and elaborate three-act opera seria in the manner of *Idomeneo,* and the experienced Prague impresario Guardasoni anticipated that. Therefore, Mazzolà's poetically sensitive rearrangement of the Metastasian libretto reduced the opera to two acts by eliminating altogether eighteen solo arias. He replaced them with only eleven new numbers: four solos, two duets, three trios, and two ensemble finales. The poetry as such is entirely Mazzolà's, of course, but the novel libretto structure with its decisive rejection of a series of solo numbers would hardly have materialized without Mozart's active participation. Moreover, "vera opera" appears not to be a quote of the librettist's words but an authentic Mozartean expression, one that underscores the composer's vital interest in producing an effective musical drama regardless of its subject, origin, or genre. Remarkably, the obvious time limitations and the burden of dealing more or less simultaneously with two operas did not lure Mozart into the expedience of merely setting a delivered text to music. His musical ethics and professional ambitions told him otherwise.

That the genesis of *La clemenza di Tito* is practically embraced by Mozart's work on *The Magic Flute* directly raises the question of conceptual connections. The distance in time between the two opere serie—*Idomeneo* of 1781 and *Tito*—is comparable to that between Mozart's two German singspiels, *The Abduction from the Seraglio* of 1782 and *The Magic Flute.* The differences in musico-dramatic approach are equally significant and notably compounded by Mozart's intervening and more recent experience with the three Da Ponte operas—*Figaro, Don Giovanni,* and *Così fan tutte*— dating from 1786, 1787, and 1789. *Don Giovanni,* especially, broke the traditional boundaries of the buffo genre and generally opened up a more flexible operatic strategy. In this regard, *Die Zauberflöte* represents the consummation of a trend—confirmed by *Tito*—that reflects Mozart's maturing philosophy of musical drama in which genre boundaries become porous and conventions increasingly irrelevant.

This is particularly evident in a comparison of the two German operas. The playbill and title page of the libretto for *The Abduction* refer to "a singspiel," whereas those of *The Magic Flute* boldly announce "Eine große Oper" (a grand opera). While *Tito* still adheres to the designations "Dramma serio per musica" (libretto of 1791) and "opera seria" (Mozart's thematic catalog), none of the original references to *The Magic Flute* even mention singspiel.[2] This word would indeed be a misnomer, because Mozart definitely aimed for something entirely different. The term "große Oper" is not only used here by Mozart for the first time; it also appears to occur here for the first time in general—not, of course, in anticipation of the French postrevolutionary genre of "grand opera" but rather in the generic sense of making the fullest use of musical and theatrical resources.[3] Naming *Die Zauberflöte* a "grand opera" defines its ambitiously comprehensive format and has a meaning conceptually analogous to "vera opera" for *Tito*. Both instances signal a departure from traditional expectations and represent major steps in a new direction. Of the two, however, *The Magic Flute*, perhaps because of its longer gestation period, demonstrates a more complex and higher degree of innovation and, therefore, offers a singularly impressive and illuminating sample of the steady forward drive so characteristic of Mozart's last year.

More than an Egyptian Opera

FROM its premiere through a sheer endless number of presentations in the fall of 1791, *The Magic Flute* was a resounding success, an absolute hit that, unlike any other, catapulted both the opera and the composer into immortality. What turned out to be Mozart's final show in Vienna became his greatest operatic triumph, a success story that continued unabated after his death. By 1800, the work had been given no fewer than two hundred times at the Vienna Theater auf der Wieden alone. Moreover, owing to *The Magic Flute*'s unusual degree of popularity, vocal scores of its single musical numbers began to appear for sale in competing editions by two Viennese publishers[4] only a few weeks after the premiere— something that had never happened before.

The first two performances on September 30 and October 1, 1791, were conducted by the composer himself; thereafter, the principal conductor of the Theater auf der Wieden, Johann Baptist Henneberg, took over. Beyond the information contained on the playbill, little is known regarding the staging, the richly decorative sets, and the costumes. A vague impression is conveyed by the two copper engravings printed in the original edition of the libretto: (1) a frontispiece depicting Egyptian imagery with pyramids and hieroglyphs, relating to the "Song of the Armed Men" in the finale of act 2 (fig. 4.1); (2) an engraving of Schikaneder as Papageno "in his actual costume," according to the caption. By the end of October the opera had been given twenty-four

4.1. *Die Zauberflöte,* frontispiece of the original libretto (Vienna, 1791) (*Vienna, Österreichische Nationalbibliothek*)

times and thus could be heard almost daily. Mozart himself visited the theater again and again and, a week after the premiere, wrote to his wife, who had been present for the first few performances but now was taking the waters in Baden near Vienna:

> I've just come back from the opera;—it was as full as ever.—The Duetto *Mann und Weib* and the Glockenspiel in the first act had to be repeated as usual—the same was true of the boys' trio in the 2nd act, but what really makes me happy is the *Silent Applause!*—one can feel how this opera is rising and rising.[5]

A week later, Mozart took the court capellmeister Antonio Salieri with his lover, the soprano Caterina Cavalieri, to his private box at the opera and reported in detail to Constanze how favorably impressed they were (see chap. 1, p. 42).

The Magic Flute, despite its tight production schedule, must have engaged the composer for a considerable period of time—at least the six months prior to the premiere and some time afterward, too—for the conceptual context of this opera extended to nearly all the works Mozart wrote after March–April 1791. As it happens, two relevant dinner dates for composer and librettist, June 7 and July 2, are mentioned in Mozart's correspondence with Constanze. In addition, Schikaneder himself reminisced in 1795 that he "painstakingly thought through the opera with the late Mozart."[6] Hence, it can be safely assumed that the two met and consulted regularly over a period of months.

Mozart was eager to influence the content of the opera and its overall dramatic design to suit his musical preferences. He apparently took an immediate liking to and interest in the subject matter of the play, not least of all its multitiered, variegated, philosophically tinged plot, and especially its highly contrasting characters. The widely read composer surely was familiar with the oriental fairy tales, mysteries, and various other literary sources on the basis of which Schikaneder fabricated his libretto.[7] It is unlikely, however, that he involved himself in the librettist's lyrics but rather focused on the big picture, the overall multifaceted character of the opera and its musical dramaturgy. The Egyptian cult of the sun, which would play such a dominating role in Schikaneder's text,[8] had already caught Mozart's fancy twenty years earlier in Tobias Philipp von Gebler's heroic drama *Thamos, König in Aegypten* (Thamos, King in Egypt), for which he wrote the choruses and entr'acte music K. 345 in 1779. His subsequent involvement with Freemasonry and its cultlike meetings would have nourished his interest in oriental mysteries even further.

Most of all, however, Mozart must have been fascinated by an important subtext in Schikaneder's libretto that he intended to strengthen: the power of music, a theme known to him from the ancient Orpheus myth and the Christian legend of St. Cecilia. At the behest of Baron van Swieten, he had in July 1790 completed and performed his own arrangements of George Frideric Handel's oratorio *Alexander's Feast* K. 591 and his *Ode for St. Cecilia's Day* K. 592. Both works were based on "A Song for St. Cecilia's Day" (1687), a set of poems by John Dryden, translated into German as *Die Gewalt der Musik* (The power of music) by Karl Wilhelm Ramler (1766) and *Die Gewalt der Töne* (The power of tones) by an unknown author. It is thus likely that it was Mozart himself who caused this particular element in Schikaneder's libretto to stand out more strikingly and with greater artistry, and that it was the composer's idea to emphasize the magical instrument in the work's title in a way significantly different from the role of music in Wenzel Müller's popular singspiel *Kaspar der Fagottist, oder die Zauberzither* (Caspar the bassoonist, or the magic zither), based on a libretto by Joachim Perinet and premiered at Schikaneder's theater on June 8, 1791. Evidently, the final wording of the title, *Die Zauberflöte*, was not fixed from the outset. Newspaper reports before the premiere report what probably was an earlier version of the title: "Herr Mozart has composed a new opera, *Die Egyptischen Geheimnisse* [The Egyptian mysteries]."[9] At any rate, prior to the work's premiere, all the references that circulated were to an "Egyptian opera." Noteworthy, too, is that the composer had no interest in contributing to the ongoing series of popular works for which Schikaneder's theater troupe was so famous, especially since its permanent move to Vienna in 1788. Instead, Mozart succeeded in pushing the impresario in a different direction because he wanted to give the traditional singspiel a fundamentally new face.

The power of music in *Die Zauberflöte* is made manifest by two starkly contrasting types of musical instruments, each with a captivating sound and spellbinding power: the transverse flute and the glockenspiel. Both are introduced and assigned to the two main characters of the opera in act 1, no. 5, who then hear the decisive lines:

Silber-Glöckchen, Zauber-Flöten
Sind zu eurem/unserm Schutz vonnöthen.
   Silver bells and magic flutes
   are essential to your/our protection

Mozart brings these two instruments into his score, for the first time and to extraordinary musical effect, in the finale of act 1—just after Tamino learns that Pamina is alive—when they are to perform their protective magic. But long before these two instruments resound, and as early as in no. 2, one hears another no less distinctive instrument, a panpipe ("Waldflötchen" in the original libretto), which a first-time listener could mistakenly take as the magic flute. With its strict limitation to a primitive five-note run, this third instrument, however, is not only the defining attribute of the nature boy Papageno, but a deliberate ploy to enhance the effect of the other magical instruments when they enter later.

While Tamino is given a golden flute in no. 5, Papageno gets a mechanical glockenspiel. In other words, the prince receives a genuine musical instrument that requires talent to play, in contrast to the birdcatcher's music box, whose operation requires no performing skills. Both instruments, however, a regular transverse flute and the *istromento d'acciaio*,[10] are performed from within the orchestra and merely mimed by the actors; only the simple panpipe (*Faunen-Flötchen*) is played by Papageno on stage. In this respect, the opera goes beyond the standard stage spectacle of a traditional *Maschinenkomödie*, or comedy of stage machinery. Nevertheless, *Die Zauberflöte* also comes up with a serpent, lions, monkeys, and other wild animals, thunder, fire, water, and a flying machine—all typical props of machine comedy; but the two contrasting musical instruments in the hands of the paired main characters are deliberately given a dramatic function to determine the course of the plot. In the hands of the protagonists, the sound of these instruments exerts an irresistible magic power.

Thus, after Tamino receives the magic flute, he uses it to placate the animal kingdom (stage direction in the 1791 libretto: "He plays, and immediately animals of all sorts come forth to listen to him. He stops playing, and they run away. The birds sing along"). Just a bit later, Papageno holds Monostatos and his gang of slaves in check with his glockenspiel (stage direction: "He strikes his instrument, and immediately Monostatos and the Slaves start singing [and] march offstage to the music"). On a different level and also in a completely different way, even Sarastro is included in the "power of music" subtext. He is assigned an emblematic musical attribute with a recurrent dramatic function and, in line with his priestly role, a striking ceremonial flavor in the form of a triadic chord played by wind instruments only (stage direction: "[the priests] sound the horns thrice"). This threefold chord, recalling a similar feature from *Thamos* K. 345 in its second version of 1779,[11] is fancifully orchestrated by Mozart for its various occurrences within the opera.

The different types of musical instruments and the emblematic function of the threefold chord represent a carefully charted variety of expressions of the power of music and give musical instruments in *The Magic Flute* a role very different from that in Wenzel Müller's aforementioned *Kaspar der Fagottist*. This singspiel is frequently mentioned in connection with *The Magic Flute* because Mozart attended a performance of this show on June 11. However, in a letter written the following day, he dismissed the work, "which is creating such a commotion—but actually there's nothing to it"[12]— a frank comment reflecting Mozart's opinion of the low-level repertoire of the Viennese singspiel, whose flavor he was well familiar with but wanted to stay clear of and pull Schikaneder away from. Instead, despite *The Magic Flute*'s colorful and fancy fairy-tale logic, Schikaneder and Mozart jointly made it play out on a very different plateau, notably by intelligently combining Egyptian mythology, Enlightenment-era philosophical motifs of reason and truth, and the Masonic ideal of charity. These elements are unified in the dramaturgically enhanced metaphorical move of the plot from darkness to light. In addition, Mozart appears to have been primarily responsible for a further dimension of the plot, the integration of the "power of music" motif from the Orpheus myth—a true operatic classic—as a particularly effective musicodramatic element. He achieved much entertaining stage magic by creatively employing three different musical instruments and the emblematic threefold chord as surface effects, resolutely undergirded and further accentuated throughout the entire opera by his refined treatment of a pronounced and subtly differentiated orchestral sound.

The Language of "Grand Opera"

IN Mozart's time, the process of translating an operatic text into the language of music went, by and large, according to a well-established typology of opera librettos, complying in particular with the three prevailing genres: the Italian opera seria and opera buffa, and the German singspiel. There existed, however, further genre categories, including melodrama,[13] serenata, tragédie lyrique, and others, offering a broader spectrum of musical solutions to various kinds of dramatic representation, and Mozart always took the more differentiated approach in his stage works. From his earliest experiences with the sacred singspiel *Die Schuldigkeit des Ersten Gebots* (The obligation of the first commandment), K. 35, and the Latin school drama *Apollo et Hyazinthus*, K. 38, he had acquired and developed a detailed knowledge of the wider range of theatrical styles and over the years put it to use.

This pertains in particular to the seven great operas, beginning with *Idomeneo*, called "dramma per musica," and proceeding in logical succession from *The Marriage of Figaro*, designated "opera buffa" through *Don Giovanni* and *Così fan tutte*, both "drammi giocosi" (humorous dramas) to *La clemenza di Tito*, a "dramma serio per musica." From the perspective of a completed oeuvre, it seems natural to view *Die Zauberflöte*, his "grand opera," as a culmination or even the teleological goal of a line of development rather than a conscious fresh start. Yet, when Mozart conceived the work, he definitely had his eye fixed on the future—albeit a future whose artistic progress and end eludes any speculation. The very fact of the novel term "grand opera," however, sets *The Magic Flute* apart from its predecessors. Although Mozart retained the singspiel convention of spoken dialogue and may even have engaged with Schikaneder in a creative give-and-take regarding ideas for the libretto and its shape, he redefined the underlying text in specifically musical terms and rechanneled it toward what he wanted grand opera to be and to mean—a type for which there were no models and which he basically defined for himself. Curiously, Schikaneder more or less continued to adhere to his tried-and-true singspiel scheme in the librettos he wrote after 1791.[14] This only underscores the critical role Mozart played in their truly joint operatic undertaking.

Die Zauberflöte not only effectively draws on the multifaceted resources of the opera traditions so richly explored by Mozart, notably in his Viennese decade, but also features elements going beyond conventional patterns, approaching a concept of total musical theater.

WORDS AND MUSIC

A comparison with *Der Stein der Weisen* (The philosopher's stone) of 1790, a singspiel written by Schikaneder, set to music by a Viennese composer collaborative consisting of friends of Mozart,[15] indicates that Schikaneder apparently acquiesced to quite a few of Mozart's dramaturgical ideas in *The Magic Flute*. In the earlier work, for example, the plot of the introduction (solo with chorus) keeps dragging on, whereas in *The Magic Flute*, maximum tension reigns from the very first bar of the introduction, anticipating Tamino's opening cries "Zu Hilfe! zu Hilfe!" (Help me! Help!). It also features three quickly changing stage scenes with different characters, each scene with a surprise turn of action: (1) Tamino pursued by a serpent, the Three Ladies killing the serpent; (2) Papageno naïvely but falsely claiming credit for the saving action; and (3) the Three Ladies punishing Papageno and rewarding Tamino with a portrait of Pamina. Though not directly comparable, *The Magic Flute* nevertheless seems to have profited from the experience Mozart had gained for devising a dramatic exposition from the Da Ponte operas, notably from the three opening scenes of *Don Giovanni*: (1) Leporello complains of his fate as Don Giovanni's unhappy servant; (2) an insulted Donna Anna wrathfully pursues Don Giovanni; and (3) her father, the Commendatore, attacks Don Giovanni and is killed.

The first act of Schikaneder's singspiel *Der Stein der Weisen* is roughly as long as that of *The Magic Flute*, but it contains eight musical numbers between the introduction and the finale: five solo arias (A), one duet (D), and two choruses (Ch) that form a loose string: A-A-Ch-D-A-Ch-A-A. In comparison, *The Magic Flute* offers a much different and musically more effective solution with only six numbers. The introduction is followed by three consecutive solo arias from the most dissimilar protagonists imaginable: Papageno, Tamino, and the Queen of the Night. The three subsequent ensemble numbers show a systematically decreasing number of vocal parts, from a quintet (Three Ladies, Tamino, Papageno) to a trio (Pamina, Monostatos, Papageno) to a duet (Pamina, Papageno), after which the drama escalates to its first finale. It is hardly imaginable that Mozart had no hand in this design, for the carefully planned sequence does not conform to a conventional play with a relatively arbitrary series of musical interpolations, typical of Schikaneder's theater pieces; rather, the work boasts a dramaturgical structure whose design is in many respects musically driven and therefore justifies the use of the term "grand opera."

The various discrepancies between Schikaneder's text for *The Magic Flute* and Mozart's score are mostly minor and suggest editorial interventions that the librettist presumably entered prior to the publication of the libretto. Some passages, however, reflect deliberate alterations made by the composer, with a representative example occurring in Papageno's first aria. There the opening line reads "Der Vogelfänger bin ich ja" (The birdcatcher am I) but then the printed libretto switches to the third person singular. However, the composer deliberately departed from this grammatical change of narrative by retaining the first-person form of the first line for the entire stanza, thereby improving the flow of the verse.

Schikaneder's libretto:	Mozart's score:
. . .	. . .
Der Vogelfänger ist bekannt	*Ich Vogelfänger bin bekannt*
Bei Alt und Jung im ganzen Land.	*Bei Alt und Jung im ganzen Land.*
The birdcatcher is known	I, the birdcatcher, am known
to old and young	to old and young
throughout the land.	throughout the land.

In another example, the Trio, no. 6, staging the unexpected encounter of Papageno and Monostatos, the musical text underlay departs from Schikaneder's words in the libretto: "Hu! Das—ist—der—Teu—fel—si—cher—lich!" (Gad! That—is—sure—ly—the—de—vil). In Mozart's score, "Hu!" is emphasized by a fermata and the stuttering declamation is then shaped in iambic verse, not regularly but accentuated by rests in a regular $\frac{4}{4}$ meter pattern with a pickup: "Das | **ist** – der | **Teu** – fel | **si** – cher- | **lich**."

Such linguistic fine-tuning bears witness to Mozart's paying very close attention to detail in the text of the libretto. This is equally apparent in his deliberate and free choice of stress and the weight given to individual words and phrases and to text repetitions not prescribed by the libretto. Mozart took advantage of interpretative license at every turn in order to place special emphasis on the words in such crucial passages as, for instance, the threefold repetition of "düstre Nacht" (gloomy night) in the final line of the "Ordeal by Fire" scene (act 2 finale, mm. 347ff.).

MUSICAL DRAMATURGY

One of the unmistakable Mozartean features of translating a libretto into music is the manner in which the characters of the dramatis personae are delineated and woven into the dramatic structure of the scenes. Yet here, too, *The Magic Flute* proves to be less a continuation of the Da Ponte operas than a fresh approach to opera design. Mozart's main concern in *The Magic Flute*—the same as it would be in *Tito*—must have been to produce a "genuine opera." To him the idea of grand opera would not imply a rejection of traditional generic types as much as their integration, combined with a fundamental interest in opening up new paths of musicodramatic design.

Given their close succession and highly divergent stylistic makeup, the first three solo arias (nos. 2–4) of *The Magic Flute* stake out the boundaries of an open-ended concept. It is almost impossible to imagine sharper contrasts than those emerging between the first and the last, Papageno's folksy strophic song "Der Vogelfänger bin ich ja," of true singspiel character, and the Queen of the Night's aria "Zum Leiden bin ich auserkoren" (I am predestined to suffer), with its roots in the two-part form (recitative–introduction) and virtuosic vocal manners of opera seria. The mediating link is

Tamino's aria "Dies Bildnis ist bezaubernd schön" (This image is enchantingly beautiful), whose musical format and stylistic makeup does not correspond to any eighteenth-century generic tradition.[16] The same applies to no. 17, Pamina's aria "Ach, ich fühl's" (Ah, I feel it), with its perceptive matching of words and music, subtly expressive melodic writing, and exquisite and diaphanous instrumental accompaniment. Even Sarastro's arias, Nos. 10 and 15, "O Isis und Osiris" and "In diesen heil'gen Hallen" (In these sacred halls), with their hymnlike declamation and solemn demeanor, and Monostatos's aria, no. 13, "Alles fühlt der Liebe Freuden" (Everyone feels the joys of love) with its demonic propulsion, stand outside conventional categories, although in both cases ties can be seen to, respectively, opera seria and opera buffa. Viewed as a whole, however, it is precisely the wide-ranging stylistic spectrum of the nine solo arias in *The Magic Flute* that manifests the novelty of its conception.

Likewise, attempts to classify the duets, trios, and quintets and to bring them in line with those in other operas falls short and reveals a matchless variety. Even vocal numbers of a similar type—the cantabile duet "Bei Männern, welche Liebe fühlen" (In men who feel love; no. 7) or the siciliano-like trio of the Three Boys, "Seid uns zum zweiten Mal willkommen" (We bid you welcome for the second time; no. 16)—are sharply differentiated. Equally, the musical numbers that adhere most closely to conventional comic typology as, for instance, Papageno's and Papagena's clownish duet "Pa-Pa-Pa-" in the second finale (scene 19) are distinctive enough to resist classification. Outside the conventions altogether is the song of the Two Men in Armor in the second finale (scene 28), represented on the copperplate illustration in the 1791 libretto (see fig. 4.1, p. 111). According to the original stage direction, "they read to him [Tamino] the transparent writing inscribed on a pyramid," apparently an inscription in Egyptian hieroglyphs. Here the composer combines an early sixteenth-century Lutheran chorale melody, which would have been foreign to his Viennese audiences, and strict Bach-style counterpoint in order to create an emblematic reference to a citation in an ancient language no longer spoken.[17] Mozart, who knew the musical theater of his day from every angle and at this point in his career was second to none in drawing on the resources of a wide-ranging musicodramatic pallet, was consciously embarking on new paths. It could be said that *The Magic Flute* encouraged him to make full use of the nearly unrestricted possibilities of a suburban theater stage that was not committed to conventions and was impervious to labels.

Operatic innovation is particularly prevalent in the so-called Speaker Scene, scene 15, which opens the first-act finale. Mozart sets Schikaneder's text in the form of an extended and variable accompanied recitative for which there is no parallel in his own music or anyone else's. This dramatic and formally open-ended musical scene in many ways exemplifies his application of novel operatic technique in *The Magic Flute*. Staged in a grove with three temples devoted to Wisdom, Reason, and Nature, this scene is also strategically positioned, unveiling the core idea of the opera's playful philosophical subject matter in fairy-tale guise, the move from dark to light and from ignorance to knowledge—on the whole a metaphor for the Enlightenment. At the end of it, immediately after the Speaker departs, Tamino is left alone onstage to pose the crucial double question that turns the entire plot around, for actors and audiences alike:

O ew'ge Nacht! wann wirst du schwinden?
Wann wird das Licht mein Auge finden?
    O, eternal night! When will you vanish?
    When will the light find my eye?

The Speaker Scene makes the exposition of the drama, now in retrospect, appear in a new light: the Queen of the Night and Sarastro, the opera's dramatic antipodes, have, in their characters as positive and negative forces, become reversed. Tamino recognizes the powers of darkness and light. In keeping with the metaphor of light in

Enlightenment thought, the passage "O ew'ge Nacht! wann wirst du schwinden?" (no. 8, mm. 141f.)[18] bears the key to the concept underlying Schikaneder's libretto: from now on Tamino's efforts will center on knowledge, reason, and truth. These ideals are accompanied by a secondary goal, the quest for pure love dissociated from the Queen of the Night's schemes of vengeance.

Given the special significance of this dramaturgically central scene for understanding both the opera's action and its meaning, Mozart took pains to find a musically appropriate solution for this challenging section. The problem was important enough to warrant extensive and detailed sketches to master the difficult task of coming up with an effective musical dramaturgy. In what is the largest of the few extant sketch leaves for *The Magic Flute*,[19] the opening section with the Three Boys, no. 8, mm. 1–28, is followed by a large continuity draft for mm. 39–85 that helped Mozart set down the larger musical development of the extended dialogue between Tamino and the Priest and to work out specific melodic and motivic details. In general, the sketch came very close to the final version of the scene.

One of the crucial compositional devices of the Speaker Scene is the careful distinction in recitative style between simple declamatory and elevated melodic speech for a lengthy text made up chiefly of rhymed couplets. The alternation between the two types of speech is unique, in that it enabled Mozart to highlight with emphatic melodic lines such maxims as "Wo Tätigkeit thronet und Müßigkeit weicht" (Where activity reigns and idleness shrinks) in mm. 50f. (ex. 4.1) or "Die Absicht ist edel und lauter und rein" (The intention is noble and clear and pure) in mm. 59f. The peculiarity of this unique style of recitative is underscored by the unusual handling of the instrumental accompaniment, which alternates between straightforward chordal textures and more sophisticated, motivically organized passages, always in line with the changing requirements of the text.

Not the least of the innovations in the Speaker Scene is Mozart's

4.1. Recitative styles in the Speaker Scene (no. 8) of *The Magic Flute*: (a) free declamatory speech (mm. 39–41); (b′) metric elevated speech, sketch; (b) metric elevated speech, final version (mm. 51–54).

subtle handling of the expansive instrumental apparatus, with thirty-five musicians in the orchestra: five first and four second violins, four violas, three cellos, three double basses, and sixteen winds and percussion—a configuration entirely atypical of the ordinary Viennese singspiel. To be sure, the sophisticated and virtuosic use of the large orchestral score is a particular hallmark of Mozart's operas ever since *Idomeneo*, but it reaches a singular culmination in *The Magic Flute*. Act 1, scene 15, presents a case in point. For the accompanied recitative, Mozart employed a range of timbres found nowhere else in this form. Moreover, his differentiated handling of the instrumentation in the orchestral score is not merely artful but purposefully laid open for the listener. The changing orchestral colors underscore the dramatic progress of the dialogue, which moves in various directions. The plain string accompaniment (mm. 39–50) at the beginning of the recitative is followed in rapid succession by nine combinations with different winds: 2 bassoons and strings (mm. 51–65); 1 flute, 2 oboes, 2 bassoons, and strings (56–61); 2 flutes, 2 oboes, 2 bassoons, and strings (62–82); 2 clarinets, 2 bassoons, and cello (88–90); strings only (91–107); 2 oboes and 2 bassoons (108–12); 2 flutes, 2 oboes, and strings (113–16); strings only (117–39); 1 oboe and strings (140–42); 3 trombones and strings (143–51); and strings only (152–59).

Mozart's choice of instruments in the Speaker Scene is intimately connected with the section's musical organization. He weaves various groups of motifs into the accompanied recitative, distinguishing between three types of motifs: singular, corresponding, and reminiscent. Singular motifs, usually marked by tempo changes, are used to accent key phrases of text such as the passages "Wo Tätigkeit thronet . . ." (Allegro; translation above, p. 123), "Die Absicht ist edel . . ." (Allegro assai), or "Der Lieb und Tugend Eigentum . . ." (Love's and virtue's property; Andante). Corresponding motifs appear particularly prominently, for example, in conjunction with Tamino's courageous approaches to the three temple doors, mimicked by the orchestra, and the violent rebuffs "Zurück!" (stand back!) in B-flat, E-flat, and A-flat major (mm. 69, 76, 83):

4.2. Recurring motives in the Speaker Scene of *The Magic Flute*: (a) instrumental (mm. 68–71); (b) instrumental (mm. 102–7); (c) vocal, with "ceremonial" accompaniment (mm. 137–39).

Particularly effective are the emotionally charged instrumental passages in B-flat minor and F minor (mm. 102–7) that draw attention to Tamino's increasing doubts about his mission on behalf of the Queen of the Night. Finally, the high tensions of the scene marked by the polarity of ignorance and knowledge are relaxed by the priestly Speaker's assurance (mm. 137–39), presented in a melody of hymnal quality with psalmodic instrumental accompaniment (and twice repeated sotto voce in oraclelike fashion by a backstage male choir), that darkness will be dispersed and Pamina will be in reach

"Sobald dich führt der Freundschaft Hand / ins Heiligtum zum ew'gen Band" (As soon as friendship's hand / leads you into the sanctuary for the eternal bond).

The nexus of close internal musical relations and cross-references at work in the Speaker Scene is unique in Mozart's operas—in its dramaturgical function, fundamentally new and different from the kind of musical correspondences elsewhere in *The Magic Flute*. One particularly obvious and often-cited example along these lines is the opening melodic phrase with the characteristic leap of a major sixth in Tamino's aria "Dies Bildnis ist bezaubernd schön" (This portrait is enchantingly beautiful; No. 3) and its repeat by Pamina at the words "Tamino mein . . ." in the brief dialogue of the recognition scene in the second finale.[20]

Recurring musical ideas that waken the dramatic and musical memory of the theatergoer and listener are not new in eighteenth-century opera and occur frequently in Mozart's mature operas.[21] What is new in the Speaker Scene and is so significant in the orchestral score of *The Magic Flute* is the pointed use of instrumentation in building musicodramatic effects. In general, the lavish orchestral writing, as opulent as it is subtle and above all functional, merits special attention as a further defining attribute of Mozart's "grand opera" approach. Although all of his operas from the Viennese decade are distinguished by the special weight he gives to the treatment of the orchestra, *The Magic Flute* crowns this trend. Its orchestra roughly approximates in size that of *Idomeneo* and *Don Giovanni* (apart from the special instruments: glockenspiel and panpipe), but, different from all opera scores except that of *Die Entführung*, it includes an alternation between regular and low-register clarinets, or basset horns. This alternation is particularly effective in Pamina's first encounter with Sarastro (no. 8, mm. 395ff.), which opens with the threefold chord in F major (heard here for the first time since the overture) and thus suggests, by purely timbral means, a change of scene not set down in the libretto.

The wide range of instrumental combinations (table 4.1) illuminates the diversified approach evident throughout the opera and makes clear how closely the orchestral sound is fitted to the character of each number. Mozart even makes changes in the string section, at various occasions dividing the violas and flexibly using the cellos and double basses for the bass line, alterations that mostly cannot be put down in tabular form. The decisive role in these different timbres is usually taken by the winds. Thus nos. 2–4, the three arias near the beginning of the opera, use contrasting combinations of wind instruments. In particular, Tamino's aria is given a strikingly different color by the addition of the clarinets to stress its mediating position. But Mozart did not proceed schematically in this regard. Hence it is immediately noticeable that Papageno— who was played originally by the theater director Schikaneder and is assigned the first and the final solo numbers of the opera—receives in the finale, no. 21, an additional flute accompaniment and thus, with the glockenspiel, transforms the scene into a deftly calculated climax. Nor is it necessary for the winds to appear consistently in pairs, as seen in particular in the treatment of the flutes. Even so, Pamina's G-minor aria "Ach, ich fühl's" (no. 17) represents an exception in this respect. Not only is it unique in its scoring for three contrasting solo winds, this same ploy also gives it a fervent translucency and a special intensity of expression, emphatically underlined by the aria's brief and poignant instrumental postlude.

The days and weeks following the *Zauberflöte* premiere left Mozart with hardly a moment to spare. In a letter of October 7, for example, he told Constanze that among the events of the preceding day "I orchestrated almost the entire Rondo for Stadler," that is, the 353-bar finale of the Clarinet Concerto, K. 622, which already existed in a draft score. The first two movements were presumably finished, for Anton Stadler was scheduled to perform the concerto in Prague on October 16.[22] The entry of this work immediately after *Die Zauberflöte* in Mozart's thematic catalog, albeit undated, is followed only by that of the Little Masonic Cantata, K. 623, of November 15. The Requiem did not find its way into the thematic

Table 4.1: Instrumental Combinations

	flute, piccolo	oboe	clarinet, basset horn	bassoon
FIRST ACT				
1. Overture	2	2	2	2
2. Introduction	2	2	2	2
3. Aria (Papageno)		2		2
4. Aria (Tamino)			2	2
5. Rec. & Aria (Queen of the Night)		2		2
6. Quintet (3 Ladies, Tamino, Papageno)		2	2	2
7. Trio (Pamina, Monostatos, Papageno)	1	2		2
8. Duet (Pamina, Papageno)			2	2
9. Finale (all but 3 Ladies & Queen)	2	2	2→2	2
SECOND ACT				
10. March	1		2	2
11. Aria con coro (Sarastro, Priests)			2	2
12. Duet (Priests 1 & 2)	2	2	2	2
13. Quintet (3 Ladies, Tamino, Papageno)	2	2		2
14. Aria (Monostatos)	1+1		2	2
15. Aria (Queen of the Night)	2	2		2
16. Aria (Sarastro)	2			2
17. Trio (3 Boys)	2			2
18. Aria (Pamina)	1	1		1
19. Chorus (Priests)	2	2		2
20. Trio (Pamina, Tamino, Sarastro)		2		2
21. Aria (Papageno)	1	2		2
22. Finale (all)	2	2	2	2

horn	trumpet, timpani	trombone	strings	panpipes	glockenspiel	flute[a]
FIRST ACT						
2	2+2	3	✓			
2	2+2		✓			
2			✓	✓		
2			✓			
2			✓			
2			✓			
2			✓			
2			✓[b]			
2	2+2	3	✓[b]		✓	✓
SECOND ACT						
2		3	✓			
		3	✓[b,c]			
2	2+2	3	✓[b]			
2	2+2	3	✓[b]			
			✓			
2	2+2		✓			
2			✓			
			✓			
			✓			
2	2+2	3	✓[b]			
			✓			
2			✓		✓	
2	2+2	3	✓[b]	✓	✓	✓

a. "Golden flute" in orchestra pit. b. Divided violas. c. Without double bass.

catalog, but Mozart worked on it mainly during the months of October and November, before the onset of his final illness on November 20. All the same, the overlap between the sketches for two Requiem movements and the overture to *The Magic Flute* indicates that at least some preliminary work on the Requiem antedated the completion of the opera. It therefore comes as no surprise that they have certain points in common, apart from instances relating to the solemn qualities shared by both.

Stylistically, the two works show, in particular, the use of uncomplicated, melodically and rhythmically smooth vocal lines and corresponding instrumental phrases (see the discussion at the end of chap. 3, p. 103). In their compositional technique, they comprise expressly contrapuntal elaboration in many sections and, in general, an innovative conceptual approach while striking out on fresh paths—away from conventional singspiel and toward grand opera, away from church music dominated by instruments and toward church music with a stronger emphasis on the voice.

Another connection between *Die Zauberflöte* and the Requiem was of a completely different nature and arose at the time of the composer's death. His sister-in-law Josepha Hofer (the Queen of the Night in the running *Zauberflöte* production) and his friends Benedikt Schack (Tamino) and Franz Xaver Gerl (Sarastro) reportedly gathered around his sickbed and sang from the still unorchestrated Requiem in short score, with Mozart himself supplying the alto part.[23] Then, shortly after his death on December 5, 1791, in view of the unexpected turn of events and the opera's great success and in a spirit of gratitude and veneration, Schikaneder and his company initiated a memorial service for Mozart and a benefit performance for his family. As one of the Viennese newspapers reported on December 16: "Herr Schikaneder had obsequies performed for the departed, at which the *Requiem*, which he composed in his last illness, was executed. Herr Schikaneder will give a performance of *The Magic Flute* in the next few days for the benefit of the widow."[24]

Thus, as early as December 1791, the Requiem and *Die Zauber-*

flöte formed a remarkable musical twosome that not only marked an initial climax of Mozart's early reception but also set in motion the continuous growth in widespread appreciation that began with his death, and this not just in the German-speaking lands. Within the briefest span of time, *Die Zauberflöte* appeared on Italian stages as *Il flauto magico*, in London alongside *The Beggar's Opera*, and in Paris for a protracted length of time in the bowdlerized form of *Les mystères d'Isis* alongside Beaumarchais' *Le mariage de Figaro*, thereby becoming "one of the sensations of eighteenth-century theatrical history."[25] Indeed, it even far surpassed its precursors and developed over generations into a long-term hit without parallel, thanks to Schikaneder's imaginative libretto, with its broad leeway for interpretative license, but thanks most of all to Mozart's ravishing music. No other work had a similar impact on the history of German opera in the nineteenth century. Although the work had less influence on, for example, such immediate Viennese "successors" as Beethoven and Schubert, it left a particularly strong and formative impression on Carl Maria von Weber and then, especially, on Richard Wagner.

In his late essay on "Das Publikum in Zeit und Raum" of 1878 Wagner made an illuminating—though in many factual details utterly misguided—comment on what had been one of his earliest favorite operas:

> That Mozart's creation so immeasurably exceeded the demands addressed to him and that here no *individual* but a whole *genus* of the most surprising novelty seemed born, we must take as the reason this work stands solitary and assignable to no age whatsoever. Here the eternal, valid for every age and all humanity (I need but point to the dialogue between the *Speaker* and *Tamino*!) is so indissolubly bound up with the absolutely trivial tendency of a piece expressly reckoned by the playwright for the vulgar plaudits of a Viennese suburban theater, that it requires the aid of a historical commentary to understand and approve the whole in its accidental dress. Analysis of the various factors of this work affords us speaking proof of the aforesaid tragic fate of the

creative spirit condemned to a given time and place for the conditions of its activity. To save himself from bankruptcy, the manager of a Viennese suburban theater commissions the greatest musician of his day to help him out with a spectacular piece designed to meet the taste of its habitual public, and Mozart sets music of eternal beauty to the supplied text. But this beauty is inextricably embedded in the work of that director, and—waiving all affectation—it remains truly intelligible to none but that suburban audience of Vienna for whose ephemeral taste it was intended.[26]

For Wagner, *The Magic Flute* represented the cornerstone of German opera. With remarkable precision, he identifies some of the decisive elements that signify the "surprising novelty" and timeless validity of Mozart's last contribution to the history of opera. He singles out the extraordinary dramaturgical role of the Speaker Scene in this regard, its impact on the quality of the libretto, and its impression left on the audience. Wagner subscribed to the long-lasting hypothesis of a fundamental libretto alteration,[27] namely "that the villain was suddenly changed to a hero, the originally good woman to a bad one, making utter nonsense of what had happened in the first act";[28] therefore, he expressed the need for "a historical commentary to understand and approve the whole." Even so, Mozart's musical genius made all the difference to Wagner in his appreciation of the opera vis-à-vis what in his view was a despicable libretto. He recognized the novelty of the music but missed the point that Mozart's concept of "vera opera"—the mutually supporting function and inseparable unity of text and music—came close to his own.

Like Wagner, virtually all the later admirers of *The Magic Flute* saw and understood the work as the crowning achievement in Mozart's operatic oeuvre, very much on a par with the last three symphonies. Yet even though nothing was to follow its premiere, the context that to a great extent produced and shaped the opera— including Mozart's apparent interest in reaching out to a broader musical public—defies any perception of a final statement. In 1791, faced with the opportunity of writing a show for the popular theater, Mozart very much continued steering a clear new course. This time, the premiere of the *Magic Flute* on September 30 and its subsequent performances demonstrated that the opera indeed topped and encompassed his own latest, most modern, and profound creations in the traditional genres—the comic *Così fan tutte* and the serious *La clemenza di Tito*—with a piece of total musical theater. What he produced was not one "vera opera" by itself but a series of works in a continuing search for new shapes of musical drama. Thus, the story of *The Magic Flute* is not that of a capstone but that of the imperial court composer stopped in his tracks by fate.

5

"The Higher Pathetic Style of Church Music" and the Requiem

——————◇ ◇ ◇——————

An Auspicious Prospect

ONE OF THE MOST IMPORTANT and far-reaching, yet often neglected biographical documents from Mozart's last year is a decree issued by the city magistrate of Vienna on May 9, 1791.[1] It states:

> The City Magistrate of the I[mperial]. & R[oyal]. Capital City of Vienna declares that Herr Wolfgang Amadeus Mozart shall in consequence of this petition be assigned as assistant to Herr Leopold Hofmann, Kapellmeister at St. Stephen's Cathedral Church, in such wise that he shall make himself liable by a legal agreement, to be deposited here, to assist the said Herr Kapellmeister in his service without remuneration, to deputize for him when he cannot appear in person, and in case this post of kapellmeister shall fall vacant, to be satisfied with the salary and with all that which the City Magistrate may decree and deem advisable.

Which is herewith imparted to the above for his information.

Jos. Georg Hörl, I & R Councillor and Burgomaster

Ex Cons. Magis. Vien. 9 May 1791

Johann Hübner, *Secret.*[2]

The prehistory of this decree remains largely in the dark but may be related to an event from the spring of 1790. Shortly after the death of Joseph II, Mozart petitioned Archduke Franz, the younger brother of the incoming Emperor Leopold II, for a second kapellmeister post at the court with specific responsibilities for sacred music (see chap. 1, p. 38). In 1782, Emperor Joseph had severely curtailed the sacred-music activities of the court kapelle and, thereby, created quite a stir so that even a far-away Berlin newspaper could announce, "At the Imperial kapelle the former church music has been abolished."[3] The new emperor, however, held a rather different view regarding religious affairs and, on March 17, 1791, officially lifted most of the restrictions regarding sacred-music practices his brother had decreed. This change evidently led to action on behalf of music at the cathedral and certainly paved the way for Mozart to file his application. His petition clearly related to the prominent church-music functions of the court kapelle prior to 1782 when Joseph II reduced its sacred-music duties. However, since a second kapellmeister post for this purpose, as suggested by Mozart, was not approved, the court may well have collaborated with the city's magistrate in devising a new, promising, and money-saving scheme for revitalizing sacred music in the capital.

However the appointment came about, it assured Mozart, by way of a temporarily unpaid yet formal interim adjunct post, of occupying in the future the distinguished kapellmeister office at Vienna's St. Stephen's Cathedral (fig. 5.1). Its incumbent, the fifty-three-year old Leopold Hofmann, had been ailing for quite some time, was no longer active as a composer, spent much of his time at his country house in Oberdöbling outside of Vienna, and continued collecting a lucrative salary of 2,000 florins.[4] The issue is not

5.1. St. Stephen's Cathedral, Vienna, engraving by Karl Schütz, 1792 (*Vienna, Österreichische Nationalbibliothek*)

irrelevant, because in the spring of 1791 someone must at last have determined that a solution was overdue and needed to be found now. The initiative could hardly have come from Mozart himself; it must have come either from the leadership of the city magistrate, from one of Mozart's aristocratic or Masonic supporters, or, most likely, from a high-ranking imperial court official who intervened on Mozart's behalf and encouraged him to submit the petition referred to in the decree.

The considerations regarding the Hofmann succession were surely not prompted by any intention of improving Mozart's financial situation, but rather by the need for finding the best possible candidate for this distinguished post in order to raise the standards at the church to meet those of the theater and chamber music, both of which were under the purview of the imperial court. At any rate, Mozart must have felt encouraged enough to draft a petition in April 1791 and have a presentation copy for the magistrate made by a professional scribe:

Most Honorable and Wise Viennese City Magistrate!
When Herr Kapellmeister Hofmann was stricken ill, I considered taking the liberty of applying for his post in view of the fact that my musical abilities and achievements as well as my compositional skills are well known abroad, my name is held in some esteem everywhere, and I have the honor of holding an appointment as composer at the Court of Vienna for several years now. Therefore, I hope not to be unworthy of this post and to gain favorable consideration by this most learned City Magistrate.

Kapellmeister Hofmann, however, has regained his health, and as I wish and hope with all my heart that he will live a long life, it occurred to me that it might be beneficial to the Cathedral as well as the City Magistrate if I were appointed as an unpaid assistant to the Herr Kapellmeister, who is advanced in years, and thereby gain the opportunity to assist this worthy man in his duties, thus acquiring the approbation of so wise a City Magistrate by my actual participation in the services for which I deem myself well qualified above others, on account of my experience in the church style.

> Your most humble Servant,
> Wolfgang Amadé Mozart
> Imperial and Royal Court Composer[5]

Mozart's petition carefully avoids making any reference to a possible future vacancy in the post. The decree as such, however, does so very clearly, and actually represents a contractual commitment. Clearly, some backroom maneuvers at the magistrate must have taken place. According to the council minutes, the petition was initially rejected at the meeting on April 28 "because the Herr Kapellmeister at St. Stephen's had not requested an adjunct," but the appointment was approved less than two weeks later, expanded by the express assurance in the decree that the initially unpaid adjunct position would eventually lead to the kapellmeister appointment at full salary. Moreover, in contrast to the imperial appointment of December 1787, which was apparently neglected by the press, a newspaper report of May 21, 1791, went even beyond the more restrained wording of the decree by stating more plainly: "The court composer Mozart has received from the local magistrate the assurance of the kapellmeister position at St. Stephen's at a salary of 2,000 florins."[6] Yet, history took a different course. Mozart died that December and the adjunct post fell to Johann Georg Albrechtsberger, court organist in Vienna, distinguished composer, theorist, and Mozart's senior by twenty years.[7] A little over a year later, the Viennese magistrate also honored the commitment previously made to Mozart and, after Hofmann's death in March 1793, Albrechtsberger became kapellmeister of the cathedral and retained that office until the end of his life in 1809.

Mozart held the adjunct post at St. Stephen's for less than seven months in 1791, but there are no concrete references, let alone documents, that shed any light on how this new but loosely defined responsibility fit into his life and work. To be sure, reports on everyday musical life at the cathedral are not normally expected unless matters depart from well-established routines or some specific event requires comment, but evidently neither of these occurred during that year. A single casual remark by Mozart in a letter of July 12, 1791, to Anton Stoll, choirmaster in Baden near Vienna, brings up that he has "been asked to conduct a Mass in a church here" and, therefore, urgently requests the return of performing parts he had loaned him for the Mass in B-flat major, K. 275, and the Gradual "Pax vobis" in B-flat by Michael Haydn. Although the cathedral is not specifically mentioned as the performance venue, it would seem plausible that Mozart routinely conducted at a number of Sunday and feast-day services there without making much fuss about it.

He may also have done so—and maybe played the cathedral organ as well—even prior to his adjunct appointment, since he always had good relations with the clergy at St. Stephen's. After all, he and Constanze were married at the cathedral in 1782, two of their children were baptized there, and the Mozarts lived in its immediate vicinity from 1784 to 1787 and again from the fall of 1790 on. Two documents shed light on the likelihood that from 1788 on, Mozart was turning his attention to church music. On August 2, 1788, he asked his sister in Salzburg to get in touch with Michael Haydn there for a special request: "I would appreciate it very much if Haydn could lend me for a little while the 2 *Tutti-Masses* and the Graduali he composed;—I would return them with gratitude."[8] In the same month, Joachim Daniel Preisler of Copenhagen reported in an August 22 journal entry following a visit with Mozart, that "he now produces church music in Vienna, and since the *operetta* has come to an end, he has nothing more to do with the theater."[9]

Most likely, the reference to the "operetta" relates to the abolition of the German singspiel (chap. 1, p. 17) rather than the Viennese production of *Don Giovanni* (premiered in May 1788) and the "production of church music" to stated intentions by the composer and perhaps also to the upcoming public performances of Handel oratorios for the van Swieten circle. It is worth speculating that the overall situation described by Preisler may have something to do with the leadership reorganization for the imperial court music in 1788 and that Mozart may have received word, directly or indirectly, about general plans for sacred music in the capital city. At least something must have encouraged him in 1788 to begin thinking about contributing to church music and preparing himself for a certain eventuality.

A more concrete substantiation for Mozart's practical involvement with sacred music in Vienna can be found in the cathedral's music collection of eighteenth-century materials. Even though this has survived only in a sadly depleted state, it once contained numerous works by Mozart from his Salzburg period. There is evidence, however, that three Masses—the Missa brevis in B-flat major, K. 275, of 1777 and two Masses in C major, K. 317 ("Coronation") of 1779 and K. 337 of 1780—as well as several other works for which Viennese performing parts from Mozart's lifetime either exist or are documented,[10] were used by the composer to fulfill his obligations as an adjunct to Leopold Hofmann and on other occasions. And most likely, the motet "Ave verum corpus" K. 618, which Mozart composed on June 17, 1791, during a short visit in Baden, was performed not only there, on or near the feast of Corpus Christi (on June 22, after he had already left town),[11] but also, given his new capacity, at St. Stephen's in Vienna.[12] Mozart wanted to join the traditional Corpus Christi procession from there to the Josefstadt "holding a candle in my hand" as he wrote on June 25 to Constanze in Baden.[13]

After having abandoned his position as cathedral organist in Salzburg under Prince-Archbishop Colloredo, Mozart apparently showed no interest in seeking a church office anywhere in Vienna, a clear stance that extended also to his prolonged hiatus from writing sacred music. The single exception to his sacred-music suspension was the work on the large-scale Mass in C minor, K. 427, which he undertook as a votive Mass in preparation for his first and only visit from Vienna to his hometown Salzburg, in the summer of 1783. There, in a service, he apparently performed the finished portion of the work. The rest of the Mass, however, with drafts of individual movements in various states of completion, remained a torso.[14] The Kyrie and Gloria parts of the C-minor Mass were later rearranged for the large-scale cantata "Davidde penitente" K. 469, and presented at a public concert in March 1785 to benefit the *Tonkünstler-Sozietät*, the musicians' pension fund.

Apart from this Mass and the work derived from it, the only completed piece of sacred music Mozart composed in the Viennese decade is the short motet "Ave verum corpus" of June 1791 mentioned earlier. Nevertheless, and independent of his cathedral appointment, Mozart's reputation as a composer of church music grew from the late 1780s on, primarily through Vienna's busiest music dealer, Johann Traeg. Traeg's sales catalogs increasingly included manuscript copies of Masses and other sacred compositions Mozart had written in Salzburg, which thus became more widely available. The Hofkapelle under Antonio Salieri also expanded its church-music repertoire with numerous Mozart works, most of them acquired from Traeg after the composer's death. It appears, however, that Salieri selected a Mozart Mass next to his own Te deum in D major for the official coronation ceremony in Prague's St. Vitus Cathedral on September 6, 1791. It has long been assumed that the work in question was the mass in C major, K. 317, but extant manuscript sources from the court kapelle point to the C-major Mass, K. 337, which apparently replaced a Mass by Koželuch originally planned for the important event of Leopold II's coronation as king of Bohemia.[15] In the manuscript score of K. 337, Salieri notated an extra viola part in the "Et incarnatus" of the Credo, filling a perceived void left by Mozart, who had scored this movement like all his other Salzburg church works for just two violins and bass.[16] Thus, he brought the work in line with the Italian custom in which the viola often doubles the continuo part.

The two solemn Masses in C major, K. 317 and K. 337, composed for the Salzburg cathedral, stand as the culmination point of Mozart's early career, the composer having devoted much of his young life to the broad spectrum of genres in sacred music—masses, litanies, vespers, motets, and other works. In 1783, Mozart once again put his hand to a Mass, this time on a work of great complexity and length, but for reasons largely unknown did not finish it. Then, after a further hiatus of more than eight years, he returned to a musical subject area that had once been at the focus of his interests by accepting the commission for a Requiem Mass.[17]

A Timely Commission

THE REQUIEM owes its origin to Franz Count von Walsegg, a music-loving nobleman who owned estates outside of Vienna and a business office in the city, and who was the landlord of Mozart's Masonic brother and benevolent financier Michael Puchberg. The wealthy count commissioned the work in memory of his wife Anna, née Flammberg, who had died on February 14, 1791, at the youthful age of twenty-one. The assignment, which Mozart accepted at some point during the summer but definitely before he left for Prague in August, was handled through an intermediary because the count wanted to guard his anonymity. Mozart surely welcomed the fee and the advance, but what must have made him particularly receptive to the idea was the chance to turn his attention to a type of sacred music that was new to him. Never before had he written a Funeral Mass and, in anticipation of his future role as kapellmeister of the cathedral, he realized that music in this category would be frequently needed, notably in the empire's capital city. He may, for example, have remembered that earlier in that very year, on February 20, the first anniversary of the death of Joseph II, Salieri conducted the Requiem in C minor by Leopold Hofmann, whom Mozart expected to succeed.

Seen in this context, the Requiem commission gained personal importance for Mozart because it provided the opportunity to compose a major liturgical repertoire piece that would mark his return to sacred music, his supposed "favorite subject,"[18] and enable him to refresh and expand his previously acquired knowledge of church style. Such consideration also lends credibility to Constanze's later statement that her husband "told her of the remarkable request [to compose a Requiem], and at the same time expressed his desire to try his hand at this genre, the more so as the higher pathetic style of church music had always appealed to his genius."[19]

There is yet a further layer in the context for the Requiem. By the time Mozart received the commission, he apparently had been thinking increasingly and seriously of sacred music—probably not only in conjunction with his duties at St. Stephen's Cathedral, but also during the years leading up to 1791. Of particular significance in this regard is his involvement from 1788 to 1790 with performances of major vocal works by George Frideric Handel and Carl Philipp Emanuel Bach, which he prepared for and conducted at Baron van Swieten's private and public concerts.[20] Although not music for liturgical purposes, these works opened up for him new perspectives on the realm and the rich tradition of sacred music in a broader sense, to which must be added his study of music by Johann Sebastian Bach. Even the ceremonial numbers in *The Magic Flute* benefited from this musical experience.

Finally, the Requiem commission fits into concrete plans Mozart had for new works of church music, all of them dating from after 1787.[21] Several manuscript fragments indicate that Mozart laid at least the groundwork for some Masses (table 5.1).[22] The only criteria available for an approximate chronology are provided by the analysis of the paper types used by the composer throughout the

Table 5.1: Fragments of Mass Movements from the Final Years

Kyrie in C major, K. Anh. 13 (Fr 1787b)[23]
 for 4 voices, 2 trumpets, timpani, strings, and organ: 9 measures

Gloria in C major, K. Anh. 20 (Fr 1787c)
 for 4 voices, 2 trumpets, timpani, strings, and organ: 26 measures

Kyrie in D major, K. Anh. 14 (Fr 1787e)
 for 4 voices, 2 oboes, bassoon, strings, and organ: 11 measures (see Fig. 6.4, below)

Kyrie in G major, K. Anh. 16 (Fr 1787a)
 for 4 voices, 2 trumpets, timpani, strings, and organ: 34 measures, completed by
 Maximilian Stadler

Kyrie in C major, K. Anh. 15 (Fr 1790a)
 for 4 voices, 2 oboes, 2 bassoons, 2 trumpets, timpani, strings, and organ: 37 measures,
 completed by Stadler

Sketch for a Credo in D major, K. deest ("Nantes" sketch leaf[24]): 13 measures; includes a
 sketch for an untexted soprano part in D minor, K. deest: 32 measures

5.2. Requiem, K. 626, beginning of "Lacrymosa," autograph score (*Vienna, Österreichische Nationalbibliothek*)

course of his creative life. In this case, most sacred music fragments were written on paper in use after 1787. Nevertheless, the possibility that in 1791 Mozart drew on an unused piece of ruled music paper from an earlier year needs to be taken into consideration. It therefore remains open whether the projected works were related to his function as adjunct at the cathedral or conceived earlier and independent of the appointment. The fragments record the basic ideas Mozart had for the music of a certain piece or movement but he lacked the time, a commission, or a specific purpose for its further elaboration. At any rate, the drafts in open score clearly indicate that the compositions were intended to be finished at a later point (fig. 5.2; for parallel instances, see chap. 6).

Some other manuscripts in Mozart's hand representing incomplete copies of works by Georg Reutter Jun., former kapellmeister of St. Stephen's Cathedral, also need to be considered. They apparently belong to Mozart's performing materials prepared for his sacred-music activities. Once regarded as early works by Mozart himself, they include a Kyrie in D, K. 186^i; "De profundis" K. Anh, A22; and "Memento Domine David" K. Anh. A23.[25] Additionally, an important work to take into account as part of this Viennese repertory is the so-called "Munich" Kyrie in D minor, K. 341,[26] an elaborate composition for four voices and a richly scored instrumental accompaniment of 2 flutes, 2 oboes, 2 clarinets, 2 bassoons, 4 horns, 2 trumpets, timpani, strings, and organ. First published by Johann André around 1825 presumably on the basis of Mozart's original score, it remains unclear if this single Kyrie movement was completed by Mozart himself or by someone like Abbé Maximilian Stadler. Moreover, in 2008 an entirely unknown sketch for a Credo in D major turned up. Although the autograph manuscript is definitely of Viennese origin yet not precisely datable, it seems intriguing to relate the Credo sketch to K. 341 and perhaps to a projected larger-scale Mass in D.

Envisioning a New Kind of Sacred Music

CONSTANZE MOZART'S reference, cited above, to "the higher pathetic style of church music" as a genre with special appeal to Mozart invites a comparison with the meaning of "pathetic style" as discussed in contemporaneous literary sources. For example, according to the definition given by Johann Christoph Adelung in his book *Über den deutschen Styl* (About the German style; Leipzig, 1785), the pathetic style "enlarges [enhances] every idea on account of vigorous [intense] pathos."[27] Similarly, Johann Georg Sulzer, in his *Allgemeine Theorie der schönen Künste* (General theory of the fine arts; Leipzig, 1779) defines pathos generally in terms of grandeur of sentiment ("Größe der Empfindung"), especially depictions that "fill the spirit with the dark emotions"—of fear, terror, and somber sadness—that art has the power, even the duty, to arouse. "In music," he writes, "it is prevalent above all in church pieces and in tragic opera, although it rarely rises to such heights. The dying chorus in Graun's *Iphigenia* is very pathetic; and there is said to be much pathos in the *Alcestis* of Chevalier Gluck."[28] Given Mozart's extensive operatic experience, and given the Funeral Mass text as an ideal vehicle for musical expressions of grand sentiments— especially strong, darker emotions—the composer's declared "desire to try his hand at this genre" can be readily understood.

The stylistic premises of the Requiem are most clearly revealed by Mozart's autograph score which, in spite of its fragmentary state, completely defines the musical substance of the work. An examination of the autograph suggests that Mozart's compositional planning and execution in the Requiem resembled closely his mature practice of writing string quartets. The Requiem score focuses primarily on the four-part vocal setting as a whole, lets it unfold in phrases and sections, and never singles out one voice over another for a longer section of the composition. The instrumental score definitely remains subordinate to the primary vocal substance. In this respect the Requiem indicates the composer's intention to explore new horizons, as it differs fundamentally from his Salzburg church music and also from the advanced and daring style of the C-minor Mass of 1783, with its virtuoso vocal solos and opulent instrumental score. Hence, Mozart took advantage of the unexpected commission as an opportunity for a fresh return to his "favorite subject" and, at the same time, to elevate it to a new level.

As for the stylistic premises of the Requiem, in particular the fundamentally transparent and coherent four-part vocal setting, Mozart applied the same general idea and approach he had used in the "Ave verum corpus" motet of June 1791. Though the Requiem is a much larger piece, more differentiated in gestures, polyphonic textures, and integration of both retrospective and decidedly forward-looking elements, it took the Corpus Christi motet, its redefinition of the proportional and functional relationship of a vocal setting with its instrumental accompaniment and its novel stylistic orientation as a point of departure for further refinement in terms of scale and contrapuntal technique. As the brief motet happens to be the first piece of sacred music undertaken and completed after his appointment at St. Stephen's, it seems as though Mozart the faithful Roman Catholic chose one of the highest feasts of his church to make a meaningful contribution to sacred music, an area in which he had been inactive for years. Moreover, he used this occasion to give sacred music a new conceptual direction in very much the same way as he had previously done, for example, with the three symphonies of 1788.

The modest motet for four voices, strings, and organ, a piece of only 46 measures in length, shows remarkable melodic and harmonic restraint, elegant and graceful simplicity as well as supple and extremely transparent polyphonic textures. This combination of features was designed to carry the liturgical text, follow its prosody closely, underscore its meaning, and significantly enhance and enlarge its overall ceremonial character and religious sentiments. The accompaniment, with its short instrumental prelude, brief interludes, and succinct postlude, supports the vocal structure, derives its declamatory identity entirely from it, and contributes no additional substance to the piece. Incidentally, a very similar conceptual approach is typical of the fragmentary Mass movements K. Anh. 13, 14, 16, and 20, but in neither the Kyrie fragment K. Anh. 15 nor the D-minor Kyrie, K. 341, suggesting that the latter two may belong to an earlier strand within the 1788-to-1791 chronological frame.

This focus on external effortlessness and expressive immediacy in the "Ave verum corpus" finds its nearest musical equivalent outside the Requiem in the melodic style and instrumental accompaniment of the arias sung by Tamino, Pamina, and Sarastro in *The Magic Flute,* on which Mozart was working at the same time. It also anticipates the kind of simple melodic elegance that adorns the thematic inventions for the Clarinet Concerto, K. 622, of October 1791, which in turn picks up similar patterns in the last piano concerto,

K. 595, and a number of other instrumental pieces (see chap. 3, p. 103). In comparison with all these, the principal musical features of the motet are reduced to a bare minimum, yet they fulfill their ceremonial function in the sacred piece very directly and particularly well. While the Requiem reflects a different degree of complexity and sophistication, its general compositional approach in terms of focusing on the vocal score resembles the principles established so clearly in the motet. They are reflected clearly throughout the Requiem, most strikingly at the point of transition from the "Confutatis" to the "Lacrimosa" movements of the "Dies irae" sequence. Here both the substance and the structure of the compositional material are carried exclusively by the vocal parts. The refined and elegant enharmonic modulation from A minor via A-flat minor and G minor to F minor with an uncanny major-mode ending (mm. 26ff.) is achieved principally through vocal part-writing:

5.1. "Oro supplex" section from the "Confutatis" movement (no. 6) of the Requiem: vocal score, mm. 25–40.

Moreover, the short instrumental opening phrase of the subsequent "Lacrimosa" (fig. 5.2) effectively prefigures the subsequent vocal textures, with the bassetto (viola) citing the initial bass line of the Introit.[29]

The only surviving sketch leaf from the Requiem contains a passage from the "Rex tremendae" and the thematic layout of a concluding "Amen" fugue for the "Dies irae" sequence and corroborates the evidence of the autograph score regarding the overall stylistic orientation of the work. Two single sketches do not permit drawing wide-ranging conclusions, but they nevertheless underscore the composer's primary focus on the four-part vocal setting which, at the same time, serves as the material source for the accompanying instrumental score. In other words, as in the motet, the instrumental substance derives its identity primarily from the defining vocal material.

Naturalness and simplicity—but not in the sense of artless naïveté—that definitely include the elegant infusion of a broad range of stirring chromaticism and other expressive devices appear as deliberate aesthetic goals. This is impressively demonstrated throughout the Requiem and is particularly evident in the exemplary "Domine Jesu" movement and its display of various complementary features, among them the evolution of its chief motif:

Do - mi-ne Ie - su Chri - ste   Do - mi-ne Ie - su Chri - ste   Do - mi-ne Ie - su Chri - ste

5.2. "Domine Jesu Christe" (no. 8) from the Requiem: modifications of vocal head motif.

The triadic melody is presented in three simple but different configurations, climactically staggered: first in the minor mode, then in major, and finally in a modal mixture of minor and major. Originally supported by a homophonic instrumental accompaniment, the latter gradually incorporates refined imitative textures without ever giving up its modest sweep.

Almost a quarter century after the Requiem was written, the composer-writer E. T. A. Hoffmann, in an influential essay of 1814, "Old and New Church Music," specifically praised Mozart's work as the ideal of a new kind of sacred music. He does so precisely because of the primacy of its vocal qualities, which he contrasts with the more playful and considerably less solemn outlook of Haydn's masses:

> In the last half of the eighteenth century increasing enfeeblement and sickly sweetness finally overcame art; keeping step with so-called enlightened attitudes, which killed every deeper religious impulse, it eventually drove all gravity and dignity from church music. Even music for worship in Catholic churches, the masses, vespers, Passiontide hymns, etc., acquired a character that previously would have been too insipid and undignified even for opera seria. [. . .] Mozart's masses, which he is known to have composed to a prescribed pattern on paid commission, are almost his weakest works. In one church work, however, he has revealed his innermost feelings; and who can remain unmoved by the fervent devotion and spiritual ecstasy radiating from it? His Requiem is the most sublime achievement that the modern period has contributed to the church. Compelling and profound though Haydn's settings of the High Mass frequently are, and excellent though his harmonic development is, there is still hardly one of them that is completely without playfulness, without melodies quite inappropriate to the dignity of church style.[30]

The primacy of the vocal structure had consequences for the scoring and instrumentation of the Requiem. Those who find the lack of oboes and flutes in the Requiem score inconsistent with Mozart's style in works from his last year, notably the two operas,[31] misunderstand the composer's intentions. In terms of their orchestral treatment, neither *Die Zauberflöte* nor *La clemenza di Tito* can be considered as stylistic and technical parallels. Their prominent instrumental scores serve an entirely different purpose. Mozart surely had no interest in an operatic dressing-up of his new style of church music. On the contrary, his reduction of the woodwinds to low-register clarinets clearly is thought of as underscoring the somber character of a Requiem Mass. There is, however, one point that both the Requiem and *The Magic Flute* have in common: the very concise design and deliberate shortness of instrumental introductions and interludes for the vocal solo numbers, a definite move away from the more generous, ritornello-like structures that prevail in the earlier works, and above all projecting the multifaceted reservoir of musical rhetoric and styles from Handel and Bach through the century and aiming at the future.

Further aspects help illuminate Mozart's new approach to sacred music. There is, first of all, the liturgical functionality of the Requiem. As he received the commission under a cloak of anonymity and secrecy, Mozart could not know the person to whom it was to be dedicated (the Countess Walsegg). Therefore, he was in no position to take individual circumstances into account except what may have been specified by the commission, and had no reason to depart from the usual norms regarding size and quality of performing forces or formal layout of the work. So he decided in favor of something at once pragmatic and consciously original as evidenced, for example, by the choice of basset horns in order to underscore the character of mournfulness. Rather than a grand and large-scale work suitable for a specific ceremonial occasion, he designed a concise, liturgically useful work of well under one hour's length—in short, he created a repertory piece of regular liturgical dimensions. Its overall form, with relatively brief individual movements, conformed to the type of a "Missa brevis et solemnis," as appropriate for a standard repertory piece but quite unlike, for instance, the monumental dimensions planned for the C-minor Mass, K. 427, of 1783.

At the same time, he gave the Requiem an individual cast of sonority (notably by involving the unusual basset horns), texture, and musical language intended to make it stand out from the traditional requiem types familiar to him. Moreover, he created an overall musical architecture[32] that closely follows the various correspondences in the liturgical text: "dona eis requiem" (associated with the principal "Requiem theme"; see ex. 5.3) occurs three times in the liturgical text and, accordingly, in movements 1, 7, and 12.

Table 5.2: Principal Formal Design Features of the Requiem

LITURGICAL SECTION	MOVEMENT	FUGUE AT WORDS
Introit and	1a. *Requiem aeternam dona eis**	
Kyrie	1b. Kyrie	Kyrie eleison
Sequence	2. Dies irae	
	3. Tuba mirum	
	4. Rex tremendae	
	5. Recordare	
	6. Confutatis	
	7a. Lacrimosa . . . *dona eis requiem**	
	7b. [*Amen**][a]	Amen
Offertory	8. Domine Jesu	
	9. Hostias	Quam olim Abrahae
Sanctus	10a. Sanctus	
	10b. Osanna	Osanna in excelsis
	11. Benedictus	
	10b. Osanna	Osanna in excelsis
Agnus Dei and	12a. Agnus Dei . . . *dona eis requiem**	
Communion	12b. Lux aeterna	Cum sanctis tuis[b]

*Requiem theme
a. Not completed—autograph sketch only. b. "Kyrie" fugue repeated (as allegedly suggested to Süssmayr by Mozart).

Second, he concludes each liturgical section—Introit and Kyrie (movement 1), Sequence (2–7), Offertory (8–9), Sanctus (10–11), and Agnus Dei (12)—with a fugue and, thereby, gives the whole work a compellingly logical overall form (table 5.2).

As for Mozart's personal definition of a "higher pathetic style of sacred music," he found it important, in the interest of continuity, to fit his own work into the tradition of church music in general and the funeral genre in particular. Significantly, however, he did not integrate the classical vocal polyphony of the Palestrina-Fux tradition into his new concept, even though this style had become an integral part of church music practices in Vienna during the later eighteenth century.[33] But Mozart looked back only as far as the generation of Bach and Handel, thereby bringing something entirely new into the Austrian tradition. Anyhow, he was not merely adopting ideas and themes or thinking of copying earlier style models as such. Rather, his primary intention was to integrate certain manners of traditional counterpoint into his music in order to enrich its stylistic vocabulary, refine its texture, and to enhance and strengthen its expressive prowess. The deliberate exploration of polyphony, in the manner of Bach and Handel in particular—as he did by combining fugue and sonata principles in the finale of the G-major Quartet, K. 387, or by playing with canonic devices in the minuet of the C-minor wind serenade K. 388, both of 1782—led to a wholly new kind of form, style, and sound image, with nothing backward-looking about it. The same is true of the Requiem, except at those points where the composer—as in the Kyrie fugue—plainly acknowledges older models. Even there, considering the way he designs the concluding cadence following a dimished seventh chord, he does not choose conventional patterns.

The opening movement of the Requiem indicates in particular Mozart's indebtedness to models that provided him with points of orientation in his search for integrating new and old ways of composing. He borrows substantive musical material from the opening chorus of Handel's *Funeral Anthem for Queen Caroline*, HWV 264,

5.3. Incipit of the Lutheran funeral hymn "Wenn mein Stündlein vorhanden ist" (from Handel's Funeral Anthem, HWV 264) and Mozart's "Requiem" theme.

of 1737. The Handelian material includes the instrumental introduction (including its staccato articulation) as well as the principal
Requiem theme with its countersubject. The chorale elaboration
in the second half of Handel's movement quotes the well-known
tune used for two Lutheran funeral hymns, "Wenn mein Stündlein
vorhanden ist" and "Herr Jesu Christ, du höchstes Gut." The first
line of this latter sixteenth-century melody supplies the Requiem
theme (ex. 5.3, previous page).

Unlike Handel, though, Mozart combines this theme with a liturgical cantus firmus for the text portion "Te decet hymnus" (Psalm
65). He picks up the idea of a psalm tone for this text segment
from Michael Haydn's C-minor Requiem, composed in 1771 for
the funeral of the Salzburg Archbishop Sigismund Schrattenbach,
a performance in which Mozart participated. Mozart, however, did
not choose psalm tone I used by Haydn, but psalm tone IX, the so-
called "tonus peregrinus,"[34] preferred in the Lutheran realm as, for
example, in Bach's *Magnificat.* The liturgical chorale along with the
German funeral chorale line—both unfamiliar to Austrian Catholic
audiences—enlarges the scope of the entire Introit movement and
actually turns it into a double chorale elaboration and a genuine
contrapuntal feat.

The material of the subsequent Kyrie fugue comes from another
Handel work, the closing chorus of the Dettingen *Te Deum* of 1743.
Mozart again borrowed both theme and countersubject, but changing the mode from Handel's D major to D minor. Abbé Maximilian
Stadler, an adviser to Mozart's widow and the first organizer of the
composer's musical estate, reported in his *Vertheidigung der Echtheit
des Mozartischen Requiem* (Defense of the authenticity of Mozart's
Requiem; Vienna, 1826) that "in the last years of his life Mozart still
had such respect for the great masters that he preferred their ideas
to his own."[35] Intimately familiar with Mozart's working materials,
Stadler was also the first to observe and report that Mozart chose
Handel "as his model in solemn vocal music" and to draw attention
to Mozart's adoption of Handelian "motives" in the Requiem:

Just as Mozart took the motif for the "Kyrie" from a Handel oratorio, so too he took the motif for the "Requiem" from Handel's anthem for the Funeral of Queen Caroline, composed in the year 1737. [. . .] He found a very apt idea for a requiem in this anthem; used it as some sheets among his papers testified, worked it out in his own style, added the "Kyrie" in the manner suggested by Handel's idea, and then, when he actually received the commission to compose a requiem, he sought out his old sketches, put everything into his new score and developed it all in masterly style.

True connoisseurs will assuredly obtain exquisite musical pleasure if they compare Handel's anthem and Mozart's Requiem. They will see how skillfully and beautifully both masters worked out their different chorale settings and developed the whole motive; they will admire them both and be at a loss to say which is the better.[36]

Stadler's account proves accurate, insofar as Mozart's use of Handelian material in the Requiem did not constitute straightforward borrowing as commonly understood, but was limited to the selection of musical motives: preexistent ideas were developed independently, linked with other materials, and augmented by essentially new material, thus achieving in the end a wholly original result. Neither the Introit nor the Kyrie fugues resemble their Handelian models in the way the material was compositionally developed and shaped. The unmistakably Mozartean trait of redefining his models is apparent from the very first bars, where he broke up the strict rhythm of Handel's string chords, modified the bass line, and transposed the contrapuntal oboe parts down to the alto and tenor registers for basset horns and bassoons, respectively. The result far outreaches Handel's original in contrapuntal complexity (including stretto treatment of the two chorales) and also in refined compositional accomplishment as a whole.

Mozart also had access to the vocal music of Johann Sebastian Bach, whose B-minor Mass and *Magnificat* were among the manuscripts to be found in the music collection of Baron van Swieten.

There Mozart could have seen, for instance, that Bach worked the ninth psalm tone into the "Suscepit Israel" movement of his *Magnificat* as Mozart would in the Requiem. Since visiting Leipzig in 1789, where he encountered Bach's vocal music, notably the motet "Singet dem Herrn," BWV 225, Mozart could regard Bach as an exemplary model for a forward-looking style of vocal polyphony (see chap. 3, p. 66). Stadler also specifically referred to Mozart utilizing Bach:

> Mozart inserted a chorale into this opera [*The Magic Flute,* song of the Two Men in Armor] that was not of his own invention; moreover, for its accompaniment he took an idea of the celebrated Sebastian Bach. I refer . . . to Kirnberger's *Kunst des reinen Satzes,* Berlin, 1774, page 243. It should be observed that Mozart had already composed a totally different accompaniment for this very chorale, which I possess in his manuscript [K. 620b = K. Anh. 78]. . . . Anyone who compares these two different versions of the chorale will see for himself the different character of this wonderful accompaniment.[37]

Although the phenomenon of Bach-style counterpoint added only an effective surprise moment to the musical dramaturgy of *The Magic Flute,* Mozart realizes the concept of persistent and varied contrapuntal polyphony throughout the Requiem. Going well beyond an emphasis on any single model, the work essentially represents a folding of Handelian and Bachian ideas and principles into Mozart's very own language of music. This concept penetrates every page of the Requiem, not only in its strict fugal passages but just as effectively in the many sections that show more loosely knit yet consistently contrapuntal elaboration as particularly notable—for instance, in the "Recordare" movement of the "Dies irae" sequence. Georg Nikolaus Nissen recognized this in his 1828 biography, where he aptly described the Requiem as a masterpiece "that unites the power, the sacred dignity of the music of the past with the rich dressing of the music of the present."[38]

To summarize, the Requiem and the "Ave verum corpus" motet definitively complement one another as examples that mark a singular culmination point in Mozart's church music. However, in the context in which they originated, they shed light on the composer's quest and his initial departure for a new style of sacred music. The departure aspect is compounded by his recent appointment as adjunct at St. Stephen's Cathedral, an assignment that had barely materialized, let alone been consummated. Therefore, the two works offer only a hint at what may have been in store for the "higher pathetic style of sacred music" and its guiding elements that the composer intended to emphasize. They included primarily:

- a concise musical format in the interest of liturgical repertory standards in the emerging post-Josephinian era;
- a focus on vocal substance and on flexible and transparent polyphony, in the interest of an intimate accord between words and music and in line with a redefinition of the role of the orchestra;
- emphasis on animated pathos, dignity, and solemnity ("so flowing, so noble, and so full of expression"),[39] aided by a seamless integration of historical models.

The Requiem opens up illuminating perspectives on broader concerns that engaged the composer at the time. A seemingly inconsequential remark, Abbé Stadler's reference to Kirnberger, cited above, brings up Mozart's study of this theoretician's influential treatise. Johann Philipp Kirnberger, a pupil of Bach's, essentially codified in his treatise his teacher's art of principled and forward-looking composition, and the book's title *Die Kunst des reinen Satzes in der Musik* (Berlin, 1774–79)[40] defines this art characteristically as pure composition. The choice of the word "pure" here reflects its use in late eighteenth-century German idealist philosophy as articulated most prominently in Immanuel Kant's *Kritik der reinen Vernunft* (Critique of pure reason) of 1781.

Neither a philosopher nor a theoretician, but a teacher and in particular a deeply reflective person, Mozart's express concern about the idea of "vera" opera regarding the dramaturgical and musical concepts for *La clemenza di Tito* attests to his awareness of, and interest in, matters true, genuine, and pure. This is not to suggest that the composer engaged in philosophical study and discourse, but implies that he did not remain untouched by fundamental contemporary intellectual issues of analytic judgment. Thus, it could be said that in his imperial period, Mozart pursued an all-encompassing idea of pure sacred music and with it even his own concept of pure composition and its practical realization.

There is hardly a more eloquent document to be linked with Mozart's musical biography than his Requiem. Following the composer to his end, it creates the awareness of both artistic consummation and irretrievable loss, a loss clearly extending beyond the Requiem fragment as such and casting a light on the much larger fragment of an abbreviated creative life. However, Mozart's unintendedly final piece, like the works in the various other genres that indicate the composer's determination to move into a new direction, leaves completely open the question of what would have happened if . . . Both Beethoven and Schubert, for example, adhered in their orchestral Masses to the symphonic style of sacred music set forth so authoritatively by Haydn in his late Masses postdating Mozart's death. They did not adopt the Mozartean alternative that E. T. A. Hoffmann in 1814 called "the most sublime achievement that the modern period has contributed to the church" (above, p. 150). Yet, even though familiar with the Requiem, which became so notorious after its first publication in 1800, they revered it as an exceptional work and a special legacy rather than as a stylistic model representing, along with the "Ave verum corpus" motet, a new path.

6

"Composed, Just Not Yet Written"—Music Never to Be Heard

————◇ ◇ ◇————

A Self-Assured Prodigy

MOZART ALWAYS COMPOSED MUSIC in his head. Even before he was able to hold a pen and write, the little Minuet K. 2, Andante K. 5b, Allegro K. 3, and Minuet K. 4 played by the scarcely five-year-old wunderkind were not merely improvised at the keyboard. Rather, they were created as essentially finished ideas and repeatable short pieces in his brain and would have gotten lost had they not been dictated by playing the notes, written down in musical notation and surely edited by his father, Leopold Mozart, who recorded them as "compositions of the little Wolfgang."[1] Only from about 1764 do pieces exist in the hand of the seven-to-eight-year-old boy, but mostly still emended and polished by his father.[2] However, Leopold's initially guiding[3]—later merely editorial—hand disappeared relatively soon after 1767 from the young composer's music manuscripts. What in principle remained unchanged, however, was the sequence of composing music first in his head and then writing it down—a process that included his testing musical thoughts at the keyboard and his sketching intricate passages on paper. Yet, Mozart's own phrase "componirt, nur noch nicht niedergeschrieben" (composed, just not yet written)[4] does not insinuate the normal mental process of thinking before doing. It rather implies that not only the basic idea for a musical composition but a whole piece or movement was more or less prefigured and essentially shaped in the composer's head before he set his pen down on paper.

This was and is by no means the typical working habit of composers, not even for the likes of Bach or Beethoven, who were known as versatile performers and could comfortably improvise entire pieces ex tempore in a play-as-you-go manner. Beethoven usually labored excessively over the creation of his compositions, from developing formative sketches—sometimes even for shaping a single theme—to working out major details of a score in his sketchbooks. Bach, on the other hand, sketched very little and wrote down even complicated polyphonic scores in the form of a more or less final draft. However, he normally did so section-by-section and, when the whole piece was done, reviewed, emended, and refined the score (see also below, p. 174).

The occasion that prompted Mozart to speak of music "composed, just not yet written" occurred toward the end of 1780, when the twenty-four-year-old composer took a leave of absence from his job as Salzburg court organist. He disliked the position and thus spent several months at the electoral court in Munich working on *Idomeneo*. The production of the most prestigious opera commission he had yet received was scheduled for the 1781 carnival season and would become a turning point in his career. During its preparatory phase, Leopold Mozart, the proud and ambitious father at home in Salzburg, kept inquiring about the progress of the opera, to be premiered January 29, 1781. But when he continually did not hear what he wanted to, namely that things were going well, he began to worry seriously. Finally, on December 30, in a failed attempt to calm down his father, Mozart wrote to him: "Everything has been composed, just not yet written down."[5]

The concerned father would, of course, hardly believe this. He probably imagined seeing nothing but blank paper in front of his son. So he continued pressuring and nagging Wolfgang in many ways, even well beyond the *Idomeneo* project—which was completed not only on time but also with success. In mid-1781, after quitting Salzburg for good and now trying to get established in Vienna, Wolfgang finally appealed to his impatient and eager father: "I beg you, my dearest, most beloved father, don't write these kinds of letters to me anymore, I beseech you, because they are of no use, except to fog up my brain and disquiet my heart and spirit.—and I, who am now constantly called upon to compose, need a clear head and a peaceful spirit."[6]

Leopold Mozart did not, and probably could not, fully understand his son's work habits. Although he would hardly have considered that his son was suffering from anything like writer's block, he certainly assumed that Wolfgang was unfocused. A performer and composer himself, Leopold had taught his son everything, including the technique of composing music. However, he could not grasp, let alone appreciate, something he had not taught Wolfgang: a method of designing and thinking through an entire piece of music before committing to paper what was literally engraved in his mind. Regarding the latter, Mozart once referred, in a letter to his father, to some orchestral music that the French impresario Le Gros had bought from him but subsequently lost: "I still have it fresh in my head and shall write it down again as soon as I get home."[7] Leopold would also not have understood how much hard labor was involved in his son's composing process that increasingly grew more complex, and how the elaboration of a draft score, which the composer often notated first, implied further serious efforts. This chapter offers an examination of working papers left by Mozart, a study that draws us closer not only to his composing desk but also to his artistry in general, as well as to his very special language of music in which compositional aesthetics and techniques are astonishingly well balanced.

The prevailing image of Mozart the composer is that of the

prototypical musical genius blessed with heavenly gifts who effort-
lessly created works of great beauty, deep expression, and exemplary
perfection. The image of the sweet magic of harmony and powerful
stream of sentiments originated with and was propelled by the early
biographers, beginning with the first obituary.[8] It became invariably
embellished in the writings of later generations and persists in the
popular realm until the present day. There is, of course, absolutely
no doubt about the extraordinary musical gifts that set Mozart apart
from even his most distinguished contemporaries—the Salieris of
his day, as it were.[9] What contributed to it from beginning to end
was the aura of the child prodigy. Mozart actually never lost this
status, neither during his Vienna decade nor after his death. Yet the
wunderkind image did not affect Mozart the composer as much
as it extended to his high visibility and great fame as a performer.
Being a stellar piano virtuoso won him the kind of stardom never
achieved by Gluck, Haydn, and others lacking a comparable stage
presence—until Beethoven, Hummel, Mendelssohn, and Liszt
came along.

As it does in the case of Bach, Beethoven, and many other
performer-composers, a congenial relationship may exist between
the performer's technical skills on the one hand and an advanced
level of compositional sophistication on the other. Mozart's steep
performance trajectory ran parallel in many ways to his maturing as a composer. An important link between the two functions
is formed by his frequent exercises in keyboard improvisation,[10]
which required him to come up with fertile musical ideas, organize
them on the spur of the moment, and explore their potential in
various elaborations. Mozart seems never to have been in doubt
about his innate musical gifts or questioned his musical destiny, and
there is no evidence that he ever involved himself in deep thoughts
about creativity.

Nevertheless, the origin of his creative prowess and native genius
was quite clear to him. As a twenty-two-year-old, he wrote to his

father in a remarkably self-assured and bold manner: "I am a composer, and I was born a kapellmeister. I must not and cannot bury
my gift for composing that a benevolent God has bestowed upon
me in such rich a measure—I may say so without arrogance because
I am aware of it now more than ever before."[11] Earlier, he described
in an enraged mood that the elector in Mannheim "has no idea
what I can do. . . . I would be glad to put it to a test. Let him bring
on all the composers from Munich, he can even invite some from
Italy and France, Germany, England, and Spain. I am willing to
compete with any one of them."[12] Mozart understood his musical
talents as God's gift[13] and he realized that his obligation to make
use of them would be tested in a highly competitive environment.

While Mozart the genius can hardly be defined, Mozart the composer can be described—at least in terms of the external compositional methods he applied. Certain critical aspects of his creative
process and of the resulting works of art can be brought to light,
notably on the basis of the rich autograph materials left from the
Viennese decade. It was a period in which he not only freed himself
from the controlling influence of his father, teacher, mentor, and
manager, but also approached composing in a more reflective and
intellectually involved manner. Mozart's compositions and composing methods took a significant turn during the early years in Vienna
when his scores became noticeably more complex, included more
polyphonic devices, and generally showed a more extended movement format. These features are best exemplified by the set of six
string quartets written from 1782 to 1785, usually referred to as the
"Haydn" Quartets.

An abundant body of autograph manuscripts that contain
compositional fragments—that is, incomplete compositions of
movements drafted in clean score format to be finished at a later
point—is available, mostly from the Vienna period. More than any
other documents, these fragments illuminate Mozart's approach to
composing. And, in line with the argument of this book, those from

the period 1788 to 1791 offer, along with his many completed works, a more concrete glimpse at what the composer considered "the gateway to his fortune," his art of musical composition.

Mozart's musical diary, the thematic catalog of his completed compositions entitled *Verzeichnüß aller meiner Werke* (Catalog of all my works), tells an important story in this regard. The little book, which begins in February 1784 shortly after the composer's twenty-eighth birthday and breaks off with the Little Masonic Cantata K. 623 of November 15, 1791, presents in its twenty-eight unfilled pages one of the most immediately touching documents of a creative life cut short. The book of nearly sixty pages was prepared for keeping track of an ambitious compositional program in the form of two-part entries on facing pages: musical incipits on preruled staff lines on the right-hand side, with corresponding dates, headings, and other verbal descriptions and explanations on the left (fig. 6.1).

6.1. Mozart's thematic catalog, folios 28v–29r, last entries, autograph, 1791 (*London, British Library*)

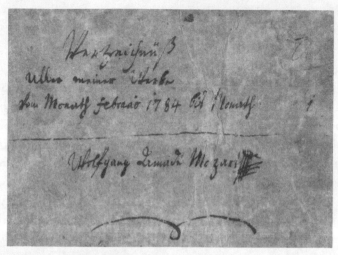

6.2. Mozart's thematic catalog, title label, autograph, 1784 (*London, British Library*)

The label on the book's cover clearly indicates the challenge the composer set for himself when he started the catalog (fig. 6.2). It shows February 1784, when the book was begun, but for the ending date it provides only the first digit, the millennium pointer "1." When Mozart wrote the label he could not be more specific because the turn of the century lay not so far ahead. The inscription can nevertheless be interpreted in two ways: first, as a pragmatic decision (would the book be filled before the end of the century?), and second, under the aspect of "God willing" (would he live into the next century?). Although Mozart took his religion seriously and was always conscious of life's unpredictability, there is no reason to assume that he warily reflected on his mortality when inscribing the cover label of his thematic catalog. In fact, had he continued composing at the pace set between 1784 and 1791, he would have run out of space before 1800.

Work in Progress: The Fragments

MOZART's thematic catalog did not include the Requiem for the simple reason that at the time of the composer's final illness, it was still a work in progress, a project that occupied him in one way or another until the very end. However, the Requiem was by no means the only musical fragment he left at his death. Even though the Funeral Mass was by far the most developed work at that time, an abundant number of unfinished works, varying in length from a few bars to several dozen or even well over 100 measures, testify to a large store of music placed in the composer's head, ready to be recalled and to be fixed on paper in musical notation. If completed, the fragments would have required filling in quite a few of the pages left empty in the catalog. As incomplete bits, however, they constitute a separate entity of the composer's creative output, a supplement to his thematic catalog as revealing as it is puzzling.

Extending over many genres, the numerous fragments left by Mozart represent an artistic monument of a scope that has neither a precedent nor a parallel in the history of music. Fortunately, Constanze Mozart carefully preserved them after her husband's death. Indeed, she considered them very important and treated them as exemplary documents of Mozart's artistry along the lines of "fragments of classical authors," as she put it in 1799.[14] This reference pertains to ancient Greek writers such as Heraclitus and Parmenides, who in the view of eighteenth-century literati provided models for "the fragment" as a literary genre *sui generis*. Contemporaneous examples for such poetic emulations could be found, for instance, in the works of the German writer Gotthold Ephraim Lessing. Now, it is unlikely that Constanze herself came up with the analogy; probably she took it from the erudite advisers assisting her in organizing the composer's musical estate in the 1790s, notably the family friend Abbé Stadler and her eventual second husband, Georg Nikolaus Nissen. Manuscript annotations by both of them show up consistently across the materials, and Stadler completed a number of fragments. Be that as it may, it remains a remarkable fact that Constanze's designation of Mozart as a "classical author" long predates the application of the terms "classic" and "classicism" to the style and period defined primarily by the music of Haydn, Mozart, and Beethoven.[15]

The large trove of extant fragments, typically single movements, altogether comprises some 140 pieces in numerous individual manuscripts.[16] The fragments document Mozart's compositional activities above and beyond the repertoire of completed works.[17] Moreover, they provide insight into the composer's working methods by complementing and clarifying information provided by the autograph scores of finished pieces. They also shed light on the compositional history of finished individual works, especially in instances where they relate to changes made during the genesis of a multimovement piece and where they reflect the cancellation or replacement of a certain movement. Finally, some fragments document the interruption or discontinuation, deliberate or accidental, of a work in progress: the aborted opera project *L'oca del Cairo*, K. 422, and the Mass in C minor, K. 427, only partially completed, figure prominently here.

Extending through much of the Viennese decade and by no means dating primarily from Mozart's final years, virtually all the fragments have one important feature in common: they notate the essence of a compositional idea that defines the beginning of a movement he had worked out in his head. The manuscript then keeps a record of the musical idea in the form of an "aide-mémoire," but the score of the movement was prepared in such a way that the composer could return to it, refresh his memory, and continue where he left off. Unlike the crossed-out, rejected short drafts of movement openings found in some of Mozart's autograph scores,[18] the fragments for the most part represent compositions that were put aside, usually for reasons unknown. The clean layout of these scores facilitated resuming the compositional and notational process. Wherever Mozart's pen stopped—at the conclusion of a section, phrase, or part—the ruled music paper and the empty staves lay ready to be filled.

It is not surprising, therefore, that some autograph scores of finished compositions by Mozart temporarily existed in a fragmentary state—as work in progress, so to speak. The scores of the opening movements of the piano concertos in E-flat major, K. 449, A major, K. 488, and C major, K. 503, for instance, could be considered "completed fragments" because, as the changing paper types in Mozart's autographs effectively demonstrate, the opening sections of their first movements were written down much earlier than the rest of the score (see chap. 3, p. 101).[19] There are probably many more instances of this kind than are presently known, but such cases are generally difficult to make out in detail, let alone verify.[20]

The order in which the fragments were kept after Mozart's death and organized by Stadler and Nissen suggests that the composer had maintained some sort of a pragmatic filing system for his unfinished works, classified by genre.[21] In other words, string quartet or piano concerto fragments were kept together, yet separate from one another. Moreover, the simple fact that Mozart did not abandon and discard them reflects his interest in preserving the material. Hence, the fragments on file and kept in reasonably good order would serve as an ingenious mnemotechnical device for storing and recalling musical ideas, be it for eventually completing the notational record of the "mentally finished" piece or simply for consultation and the stimulation of perhaps even better musical thoughts. The latter certainly pertains to the few fragments whose manuscripts bear markings and annotations completely unrelated to the music in question.[22] However, the fact that Mozart did not dispose of such obviously rejected material indicates that he wanted to keep it as a reminder of a failed, problematic, but perhaps somehow redeemable musical idea.

At any rate, the fragments are not to be understood primarily as documents of the composer's creative exuberance (an undeniable

Mozartean phenomenon), for which the finished works provide much more eloquent evidence. Rather, they corroborate an intrinsic feature of Mozart's mature style by revealing a resourceful musical mind constantly challenged by critical choices. When starting an instrumental work in a specific genre, it is clear that Mozart often pursued and seriously thought out various alternatives and notated the pertinent outlines in the form of draft scores on music paper. The process of going forward may then have been interrupted by external causes or by a commission for another piece that changed his priorities. At any rate, when continuing on what was begun earlier, he knew whether the completion required merely mechanical execution or considerably more substantive compositional elaboration because of deliberate and well-calculated decisions made by settling on a more challenging alternative.[23]

In their function as working scores, the fragments represent various types of shorthand notation that largely depend on the nature of the composition and genre. In their notational appearance, they fall into four basic categories—with many variants—as the following representative examples elucidate:

Type 1: One-line notation in a multiple-stave score. Only the leading upper part of the composition is fully developed and written out. The other parts are to be entered later in the prepared score, but the staves are temporarily left empty. This type works well for dancelike compositions determined by the shape of a single melody, with harmonically unspecific, implied accompaniment. *Example:* Rondo fragment in F major (divertimento movement) for strings and two horns, K. Anh. 108 (Fr 1787m), fol. 1r. (see fig. 6.3).

Type 2: Notation of the essential parts in a multiple-stave score. A fully developed choral score appears together with the framing and intermittent "outer" parts, typically first violin and bass. The remaining, inessential score parts are left to be filled in later. This type is particu-

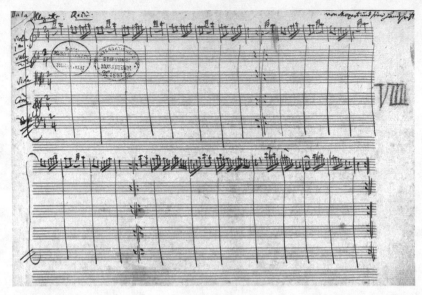

6.3. Divertimento in F major, K. Anh. 108/Fr 1787m, autograph score
(*Salzburg, Stiftung Mozarteum*)

larly suitable for concerto, aria, and vocal movements where the solo or
choir parts carry most of the substance of the work but are embedded
in a clearly defined score frame. *Example:* Kyrie fragment in D major
K. Anh. 14 (Fr 1787e), fol. 1r. (fig. 6.4).

Type 3: Notation of multiple parts in a skeleton score. The leading parts,
accompanimental detail, and transitions are indicated in order to provide internal continuity. This type serves more complex compositional
structures, primarily in chamber music. *Example:* Rondo fragment of a
quintet in A major for clarinet and strings, K. Anh. 88 (Fr 1790g), fol.
1r. (fig. 6.5).

Type 4: Full notation of all parts, with only nonessential portions left out.
This type implies that all parts of the score are essential in defining
the melodic and rhythmic texture, contrapuntal structure, and character of the composition. Virtually all keyboard music and complex

6.4. Kyrie in D major, K. Anh. 14/Fr 1787e, autograph score, pages 1–2
(*Salzburg, Stiftung Mozarteum*)

6.5. Rondo of a clarinet quintet in A major, K. Anh. 88/Fr 1790g, autograph score (*Salzburg, Stiftung Mozarteum*)

6.6. String quartet in G minor, K. Anh. 74/Fr 1789i, autograph score, rejected draft (*Salzburg, Stiftung Mozarteum*)

chamber-music movements require this kind of notation. *Example:* Fragment of a quartet movement in G minor, K. Anh. 74 (Fr 1789i) (fig. 6.6).

Comparing the manuscripts of fragments with those of completed works helps to understand Mozart's special way of getting to the finished product. The discontinued written scores cannot, of course, document the all-important mental process of forming an initial musical idea through the ripening of the material and up to the conceptual development of an entire piece in the composer's head. However, fragmentary and completed manuscripts taken together reveal how the process of committing musical thoughts to paper often involved no fewer than three rather distinct stages: first, notating the nearly complete skeleton outline of the "defining" initial section of a movement; second, carrying on the continuity draft of the complete skeleton score for the entire movement or at least for its major sections; and third, filling in the missing inner parts and working out final details of the full score.[24] Yet even the fragment of the G-major trio K. Anh. 66 (see fig. 6.7, below) clearly exposes a two-step process: first, the notation of an outline in light brown ink for the first 32 measures; then, the continuation and completion of the three-part texture in black ink.

Mozart's scores were generally written very fast, and this is true of the initial outlines as well. When working on his opera *Idomeneo*, he told his father, "I must write at breakneck speed."[25] Immediately thereafter he provides the reason for writing so fast: it is because, as cited above, "everything has been composed, just not yet written down." This implies that the basic musical substance of a planned piece was preconceived and shaped in his head. Mozart apparently had no trouble coming up with musical ideas, formulating and ordering them in his head, and thinking out a complete movement. He then needed to fix its outline quickly on paper in order to keep pace with what rolled off in his inner ear. The subsequent fleshing out of the charted skeleton score then represented a second run-through, an important act of elaboration that required considerable additional compositional efforts and attention to detail (cf. fig. 6.7).

For Mozart, the act of composition unfolded in a way that differed significantly from that of other composers. Bach, for example, also shaped thematic ideas in his head but generally worked on all parts of a score more or less simultaneously. No thematic sketches by him are known, and he probably thought carefully about the compositional consequences resulting from his choice of musical material before putting anything on paper. He then wrote out the score in a fairly systematic manner section by section until the piece was completed.[26] Beethoven, on the other hand, found it extremely difficult, indeed at times agonizing, to forge an initial musical idea into a suitable theme. He hesitated before settling on a final solution, and this procedure of elaboration typically extended well beyond the invention of the thematic-motivic substance and its development over the entire composition.[27] Extensive sketching by Beethoven documents his relatively slow process of bringing a work to completion. Mozart, however, thought through an entire movement in advance, quickly formulated an incipit as a mnemonic device, drafted the contrapuntal contours in a skeleton score of the whole piece, and finally filled in the missing details, which were often decisive for the sound of the piece.

After Mozart's move to Vienna, the growing intricacies, contrapuntal complexities, and expansive formats in his music become progressively perceptible along with the continuing and dominating melodic elegance and rhythmic fluency. The art of composition had become a more challenging and strenuous task. The pace of creating new works slowed down; structures and textures display greater density and sophistication, and the harmonic language shows more differentiation. In general, the intellectual depth of musical composition increased significantly, and the act of composing simply took more time. In 1785 when Mozart dedicated to Haydn the set of six quartets he had worked on for over three years, he expressly referred in the preface to "the fruits of long and laborious efforts."[28]

Mozart's "Haydn" Quartets, more than any other group of works, reflect a deliberate and intensive realignment of compositional parameters, especially in their embrace of traditional contrapuntal techniques. The finale of the first "Haydn" quartet, K. 387, presents a case in point in that it combines retrospective polyphonic technique of an old-style fugue in slow motion, in other words, white notation, with the contrasting fast-moving material in black notes. This technique created a distinctly modern musical language, thereby defining a new direction. Here Mozart gave historical strands of compositional technique a decidedly contemporary touch, a process that necessitated extensive corrections and sometimes even required sketching, a practice used sparingly by Mozart. His sketches are scarce and were invariably employed in finding solutions to local compositional problems in movements that were mostly contrapuntal or harmonic, often at critical junctures such as the opening of a development section or in movements requiring a larger overview that would be aided by a continuity sketch.[29]

Two characteristic examples of such sketches can be found among the few altogether that exist for the Requiem. In the "Rex tremendae" movement, Mozart recorded possibilities for stretto imitation, that is, for overlapping thematic entries in close succession—the kind of passage that would benefit from trying out alternatives on a keyboard or in written form. The crossed-out sketch of four measures at the foot of the page pertains to measures 7–12 of the final version of this movement, which in the end comes out quite differently yet demonstrates the sure hand of the composer in judging the alternatives.[30] On the same piece of scrap paper, just above this sketch, Mozart used another brief sketch to design the beginning of an "Amen" double fugue, which he did not get to enter in the autograph score.[31] Both subject and countersubject for the double fugue were, however, clearly shaped in the composer's head before he put them on paper. Therefore, the sketch reflects nothing but the quest for the best possible combination of subject and countersubject for their simultaneous entries at the beginning of the concluding movement of the "Dies irae" sequence.

Generally speaking, sketches and fragments complement one another as sources of information about the genesis of a work, but for Mozart they served entirely different purposes. Whereas the sketches document a moment in the process of solving a specific compositional problem, the fragments primarily represent mnemonic devices for compositions conceptualized in his head. As the sole surviving incomplete yet tangible evidence, they stand, in a way, for music "composed, just not yet written." Neither Constanze Mozart nor her helpers Stadler and Nissen had a sense of, or interest in, the chronological origin of the many fragments left by the composer. Only recent research made it possible to date the well over one hundred manuscripts fairly accurately.[32] Since Mozart's handwriting style does not significantly change during the Viennese decade and therefore cannot be used as an additional dating criterion, the dating process is based on a census of all the individual paper types used by the composer. Datings on the autograph manuscripts and within Mozart's thematic catalog reveal the earliest and latest documentable use of each paper type and hence the approximate time span over which it was used.[33] Thus, an autograph fragment will have a presumptive dating between the earliest known use of that paper and the latest one. Finally, there remains the possibility that a given undated fragment might pre- or postdate the earliest or latest surviving dated work, resulting in a chronological ordering that is by necessity both relative and approximate.

Table 6.1 presents an overview, grouped by genres and scorings, of fifty-four fragments of individual movements that can be dated fairly securely to the years 1787 to 1791.[34] A further breakdown by year is problematic because Mozart used some paper types for a longer time. It can be observed, however, that fewer fragments apparently fall into 1788, the strikingly productive first year after

Table 6.1: Fragments of Movements by Genre and Scoring, 1787–91

Sacred music	6
Arias and songs	4
Music for piano or mechanical clock[35]	13
Chamber music with piano	4
Chamber music with winds	12
Chamber music for strings	13
Orchestral music	2

the imperial appointment, marked by many completed works (see table 1.2): three symphonies (K. 543, 550, and 551); one piano concerto (K. 537); three piano trios (K. 542, 548, and 564); two piano sonatas (K. 533 and 545); one string trio (K. 563); and one violin sonata (K. 547).

Windows Ajar: Fleeting Sounds of Chamber Music

WHAT found its way onto Mozart's composing desk must generally be divided into two basic categories: works commissioned or destined for a specific function and music he wrote primarily out of his own interest. In the case of an opera, the dividing line is clear, but not so when it comes, for instance, to chamber works. While the three string quartets K. 575, 589, and 590 were clearly commissioned by and written for Prussian king Friedrich Wilhelm II,[36] the situation is hazy for most of the chamber repertoire. The string Divertimento (trio) K. 563 presents a case in point. According to a note in a letter, Mozart "wrote it for" his Masonic brother Puchberg,[37] yet neither his thematic catalog nor the first edition of spring 1792 make any reference to a work commissioned by Puchberg. It seems plausible, however, that Mozart, as court composer whose appointment was based in the *k. k. Kammermusik*, devoted much of his creative energy to this area of composition, even while the imperial chamber music in wartime Vienna was going through a lackluster period. And when Mozart referred, for instance, to K. 581 as "Stadler's Quintet,"[38] it doesn't mean that his clarinetist friend ordered the piece. Stadler premiered it, but he did so as a salaried member of the imperial chamber music ensemble. Hence, there can be no question that Mozart's deliberate orientation toward chamber-music composition is directly related to the courtly home of his imperial appointment. He seems to have planned and counted on the possibility that, if Joseph II had lived on, the emperor would have regularly called upon the private services of his chamber composer-pianist-violinist.

Mozart's evident devotion to chamber works also demonstrates a particular interest in widening the scope of chamber music and branching deliberately into nonstandard types of composition. He emphatically turned to the piano trio, string trio, and string quintet, genres he had previously either not engaged in or only marginally explored. In all three categories, he now makes decisive leaps forward. Notably, the three piano trios of 1788 complement the three symphonies of the same year by lifting the genre onto an entirely new level (see chap. 3, p. 87) and underscoring the composer's intention of moving in a new direction. Similarly, in the six-movement Divertimento K. 563, also of 1788, and Mozart's first essay into string trio writing, he immediately moved to a remarkably high plateau of musical sophistication. Moreover, the two last string quintets, K. 593 and 614, build on the stylistic achievement and differentiated sound quality of their predecessors, K. 515 and 516. They are tremendously more demanding technically, K. 614 especially, and contain radical expansions of Mozart's stylistic horizon, particularly as shown by the development section of the slow movement of K. 593. Finally, the Clarinet Quintet, K. 581, of 1789 adds a further new dimension to the quintet genre, not only by way of its elegant melodious features but also by integrating the alto timbre of the clarinet and the instrument's idiomatic figuration into the four-part string score. The glass harmonica quintet K. 617

Table 6.2: Fragments of String Chamber Music, 1789–91

Trio movement	Allegro in G, K. Anh. 66 (Fr 1789g)
Quartet movements	Fuga in C major, K. Anh. 77 (Fr 1789a)
	Allegro in E minor, K. Anh. 84 (Fr 1789b)
	[Rondo] in B-flat major, K. Anh. 71 (Fr 1789c)
	[Allegro] in G minor, K. Anh. 74 (Fr 1789c)
	Menuetto in B-flat major, K. Anh. 75 (Fr 1790c)
	[Allegro] in F major, K. Anh. 73 (Fr 1790d)
Quintet movements	Andante in F major, K. Anh. 87 (Fr 1791b)
	Allegro in A minor, K. Anh. 79 (Fr 1791c)

of May 1791 must be included here as well. Although the composer recognized the limitations of the glass harmonica, an instrument invented by Benjamin Franklin in 1761, he enhanced the expressive qualities of the work's delicate and transparent scoring for flute, oboe, viola, and cello by the harmonica's ethereal sonorities, notably in the C-minor Adagio opening.

The chamber music for strings only—trio, quartet, and quintet—with its balanced and homogenous sound unambiguously reveal the stylistic features that emerge in, and are characteristic of, Mozart's imperial period and illustrate them in an exemplary way: notably the expansive trend, rich and complex textures, clear-cut melodic approach, and more explicit and rigorous polyphony. This is no less true of the fragments, which complement the image presented by their finished counterparts (table 6.2). The last completed string chamber work is the Quintet in E-flat, K. 614, dated April 12, 1791, but it would be misleading to see this piece either as an isolated final statement or as a mere sequel to the preceding D-major Quintet, K. 593, of December 1790. The overall context exhibits that the composer more or less simultaneously pays equal attention to all three string genres: trio, quartet, and quintet.

The sizable fragment of a G-major trio, K. Anh. 66, extending over 100 measures, did not originate before the E-flat-major Divertimento K. 563 of 1788 but followed it. Likewise, quartet composition was by no means a closed chapter marked by the three so-called "Prussian" Quartets published shortly after Mozart's death. The fast Rondo in $\frac{2}{4}$ time, K. Anh. 71, and the Menuet, K. Anh. 75, may well be linked to the "Prussian" Quartet in B-flat major, K. 589, completed in May 1790, for which Mozart chose other solutions. Similarly, the melodically and rhythmically vibrant fragment K. Anh. 73 might form a corresponding association with the F-major Quartet, K. 590, completed in June 1790.[39] However, Mozart did not dispose of the alternative movements; he saved them for further use. The fragments of two opening movements, K. Anh. 84 and 74, however, open up a broader picture, as they relate to two separate quartets in the minor mode. The G-minor fragment, however, was scrapped by the composer (as mentioned above), while the E-minor work remained ready for completion. The short fragment containing the thematic outline of a quintet in F major, K. Anh. 87, and the five-page manuscript of an A-minor quintet, K. Anh. 79, apparently originate from about the spring of 1791, the time of the last E-flat-major quintet, K. 614. Mozart, getting involved with the *Magic Flute* project at that time and facing an extremely busy spring and summer in 1791, probably decided it would be better to hold off completing further chamber works.

At any rate, the chamber-music fragments, notably those representing first movements—which ordinarily determine the character of a multimovement structure—exemplify the breadth and depth of Mozart's rich arsenal of ideas and his technical and structural approaches to trio, quartet, and quintet writing. Three representative fragments allow a glimpse at what the composer worked out in his head before notating the opening section or sections. They capture, if only partially, the basic substance and defining moments of instrumental movements to come, of music that once existed in the composer's mind.

• *Trio fragment for violin, viola, and violoncello in G major,* K. Anh. 66 (Fr 1789g): the autograph score of an exposition of an opening Allegro of a G-major string trio, dating from 1789 or later[40] (fig. 6.7a–c, http:// books.wwnorton.com/books/mozart-at-the-gateway-to-his-fortune/).

A setting for three string instruments—one each for high, middle, and low register and very different from the Baroque trio of two violins and bass[41]—presents a particular compositional challenge. When comparing trio and quartet textures, for instance, the omission of a second violin strips the score of the possibility of enriching its sound by another complementary treble voice. The technical implications become clear by considering that a triad played by a quartet can be spaced in different ways because one of the three notes is doubled, whereas in a triad played by only three instruments the spacing is much more limited. The vertical structure of the musical setting is essentially reduced to three-part harmony. Without doublings provided by a fourth instrument, the need to create complete harmonic textures requires great adroitness of voice leading,[42] except when the use of double stops permits creating momentary solutions of more than three parts. Mozart apparently found it intriguing to deal with the challenge of properly balancing a score for only three string registers. He had essentially created the new genre of string trio in 1788 with the Divertimento in E-flat major, K. 563. The fragment K. Anh. 66, which extends over three pages for a total of 100 measures, includes the complete exposition and even the beginning of the development section. It represents a viable counterpart to the completed earlier trio and continues the path of exploring the manifold challenges of a trio score comprising three homogeneous yet distinct string parts.

FURTHER NOTES ON THE TRIO K. ANH. 66

The autograph reflects two layers of compositional activity: the outline of the first 32 measures, up to the C-sharp in the violin (brown ink), then the filling in of missing parts like viola and cello in mm.

6.7a. String trio in G major, K. Anh. 66/Fr 1789g: mm. 1–44 (*Cambridge, Fitzwilliam Museum*)

7–8 as well as the continuation of the piece beyond the double bar in m. 91 (black ink). The intricacy of the compositional undertaking and Mozart's attention to every detail is directly reflected in the exacting notation. The careful dynamic marks and the detailed articulation indicated by slurs and staccato dots through the very last measure are characteristic of a high degree of elaboration.

Written like its predecessor, K. 563, for an ensemble of virtuoso players, the trio takes, as its point of departure, a plain G-major chord reinforced by a triadic cello ascent *G-B-d-g*. The *forte* chordal opening finds an immediate contrasting response in a brief and unaccompanied conjunct *piano* melody in the violin line that ends in an accompanied chromatic gesture on a dominant seventh chord, a quasi-dissonant echo of the opening triad. The first thematic group grows out of the initial

6.7b–c. String trio in G major, K. Anh. 66: (b) mm. 45–82;
(c) mm. 83–100

six-measure statement and spins out melodic, harmonic, and rhythmic elaborations, figurations, and modifications, and reaches a virtuosic display of extended figurative triplets over the third *forte* cello ascent in m. 21 with its pointed augmented fourth (A–D-sharp).

The second thematic group (from m. 42), with its idea essentially derived from the first theme, again plays with the triad, offering dynamic contrast and a chromatic twist, but presents it in a very different way—for example, by underscoring the second theme in the cello with a *staccato* ascending scale, picked up by the violin (m. 47). The close structural relationship between the first and second thematic groups, both with a focus on opening triadic and closing chromatic gestures, and their intricate contrapuntal elaboration becomes a hallmark of Mozart's chamber music in the final years. The imitative figures of triads and modified triads (from m. 737) emphasize a three-way contrapuntal dialogue that is carried out to perfection in this extraordinary exposition of a first movement. The fragment then breaks off after the double bar, a few measures into the development section, which starts out in opaque D minor and quickly turns to the E-flat subdominant of B-flat major.

- *String Quartet fragment in E minor,* K. Anh. 84 (Fr 1789b): the autograph score of the exposition of an opening Allegro for an E-minor quartet, dating from late 1789 to 1791[43] (fig. 6.8a–b, http://books.wwnorton. com/books/mozart-at-the-gateway-to-his-fortune/).

The score, notated on two pages, comprises 54 measures and encompasses almost the entire exposition but without quite reaching the double bar (which would have meant starting a new page). Its second thematic group (from m. 17) constitutes a major-mode variant of the head motif of the first theme, following the model of Haydn but for Mozart an extremely rare example of a quasi-monothematic sonata form exposition.[44] Not in unison form but with a contrapuntal accompaniment, it firmly establishes the relative key of G major by m. 20. One of the most immediately noticeable features of the fragment, however, is the deliberately exposed virtuosic violin part, notated

6.8a–b. String quartet in E minor, K. Anh. 84/Fr 1789b: (a) mm. 1–28; (b) mm. 29–54 (*Salzburg, Stiftung Mozarteum*)

over many measures without its accompaniment. This indicates the primary role to be played by the first violin and moves the quartet into the realm of the "quatuor concertant," the type Mozart approximated but would not quite attain in the quartets of 1789–90 dedicated to the King of Prussia. Moreover, different from the "Prussian" Quartets and their emphasis on the cello part, K. Anh. 84 focuses on the violin and suggests that Mozart was interested in exploring this quartet type in a broader fashion.

FURTHER NOTES ON THE QUARTET K. ANH. 84
AND ON THE ABANDONED QUARTET K. ANH. 74

The virtuoso treatment of the violin finds itself integrated in a structure of extraordinary sophistication that becomes only gradually noticeable as the score unfolds. The key role here is played by the principal theme of 8-measure length, symmetrically organized in four corresponding two-measure phrases ABA'B' and presented entirely *piano*. The antecedent A consists of a unison melodic phrase; the consequent B is harmonized (without cello). A', with its downward leap of a seventh, and B', with its initial jump over more than an octave up to the e" of the first violin, increases the spacing of the sound that is pursued further in m. 9 with the third—and for the first time harmonized—statement of A and highlighted by the subsequent *crescendo*. Then, in m. 18 of this monothematic exposition, the second thematic group appears as a contrapuntal variant of the first. The contrapuntal treatment of phrase A begins in the viola and the second violin and, after a solo violin interlude, is pursued further in all voices, including imitation in contrary motion in violin II, mm. 33–36, and with a sudden harmonic shift into a flat-key area—the parallel minor of the relative major.

The fragment breaks off after a double statement of phrase A in violin I (mm. 49–53) and a chromatic tail that returns to the relative G major shortly before the end of the exposition, which as such is left out. This quartet exposition is unusual in its proportional distribution of the thematic materials based on one and the same melodic idea for both the first and second groups. Mozart limits the presentation of the E-minor principal theme, which begins and ends in unisons, to a mere sixteen measures and then focuses on a variety of short polyphonic elaborations of the opening head motif with intermingled virtuoso figuration in G major. Hence, the second thematic group in the relative major takes up more than twice the space claimed by the minor-mode principal theme. For the sake of comparison, it should be noted that the abandoned quartet fragment in G minor K. Anh. 74 (see fig. 6.6, above)[45] of 1789–90 is also of the "quatuor concertant" type with a focus on violin I, although its accompanimental underpinning is more clearly defined. The G-minor fragment also begins with a *piano* unison statement (as, incidentally, does the last Prussian Quartet, K. 590) and builds a similar dynamic climax in the second 8-measure statement, but its contrapuntal texture sets in earlier than in the E-minor fragment by applying voice exchange between violin I (mm. 5–8) and cello (mm. 11–14). The deceptive cadence to E-flat major (m. 10), followed immediately by the sounds of A-flat major and E-flat major triads and then by a diminished seventh-chord on C-sharp before returning in m. 16 to G minor, perhaps introduced harmonic intensity too prematurely and might have contributed to the composer's decision not to continue after 24 measures, but without throwing the promising idea away.

• *Quintet fragment in A minor,* K. Anh. 79 (Fr 1791c): the fragment of an entire exposition for an Allegro moderato opening movement of an A-minor quintet, dating from March 1791 or later[46] (fig. 6.9a–e, http://books.wwnorton.com/books/mozart-at-the-gateway-to-his-fortune/).

This fragment, along with that of an F-major Andante K. Anh. 87 and the E-flat-major Quintet K. 614, completed April 12, 1791, apparently represents Mozart's very last statement in chamber music for strings. The exposition of the A-minor movement extends over 72 measures and is essentially complete. Its notated score is limited, however, to material of structural relevance and omits all subsidiary accompanimental voices and textures—a decision that differentiates between the *obbligato* and the *ad libitum* elements in the compositional design. The first thematic group is clearly defined by the virtuosic *concertato* impetus provided by violin I, which gradually affects the entire five-part texture. Different from the concept of the quatuor concertant, which puts the spotlight exclusively on the first violin, the other parts of the quintet are to some extent drawn in as well. In its overall character and technical demands, the virtuosic design of the A-minor fragment goes well beyond the earlier quintets K. 593 and K. 614.

FURTHER NOTES ON THE QUINTET K. ANH. 79

The fragment devotes 30 measures to the first thematic group. After this opening of the exposition, a sudden and strong rhythmic and dynamic contrast is established by the second thematic group in C major (from

6.9a. String quintet in A minor, K. Anh. 79/Fr 1791c: mm. 1–13 (*Bergamo, Biblioteca Donizetti, Legato Piatti-Lochis, fols. 1–2*)

6.9b–c. String quintet in A minor, K. Anh. 79: (b) mm. 14–27;
(c) mm. 28–44

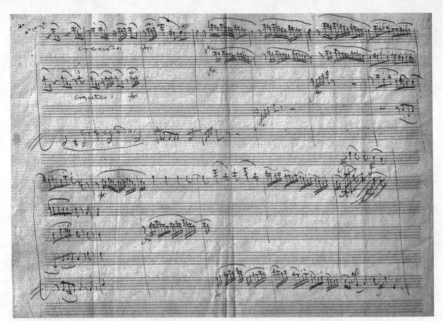

6.9d–e. String quintet in A minor, K. Anh. 79: (d) mm. 45–57;
(e) mm. 58–72 (*Salzburg, Stiftung Mozarteum, fol. 3*)

m. 31) and its gradually unfolding, chromatically inflected contrapuntal elaboration. Again, throughout the exposition, Mozart displays his fine sense of dynamic contrast, refined articulation, and differentiated sonorities. Particularly noticeable in the A-minor fragment is the quiet beginning with its violin opening phrase played *legato* and the sharply contrasting articulation in m. 3, all under *piano* cover. It is followed by the edgy *sforzato* syncopations in the concertato violin (mm. 15–16), with the cello *pizzicato* effect underneath, all within a *forte* dynamic, and by a restatement of the opening material, underpinned by a new homophonic harmonization, again all in *piano*.

The fragment as a whole, that is, the image of the not-fully-executed and l-notated score, exhibits the delicate profile of a particularly imaginative, finely shaped, and highly expressive quintet exposition and represents an informative blueprint for the unity of rhetoric, character, structure, and narrative so typical of Mozart's mature style. Reasonable guesswork can compensate for the nonessential components Mozart had not filled in, thus revealing an electrifying quintet exposition but, at the same time, raising the expectation of a suspenseful continuation and conclusion of the musical discourse. Even the fully notated "finished" portions of the fragment contain trio and quartet features. Particularly noteworthy in this regard is the true quartet beginning—with 2 violins, viola, and cello—of the second thematic group (mm. 31–38), which after only eight measures unfolds into quintet texture.

Epilogue

IT IS HARD to find, let alone define, a common denominator for the musical style of Mozart's last years, the years in the service of the emperor. There are some general elements that are prevalent in much of the music of this period: grand and sublime statements as realized in the three last symphonies and an ambitious increase in the musical format of movements; a more restrained and mellow, yet no less effective approach toward concerto writing, as seen in the last two piano concertos and the clarinet concerto; and, generally, a more open, more adventurous, and more varied application of polyphonic designs as well as truly unusual and untested harmonic processes such as modulations gliding in and out of distant realms and creating shocking expressive effects.[47] Above all, a zeal for innovative compositional approaches is noticeably dominant. This holds true not only for genres that came to be significant for Mozart, like the piano trio that attained a radically new face through the 1788 publication of the set with K. 502, 542, and 548. It even affects the chamber music for strings, in which he adopts an entirely fresh approach. During the last four years of his life, unlike the time when the "Haydn" Quartets came into being, Mozart dealt with trio, quartet, and quintet in parallel, and in such a way that each of the three types shows a more sharply defined identity and all three benefit from considerable cross-fertilization.

This is particularly evident in the conceptual design of the last quintets.[48] Here the A-minor fragment (fig. 6.9), discussed at the end of the previous section, provides a singular glance at Mozart's workshop and demonstrates, in the picture of its score alone, how the composer organized the structure of a quintet both horizontally and vertically. Various score segments, from single lines to all kinds of combinatorial two-, three-, and four-part textures, serve in the construction of a continuous web of musical thoughts designed to form a whole. But this whole is made up of different components— duo, trio, and quartet elements—that feed into a multiplicity of exchange patterns and establish a dynamic interplay laid open by the informative notation of the fragment, informative by the selective display of musical thoughts. It becomes particularly evident that in the chamber music for strings, where the rich and colorful resources of the orchestra are not available, Mozart nevertheless manages to explore new horizons. The fragments help to identify this particular trait, and a pertinent remark by Goethe, one of the first to undertake examinations in genetic development, as it were, illustrates this point: "Works of nature and art cannot be recognized when they are finished; one has to catch them in the making in order to more or less understand them."[49]

There is no question that Haydn provided the keystone for the string quartet genre and for what can justifiably be called Viennese quartet culture. But there is also no question that Mozart's imaginative response to Haydn's op. 33 in his own quartets— later dedicated to Haydn—solidified the older master's achievements and essentially set a new threshold. The imperial chamber composer then not only raised this threshold further with the "Prussian" Quartets but aimed at a more expansive compositional context, as the Divertimento K. 563 and the string quintets show, and eventually the piano trios as well. Hence, it is not merely the quartet genre as such but Mozart's combinatorial approach to chamber music and his thirst for adventure that proved to be the ultimate challenge to Beethoven, Hummel, Schubert, and their successors in this area. Moreover, the shadow cast by Mozart's methods and language on the future of music extended well beyond the narrower domain of the *Kammer Kompositor* because of his innate tendency to transgress conventional limits and his deliberate goal of rising above them. His grip on harnessing an extraordinary diversity of motives, rhythmic textures, harmonic ideas, and other compositional devices in whatever genre into a focused, organic whole show an astonishing and truly magisterial command of artistic power.

Mozart's imperial period, a time in which strategies aimed at new artistic perspectives played such a major role, epitomizes a culmination point in the composer's creative career. It was a time full of external disadvantages and difficulties, a period that after all could produce as forlorn a piece as the B-minor Adagio, K. 540, for piano. It was not, however, a time determined by resignation, hopelessness, and desolation, as evidenced by a stream of abundant productivity. Not meant to be the end, it was a new beginning. What the A-minor string quintet fragment signaled only inadequately in the spring of 1791 resonates more strongly in the much larger projects of the final year, the music of *The Magic Flute*, the Clarinet Concerto, and the

Requiem. These works represent a point of departure for genuinely new horizons. Yet the image of Mozart the composer looking ahead is, in a meaningful way, complemented by the repertoire of works in progress, documented by a collection of pieces composed in his head but notated only in abbreviated form and kept for reference and future use. In this way, the fragments permit a glance at fleeting sounds and, by the same token, at the other side of what Mozart would have perceived as "the gateway to his fortune."

Offering surprises, taking new turns, and revealing a strong forward drive had been consistent patterns throughout Mozart's creative life. Even throughout his imperial employment, fresh points of consummation were reached—up to the moment that fatefully reversed everything. Yet what was an incredibly rich and much more than promising new beginning turned into an abrupt and absolute end: a loss compounded by music left unfinished for posterity, but as evidenced in particular by the preserved fragments at least to some extend actually "composed, just not yet written down" and, therefore, never to be heard.

6.10. Mozart's thematic catalog, folios 29v–30r (*London, British Library*)

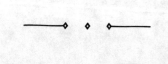

Appendix:
Currency and Monetary Values

Standard monetary units in eighteenth-century Austria

kr. (x)	kreuzer, copper coin	
fl.	florin (Gulden), silver coin	= 60 kr.
th.	thaler, silver coin	= 2 fl.
dukat	ducat, gold coin	= 4½ fl.

The value of eighteenth-century money cannot reliably be converted into current equivalents. According to a rough estimate of comparative purchasing power, 1 florin is worth today approximately 65–85 U.S. dollars or 45–60 euros.

The following information on earnings and prices in Mozart's Vienna was kindly provided by the Mozart Institut of the Mozarteum Foundation Salzburg:

Median annual incomes

Maid	10–30 fl.
Court musician	150–450 fl. (concertmaster: 450 fl.)
University professor	300 fl.
Civil servant (mid-level)	500–1,000 fl.

Food prices

1 loaf of bread	6 kr.
1 pound of beef	7–12 kr.
1 pound of butter	16 kr.

Rental fees

Average apartment	60 fl.
Apartment in top location	230 fl.
Luxury apartment	up to 2,000 fl.

Music

Music lesson (L. Mozart)	12 kr.
Music lesson (W. A. Mozart)	2 fl. (ten times his father's fee)
Copyist fee for an opera	18–36 fl.
Violin	27–45 fl.
Clavichord	up to 100 fl.
Fortepiano (A. Walter)	50–120 fl.

Notes

Prologue

1. Braunbehrens 1989, 406–13, surveys and comments on the anecdotes.
2. Landon 1988, 10.
3. See Wolff 1994, 1–7.
4. Zaslaw 1990, 117f.
5. Edge 1996, 66–70.
6. Solomon 1995 devotes nine chapters to this period.
7. Ibid., 473.
8. Bär 1972 presents the most detailed study of Mozart's medical history, his final illness, and his doctors; see also Werner 1996.
9. In April 1787, Mozart was seriously ill and apparently suffering from kidney problems. They may have had their origin in urinary tract deformities related to Mozart's abnormally shaped left ear (Fig. 2.2); see the discussion on p. 55.
10. B-D, no. 1079.
11. Bauer 2009, summing up and adding significantly to all previous studies, presents a well-researched and up-to-date account of the available data pertaining to Mozart's earnings, spending, and loans.
12. Over the years, Mozart asked Puchberg for well over 4,000 florins but always received much less than he asked for, altogether 1,415 florins.
13. Brauneis 1991. The suit over 1,435 florins and 32 kreutzer was apparently dropped after Mozart's death.
14. "Seine Fehler waren, daß er das Geld nicht zu dirrigieren wuste" (B-D, no. 1213).
15. Letters of July 3 and 9, 1778 (ML, 163, 165).
16. ML, 390.
17. "Nun stehe ich vor der Pforte meines Glückes" (B-D, no. 1120). Anderson translates, "I now stand on the threshold of my fortune" (Anderson, 936), and Spaethling, "I am standing at the threshold of my fortune" (ML, 417).

18. See the chapter "The Emperor at War," Braunbehrens 1989, 310–16.
19. ML, 417; B-D, no. 1120.
20. Ibid.
21. Ibid.
22. Probably in conjunction with van Swieten's invitation to Mozart for preparing and conducting a series of Handel oratorios for his private music society; these performances began with the pastorale *Acis und Galathea*, K. 566, on December 30, 1788.
23. *Georg Friderich Händels Lebensbeschreibung*, trans. Johann Mattheson (Hamburg, 1761). Because Mozart gave it away, the Mainwaring-Mattheson book is not included in the estate catalog, "Verzeichniß und Schätzung der Bücher des verstorbenen Tl. Herrn W. A. Mozart Kays. Kapell-Meister" (1791); Konrad and Staehelin 1991, 118, lists it under no. 78 as not identified.
24. Most likely involving some kind of gambling; see Bauer 2003. The confidential correspondence with Puchberg indicates that the latter was entirely aware of the reasons for the composer's persistent financial misery, the dramaturgy of which Mozart could handle much better than its grounds. But his disarming honesty toward Puchberg is documented, for example, in a letter of early May 1790, which reads at the end: "So now I have confessed everything, and I beg you to do whatever is within your ability" (ML, 418).
25. Mainwaring 1987, 110f. (the English original of 1760 adjusted to match Mattheson's translation).
26. Valentin 1942; Bauer 2009, 318.

Chapter 1: Imperial Appointments

1. Dedication for *Alceste* (1776); quoted from Oliver Strunk, ed., *Source Readings in Music History* (rev. ed.), ed. Leo Treitler (New York, 1998), 933.
2. Croll and Croll 2010, 189.
3. See his letters from Paris (e.g., ML, 142, 167).
4. Letter of June 27, 1781 (ML, 270).
5. Mozart suggested in a letter of January 30, 1782, that these performances had a negative impact on the completion of his own work: "My opera has not gone to sleep;—but it has been delayed because of Gluck's big operas" (ML, 302). Most of the singers for *Die Pilger von Mekka* were also used by Mozart.
6. ML, 321. Mozart attended the performance of Gluck's *Alceste* at Schönbrunn Palace on December 15, 1781, and (according to Croll and Croll 2010, 256) ten days later Gluck may have been present at Mozart's performance in competition with Muzio Clementi on December 24.

7. Letter of June 27, 1781 (ML, 326).

8. Letter of March 11, 1783 (ML, 345).

9. Appointed in 1774 to this post by Joseph II after the death of Florian Gassmann, but his salaried position was that of a *Kammerkomponist,* a composer in the direct service of the emperor. The Kammer Musici were "personal attendants to Joseph, who regularly made music with him in his private chambers" and "enjoyed employment for life" (Link 2003, 22). For further details, see Rice 1998, 48, and Link 2005, 157. Link 2005 and Brauneis 2006 present a detailed overview and analysis of the complicated Viennese court music scene with its many overlapping appointments and responsibilities.

10. Rice 1998, chap. 12. Note also Salieri's title "Maître de la Musique de sa Majesté Imperiale et Royale et des Spectacles de la Cour de Vienne" in the printed score of *Les Danaïdes* (Paris 1784).

11. Link 2005, 175, provides the full text of the decree.

12. For the memorial service, the Tonkünstler-Sozietät organized a Requiem Mass at the court parish church of St. Michael's. Salieri conducted the Requiem by Niccolò Jommelli (with oboes, bassoons, and trombones added by Salieri) as well as Gluck's own "De profundis" motet, performed in the place of the "Domine Jesu" of the Requiem (Black 2007, 348; Croll and Croll, 2010, 274). It is likely that Mozart attended although there is no record of it.

13. Quoted from Braunbehrens 1989, 302.

14. NMA II/5: 17 (W. Plath and W. Rehm), preface.

15. Ibid.

16. For the full citation of the decree, see below, chap. 3, p. 74.

17. After Mozart's death, no successor was named by Leopold II.

18. Link 2005, 176f.

19. The ordinary (*gewöhnliche*) chamber music took place three times a week after dinner; Brauneis 2006, 561.

20. Through an invitation arranged by Nancy Storace, Thomas Attwood, and Michael O'Kelly, three English friends in Vienna, Mozart had planned a concert tour to England in 1787, but he was first discouraged by his father (letter of March 2, 1787, B-D, no. 1036) and he then postponed it, probably on account of the *Don Giovanni* commission. According to a London newspaper, the invitation was renewed in late 1787; see Dok-Add.2, 48, 50, and 55f.; also Braunbehrens 1989, 284–90.

21. Issued by the "Musikgraf" Johann Wenzel Ugarte, appointed by Leopold II; Dok, 378.

22. Rice 1998, 22–26.

23. Letter of March 29, 1783 (ML, 346).

24. ML, 348.
25. For a detailed overview of the longer-term court opera developments, see Link 1998.
26. Link 2005 and Brauneis 2006. The (first) Hofkapellmeister was charged with oversight over the Hofkapelle (singers and instrumentalists) with primary responsibility for the opera; the chamber music constituted a subgroup serving the emperor privately. Prior to changes made by Joseph II in 1782, the kapelle was also involved in church music. Bonno died shortly after he retired, on April 15, 1788.
27. Salary figures pertain to the respective court offices but do not reflect the total earnings of their recipients.
28. For merely formal reasons: Mozart could not present the obligatory baptismal certificate and, therefore, never completed the application he intended to file in 1785 (Dok, 209; see also Link 2003, 33f.). In a letter to Emperor Leopold II of December 11, 1791, Mozart's widow, Constanze, refers to the regretful fact that her husband had never joined (B-D, no. 176). Gluck, incidentally, also never joined the society. The cantata *Davidde penitente*, K. 469, was presented and conducted by Mozart on March 13 and 15, 1785, at the Burgtheater for the society; later he also presented piano concertos at the society's events.
29. Rice 1998, 460.
30. Letter of February 13, 1785 (ML, 323).
31. Link 2005, 168. Only when court kapellmeister Bonno, who held the post 1739–74, had received the same salary of 800 fl. (Brauneis 2006, 506).
32. ML, 369.
33. Letter of August 2, 1788 (ML, 401). The twelve chamber musicians earned either 250 or 300 fl. (Link 2005, 158).
34. For further details regarding the war's political and economic impact, see Braunbehrens 1986, 310–15; Beales 1996; and Brauneis 2006, 560.
35. Dok-Add 1, 58.
36. Rice 2003.
37. Rice, 421f., 601.
38. For further details, see p. 39 below.
39. Jahn 4: 751–55, provides a complete listing of the opera performances at the Burgtheater, 1783–91. Dexter Edge has analyzed in detail further information obtainable from the box-office receipts for the years 1788ff. (Edge 1996, 99f., 105).
40. See K. 625 and the preface to the edition of the work by David Buch (A-R Editions, 2007).
41. For Salieri's output, see the worklist in GMO. According to Rice 1998, 601, Salieri composed two operas each in 1788 and 1789, none in 1790 and 1791.

42. For the few omissions, see the commentary by Alan Tyson in the facsimile edition (NMA X/33:1), 14–24.

43. Letter of September 30, 1790 (ML, 423).

44. See also chap. 3, table 3.2.

45. Brauneis 1991.

46. Estimated at 1,415 florins (ibid.).

47. ML, 198.

48. The estate documents after Mozart's death indicate that he was in debt then, but within a relatively short time Constanze was able to pay off everything (Eisen and Sadie, "(3) Wolfgang Amadeus Mozart," GMO).

49. Braunbehrens 1986, 140.

50. The Mozarts had six children, of which only two reached adulthood. The first child, Raimund Leopold, was born June 17, 1783 (d. August 19, 1783); there followed Karl Thomas "Carlo" (September 21, 1784–October 31, 1858), Johann Thomas Leopold (October 18, 1786–November 15, 1786), Theresia Constanze Adelheid Friderike Maria Anna (December 27, 1787–June 29, 1788), Anna Maria (November 11, 1789), and Franz Xaver Wolfgang, "Wolfgang Amadeus junior" (July 26, 1791–July 29, 1844).

51. Mozart himself complained occasionally about toothaches, headaches, and rheumatism, but without referring to any expenses for medical treatment. LM, 418.

52. On expenses for servants, gala clothing, fine cuisine, champagne, coffee, instruments, gifts, etc., see Bauer 2009.

53. See Bauer 2003.

54. See Prologue, p. 7.

55. See Braunbehrens 1986, 136–41, and Brauneis 2006, 560.

56. For the pertinent financial calculations, see Solomon 1995, 523, and Bauer 2009, 51–70.

57. Letter to Puchberg of June 17, 1788 (ML, 400).

58. Information based on the chronological survey by Haberkamp 1986, 1: 420f.

59. Ibid.

60. ML, 398.

61. Mentioned in Constanze Mozart's petition to Emperor Leopold II of December 11, 1791 (B-D 4: 176).

62. See B-D, nos. 1087, 1126, and elsewhere.

63. Anderson, 82.

64. For details, see the preface to NMA II/5:2 (R. Angermüller and W. Rehm, 1983).

65. Anderson, 88.

66. The opera received its premiere at the beginning of May 1769 in Salzburg.

67. B-D, no. 529.

68. Anderson, 693.

69. Letter of April 11, 1781 (ML, 242f.).

70. ML, 429.

71. Salieri's *Semiramide*, commissioned for the Munich carnival one year after *Idomeneo*, was also not performed in Vienna. A competitive Mozart eagerly inquired on May 8, 1782, from his father: "Please let me know how you liked the Salieri opera in Munich.—I am quite certain you saw it; if not, you probably know how well it was received" (ML, 311).

72. Rice 1998, 305.

73. Letter of July 2, 1783 (ML, 358).

74. Rice 1998, 464.

75. Salieri's work is discussed in Rice 1998, 376–84. Mozart received 50 ducats for his work, Salieri 100 ducats, not exactly an evenhanded remuneration, but it is not known whether Mozart knew of Salieri's honorarium.

76. B-D, no. 1124; Anderson, 938f. (trans. adjusted). The final version of the letter is unknown and, therefore, it remains unclear how and when Mozart approached Archduke Franz about this matter.

77. He devoted himself to church music primarily in his later years.

78. For the performance dates, see Edge 1996, 95ff.

79. Da Ponte uses virtually the same line in his libretto *Le nozze di Figaro*, "Così fan tutte le belle" (see the discussion in Heartz 1990, chap. 14).

80. This important fact had not been known in Mozart scholarship until the research of Bruce Brown and John Rice (Brown and Rice 1996); Rice 1998, 474–79, contains a discussion of Salieri's settings of *La scuola degli amanti* by Da Ponte.

81. Salieri used partly the same paper type as Mozart (Rice 1998, 475).

82. Rice 1998, 429–49 and 478f. Rice relates Salieri's not completing *La scuola degli amanti* to a period "characterized by artistic indecisiveness, a relatively low level of creative energy, and varying degrees of dependence on earlier music" (479).

83. ML, 416 ("die aber alle schon zu Wasser geworden sind"; trans. adjusted). That there must have been some serious disagreements between the composers is also reflected in what Constanze Mozart recalled in 1829, when she told the Novellos that "Salieri's enmity arose from Mozart's setting *Così fan tutte*, which he had originally commenced and given up as unworthy of musical invention" (Rice 1998, 474). However, the supposed libretto problem ("unworthy of musical invention") is unlikely because Salieri would have recognized such deficiency right away and not written a single note. Constanze's

recollections seem colored by the anti-Salieri affect arising after Mozart's death.

84. Rice 1998, 458, 493–505.

85. ML, 442.

86. Angermüller 2004, 338.

87. Brauneis 1991; Wolff 1994, 4.

88. The same church where the memorial service for Gluck took place on April 8, 1788 (see above, n. 12).

89. Brauneis 1991.

90. December 16, 1791; Dok, 374. Incidentally, the entire—by then published—Mozart Requiem was performed in 1809 at the memorial for Haydn, conducted by the Mozart pupil Joseph Eybler, then court kapellmeister in Vienna.

91. Wolff, 1994.

Chapter 2: Explorations Outside of Vienna

1. Letter of September 11, 1778 (ML, 184f.).

2. Bauman 1987, 103f., presents a complete listing of all first performances during Mozart's lifetime.

3. The suburban Kärntnertortheater in Vienna picked up *Die Entführung* in 1785.

4. See chap. 1, n. 20.

5. ML, 425.

6. Angermüller 2004, 2: 317.

7. Six rooms, two kitchens, a cellar, plus attic space.

8. ML, 423f. Mozart pawned his furniture and other possessions; his publisher, Hoffmeister, apparently assisted in securing the loan. The borrowed sum (to be paid off within two years) is not listed in Mozart's outstanding debts at his death, so he probably paid it back in full relatively soon after his return from Frankfurt.

9. Angermüller 2004, 2: 317.

10. Dok, 332.

11. Angermüller 2004, 2: 318.

12. Dok, 329.

13. ML, 426.

14. Letter of November 4 (ML, 428).

15. ML, 422.

16. ML, 425.

17. ML, 422.

18. For a detailed account of the trip, see Angermüller 1995; Solomon 1995, chap. 28, provides an in-depth interpretation. A summarizing itinerary (*Stationen einer Reise*) in Richter and Oehme 1991, 157f.

19. Braunbehrens 1989, 439.

20. ML, 403. The opening lines read in German (B-D, no. 1088):
    Wenn ich werde nach Berlin ver-Reisen
    Hoff' ich mir fürwahr viel Ehr und Ruhm

21. ML, 411; see also p. 71.

22. Mozart kept a postal logbook, which he compared with Constanze's replies to the letters that made it into her hands; see his letter of May 23 (ML, 419). According to his log, he wrote from Dresden (April **13** and **17**), Leipzig (April 22), Potsdam (April 28 and May 2), Leipzig (May 9 and **16**), and Berlin (May 19 and **23**); letters not lost are boldfaced. Solomon 1995 (chap. 28) speculates that Mozart deceived his wife and hypothesizes that on the trip he had an affair with Madame Dušek.

23. Letter of May 16, 1789 (ML, 409). Cf. the similarly phrased report from Frankfurt in 1790, p. 48.

24. Richter and Oehme 1991, 70.

25. For unknown reasons, almost half of the audience had free tickets (ibid., 63).

26. Angermüller 1995, 165f.

27. Scribal identifications by the late Wolfgang Plath in a letter to the author of April 2, 1984. The way the drawing ended up in Cambridge, Massachusetts, is a story in itself. It was faithfully copied for a "souvenir shop" run by Franz Xaver Jelinek, former curator of the old museum in the Salzburg Mozarteum, who for fundraising purposes had quite a few items from its collections duplicated. Apparently by mistake, Jelinek sold the original instead of the copy in 1879 to Cora Kennedy Aitken, whose autograph collection came to the Houghton Library at Harvard University in 1943; the copy remains in the Mozarteum.

28. For the first extensive examination, see Moritz Holl: "Mozarts Ohr: Eine anatomische Studie," *Mitteilungen der anthropologischen Gesellschaft in Wien* 31 (1901): 1–12. On the pathology, see Bähr 1972, 119–25; Dieter Kerner, "Mozarts äußeres Ohr," *Zeitschrift für Laryngologie-Rhinologie-Otologie* 40 (1961): 475–78; and Edwad N. Guillery, "Did Mozart Die of Kidney Disease? A Review from the Bicentennial of His Death," *Journal of the American Society of Nephrology* 1992: 1671–76. See also Daniel J. Wakin, "After Mozart's Death, an Endless Coda," *New York Times*, August 25, 2010, sec. C, p. 1.

29. Dok, 298.

30. Angermüller 1995, 183.
31. Letter of May 16, 1789 (ML, 409).
32. ML, 411.
33. For details on Rellstab, see Elvers 1957.
34. Anonymous, *Bemerkungen eines Reisenden ueber die zu Berlin vom September 1787 bis Ende Januar 1788 gegebene oeffentliche Musiken, Kirchenmusik, Oper, Concerte und Koenigliche Kammermusik betreffend* (Halle, 1788); see Roeder 2009, 150–52.
35. Dok-Add 2: 63. There is no basis for Cliff Eisen's assumption that Rellstab planned to undertake the enormous and unprecedented task of publishing a complete Mozart edition (*Journal of the American Musicological Society* 39 [1986]: 615–32).
36. Dok, 306.
37. On Madame Levy, her salon, and her music collection, see Wolff 2005 and especially Wollny 2010.
38. Ennobled in 1795 by Emperor Franz II; thereafter, Nathan Adam, Freiherr von Arnstein.
39. Anderson, 762.
40. They paid 2,690 florins for rent (Braunbehrens 1989, 65).
41. For her music collection, see Wollny 2010.
42. Dok, 485.
43. Hertz 1988, 94. Another sister of Sara Levy's, Zippora Itzig Wulff—later Caecilia von Eskeles (1760–1836)—lived in Vienna beginning in 1799. Her second marriage, to Bernhard Freiherr von Eskeles, Arnstein's banking partner, occurred many years after Eskeles divorced his first wife, Eleonore, who had received a most unfavorable mention in a Mozart letter of 1782 (ML, 329).
44. Lichnowsky followed in the footsteps of other members of the Austro-Bohemian nobility who prepared themselves for government and political service at the University of Leipzig. They all were attracted primarily by the most famous scholar of history and constitutional law of the time, Professor Johann Jacob Mascov (1689–1761). Several of Mascov's aristocratic students also took lessons with Johann Sebastian Bach, among them the imperial counts and princes Franz Ernst von Wallis, Heinrich Ludwig Carl von Hochberg, Eugen Wenzel Joseph von Wrbna-Freudenthal, Ludwig Siegfried von Vitzthum zu Eckstädt, and Franz Ludwig von Dietrichstein, grandfather of Moritz von Dietrichstein who served as *Musikgraf* in Beethoven's Vienna.
45. Angermüller 1995, 110f.
46. B-D, no. 780; Blanken 2011.
47. Bach-Dokumente, III, no. 780.

48. Letter of March 20, 1784 (B-D, no. 780); Blanken 2011, vol. 1, pp. xvi–xix.

49. Letter of March 24, 1781 (ML, 236). B-D (and subsequently ML) misidentify "Baron Braun" in various places as Peter and Johann Gottlieb von Braun, respectively—two very different people.

50. *The New Bach Reader*, ed. H. T. David, A. Mendel, and C. Wolff (New York, 1998), no. 360.

51. Letter of August 17, 1782 (ML, 126).

52. Kaunitz knew Mozart since 1767; Mozart played at least one house concert for Kaunitz on April 10, 1784.

53. Ibid.

54. He was probably guided by Friedrich Wilhelm Marpurg's *Abhandlung von der Fuge* (Berlin, 1753), as the rather sophisticated yet incomplete Fugue in G minor, K. 401, originating from around 1772, suggests.

55. ML, 307

56. Wolff 2009–10.

57. Regarding the authorship issues of K. 404a, see Wolff 2009–10.

58. Letter of December 6, 1783, Anderson, 862.

59. Richter and Oehme 1991, 145–56.

60. Ibid., 145.

61. Ibid., 158.

62. Reported in 1805 by C. F. Michaelis; see Richter and Oehme 1991, 145. On Platner, see Dok III, commentary; also E. Bergmann, *Ernst Platner und die Kunstphilosophie des 18. Jahrhunderts* (Leipzig, 1913).

63. Lecture notes from 1777–78 (*Bach-Dokumente*, ed. Hans-Joachim Schulze, vol. III [Leipzig, 1973], 321).

64. Bey 2005, chap. 2.

65. This quote and the following are taken from the account given by Christian Friedrich Michaelis in 1805, which appears to be less embellished than the one by Friedrich Rochlitz (Schulze 1991, 51).

66. A manuscript score of BWV 225 from van Swieten's collection contains annotations by Mozart, who evidently acquired other scores as well, including "Jauchzet dem Herrn alle Welt," BWV Anh. 160; see Schulze 1991. For a list of Mozart's Bach manuscripts and their present location, see Kobayashi 1992, 42, and, with updated information, Blanken 2011.

67. Forner 1991, 29. The identification of the symphonies on the program is possible on the basis of the early pencil annotations on the Leipzig copy of the playbill reproduced as fig. 2.2; see also Angermüller 1995, 184 (there, however, the unlikely assumption appears that the symphony in C might have been

K. 338). The pencil entries on the printed program appear to be by the same hand (C. I. Engel?) as the manuscript printer's copy of the playbill kept with the Leipzig exemplar.

68. Wolfgang Plath, in his preface to NMA IX/27:2 (1982), xii, presents a different view. He assumes that K. 574 was composed and entered into the album on May 16 and that the date "May 17" of the entry in Mozart's work catalog is mistaken. However, apart from the fair copy character of the album entry, it is more plausible that Mozart based the catalog entry on his autograph composing score and entered the little work there before leaving for Berlin on May 17.

69. Haberkamp, 1: 324.

70. Wolff 1994, 138.

71. Ibid., 116. The first edition of the Requiem was published in 1800 by Breitkopf & Härtel of Leipzig.

72. The relevant documents were completely unknown before 1991; see Brauneis 1991, 159–63.

73. *Thayer's Life of Beethoven*, ed. Elliot Forbes (Princeton, 1967), 402–3.

74. The full degree of the surprisingly extensive distribution of historical Bachiana in Vienna and the old Hapsburg lands did not emerge until after the Leipzig Bach Archive completed in 2010 a critical survey of the extant materials; the resulting catalog comprises two volumes (Blanken 2011).

75. B-D, no. 1080.

76. Biba 1992, 29.

77. The piece is lost, but mentioned in *Verzeichniß des musikalischen Nachlasses des verstorbenen Capellmeisters Carl Philipp Emanuel Bach* (Hamburg, 1790), 65.

78. *The New Bach Reader*, no. 373.

79. See chap. 3, p. 78.

80. *The New Bach Reader*, no. 374.

81. Blanken 2011, vol. 1, pp. 3–4.

Chapter 3: Grand Ambitions

1. Doc-E, 306 (translation adjusted); German original: Dok, 269f. See also the corresponding note from the High Chamberlain to the High Steward's Office as well as the minutes of the Imperial Chancellery, December 6–7, 1787 (Doc-E, 305f.).

2. ML, 240.

3. ML, 326.

4. The official court almanac (see fig. 1.1) lists changes retrospectively and serves for the court's internal use only.

5. Quoted above, chap. 1, p. 20.

6. Thematic catalog, fol. 14v–15r.

7. Listed misleadingly as K. 533/494 in all editions of the Köchel catalog, also in the NMA (see Wolff 2006). As Mozart considered the Sonata in F major a three-movement work, K. 533 designates in this book the F-major Sonata in the form in which it was published in 1788.

8. Haberkamp 1986, 1: 301. K. 494 in its original version of 1786 was published by Boßler in Speyer, Germany.

9. Haberkamp 1986, 1: 211ff. See also above, chap. 1, p. 31.

10. See Dok, 274–77. A few examples: On February 26 and March 7, 1788, Mozart the "kaiserl. königl. Capellmeister" conducted C. P. E. Bach's cantata *Die Auferstehung und Himmelfahrt Christi*. The newspaper *Wiener Zeitung* announced the publication of the new "Kriegslied" (War song), K. 539, by "Herrn Kapellmeister Mozart in wirkl. Diensten Sr. Majestät des Kaisers." The same paper advertised on April 2, 1788, the subscription of a set of three quintets (K. 406, 515, and 516), signed by "Kapellmeister Mozart in wirkl. Diensten Sr. Majestät," reprinted also by a newspaper in Weimar, Germany. The posters for the Viennese premiere of *Don Giovanni* on May 7, 1788, indicate "Die Musik ist vom Hrs. Wolfgang Mozzart [*sic*], Kapellmeister in wirkl. Kaiserl. Diensten."

11. ML, 401; Anderson, 919.

12. The Fantaisie et Sonate in C minor (K. 475/457) of 1785 served as a model for a stand-alone sonata publication, but it consisted of altogether four movements. Mozart's first Viennese sonata print consisted of a set of three, K. 330–332, published by Artaria in 1784 as op. VI. Haydn's first single piano sonata of 1789–90 (in E♭ major, H. XVI/49) was published in 1792; Beethoven's first piano sonatas op. 2 (1796) were still published as a set of three. Previous single-sonata issues by J. A. Štěpán, F. X. Dušek, and L. Koželuch usually were offprints from sets.

13. Joseph II apparently disliked and discouraged dedications, at least after his ascent to the throne in 1780. The only musical dedications to him seem to be Josef Antonín Štěpán's six sonatas op. 2 (1760) and Florian Gassmann's opera *Ezio* (1770), information kindly provided by Ulrich Leisinger.

14. See Rice 2003, 3, 18.

15. ML, 237. On Joseph II's predilection for fugal style, see Kirkendale 1979, 17, 60.

16. This Hoffmeister print also carried the announcement "in attuale Servizio di S. Maesta I. è R."

17. Abert-Jahn, II: 354 (Abert 2007, 1146n69 mistranslates Abert's original text and completely reverses its meaning).

18. A more detailed discussion of the thematic structure and the various drafts for finale movements is in Wolff 1988; for a comparative study of K. 533/494 and K. 457/475, see Wolff 2007.

19. Dahlhaus 1982, without any reference to Mozart, discusses two sonatas by Clementi from the 1790s with rudimentary "third themes" that are not as integrated in the form of the sonata discourse as they are in K. 533.

20. The German word "Einheit," according to Johann Christoph Adelung (1793), was coined and introduced into the philosophical discourse by Gottfried Wilhelm Leibniz and Christian Wolff; related discussions of "unity" may be found in the writings of George Berkeley and David Hume. See E. Heintel, "Eine (das), Einheit," *Historisches Wörterbuch der Philosophie*, ed. Joachim Ritter, vol. 2 (Basel, 1972), col. 377.

21. A late short article on "Einheit" appears in Hermann Mendel's *Musikalisches Conversations-Lexicon*, vol. 3 (Berlin, 1873), 336f. However, after 1800 the issue penetrates discussions of cyclic form and related topics.

22. Ibid., 518f.

23. Johann Georg Sulzer, *Allgemeine Theorie der schönen Künste,* 2nd ed. (Leipzig, 1778), 2: 24–26 (note added).

24. See Bauer 2009, 71–86.

25. Lorenz 2010.

26. ML, 399.

27. Lorenz 2010.

28. ML, 399.

29. Cf. the preface to NMA IV/11:9 (ed. H. C. Robbins Landon, 1957): vii.

30. Haberkamp 1986, 1: 272.

31. Letter of April 16, 1789, ML, 407.

32. On the probable performance of K. 551 in Leipzig, see chap. 2, p. 67.

33. Graz, Hochschule für Musik und darstellende Kunst: call no. 40600 (olim L 39).

34. Jonášová 2011.

35. Van Swieten is the most likely but nonverifiable recipient; the first known owner of the autograph is Maximilian Stadler, whose active musical role in Vienna did not begin until 1796. Cf. the preface to C. P. E. Bach, *The Complete Works,* III/3 (ed. David Kidger, 2005): xvf.

36. Blanken 2011.

37. Dok, 273. Mozart apparently made adjustments to the wind parts of the choruses in the oratorio as well; see NMA X:28/2.

38. For an illuminating discussion of style phases in Mozart's music and the particular problem of the "Gleichzeitigkeit des Ungleichzeitigen" (concurrency of the asynchronous), see Konrad 2005, 167–70. Konrad has the last phase begin in either 1787 or 1789 and defines "Spätwerk" (late works) in an aesthetic rather than a biographical sense. The proposal of an imperial style period that begins with Mozart's court appointment fits not only well into Konrad's scheme but also gives it a specific focus.

39. The pieces were circulating even more widely in keyboard reductions, predominantly not by Mozart; see Haberkamp 1986.

40. For the printed edition of the six "Paris" Symphonies, Haydn gave specific instructions for changing the order of pieces, to Hob. I: 87, 85, 83, 84, 86, and 82, which Artaria did not follow (see Hob. I, p. 133). For an informative comparative analytical discussion of Haydn's "Paris" Symphonies and Mozart's last symphonies, see Bey 2005 (pp. 125–37, 173–83, and 213–30), which does not, however, address the specific relationship between Mozart's three symphonies and Haydn's *Trois Simphonies,* nos. 82–84.

41. See Gülke 1998, 126–37.

42. Based on different and more elaborate analytical arguments, Gülke 1998 presents a particularly persuasive case for the manifold interconnections of the three symphonies.

43. Representative: Zaslaw 1990, 117.

44. NMA V/15:8, preface (W. Rehm), xix.

45. Tyson, introduction to the facsimile edition of K. 537 (Pierpont Morgan Library, New York, 1991): viiif.

46. As Wolfgang Rehm (ibid.) has shown, the trumpets were added to the woodwinds soon after the work was begun, not on the occasion of a later performance. This indicates that the grand sound of the orchestral accompaniment was planned from the beginning as an alternative.

47. Its left-hand part was never fully worked out in the autograph score.

48. See above, p. 90, and n. 10.

49. Landon 1988, 192.

50. See p. 53.

51. The exact dates can be determined on the basis of the paper type used by Mozart for the first and second movements and the beginning of the third; see Tyson 1987, 33 and 135.

52. Irving 2003, 250.

53. First drafted in 1789 as a basset-horn concerto (K. 589a).

54. The completion of the single concerto movement K. 514 is by Franz Xaver Süßmayr; see Tyson 1787, chap. 16.

55. Levin edition NMA V/14:5, 89.

56. On K. 488, see Levin 2008.

57. Sulzer (note 23, above), 4: 247.

58. Dok, 275; 1788 is the only year in which this opera was performed in Vienna during Mozart's lifetime.

59. Niemetschek 1808, 27.

60. In the first version of K. 550, with oboes rather than clarinets.

Chapter 4: "Vera Opera" and The Magic Flute

1. Thematic catalog, fol. 28v–29r.

2. Thematic catalog, fol. 28v, refers to "eine Deutsche Opera."

3. A few of Schikaneder's later librettos—e.g., *Der Zauberpfeil, oder Das Kabinett der Wahrheit* (1793) and *Der Königssohn aus Ithaka* (1795)—bear the designation "große Oper," but without reflecting Mozart's musical definition.

4. Both Artaria's and Koželuch's editions consist of 38 numbered fascicles; Haberkamp 1986, 1: 354ff.

5. October 7 (ML, 439).

6. NMA II/5:19, preface, xiii.

7. Branscombe 1991, chap. 1.

8. Assmann 2005.

9. NMA X/31:2, 71.

10. An instrument with keyboard-operated steel bars (ital. *acciaio* = steel), as referred to in Mozart's autograph score. (The original libretto refers to "eine Maschine wie ein hölzernes Gelächter," that is, a keyboard-operated xylophone; see Curt Sachs, *Reallexikon der Musikinstrumente*. Berlin, 1913: 188). Mozart had fun playing it himself in a few performances during the fall of 1791 and supposedly driving Schikaneder onstage into a rage with his antics.

11. The *maestoso* threefold chord in *Thamos* (no. 2, in conjunction with the enthronement of Prince Pheron) presents two C-minor triads and one G-major sixth-chord, each with only two beats (all winds plus strings), whereas the three-beat chords in *The Magic Flute* repeat an E-flat-major triad.

12. ML, 432.

13. An element of melodrama occurs in the spoken dialogue prior to the first appearance of the Queen of the Night (No. 4), where Mozart has the orchestra sound "a terrible chord" (autograph score: "ein schrecklicher Akkord"; original libretto: "ein heftig erschütternder Akkord").

14. *Der Renegat, oder Anton in der Türkei* (1793), *Die Eisenkönigin* (1792), *Der wohltätige Derwisch* (1793), and many others; but see also above, n. 3.

15. Published in the series *Recent Researches in the Music of the Classical Era,* vol. 76, ed. David Buch (Madison, WI, 2007). Mozart contributed the comic duet "Nun liebes Weibchen," K. 625, to the work. Most of the members of Schikaneder's troupe who performed *The Magic Flute* also took part in the 1790 production of *Der Stein der Weisen*; the principal conductor for both operas was Johann Baptist Henneberg, who was one of the composers of *Der Stein der Weisen*.

16. It may be understood, however, as generally related to a prototype like Belmonte's first aria, "Hier soll ich dich den sehen, Constanze?" in *Die Entführung,* but with greatly reduced melodic embroidery and accompanimental fancy.

17. For a discussion of the broader context, see Konrad 2008.

18. Melodically and rhythmically identical with the Queen of the Night's opening phrase in the recitative "O zittre nicht, mein lieber Sohn" (no. 4, mm. 11f.), which, however, is in a major key.

19. Facsimile in NMA X/30:3 (ed. Ulrich Konrad, 1998): 92 (Sk 1791a).

20. For a general discussion of this phenomenon, see Waldoff 2006, 57–62 and throughout her study.

21. See the symposia "Tonartenplan und Motivstruktur (Leitmotivtechnik) in Mozarts Musik" and "Das Problem der Leimotivtechnik in den Opern," *Mozart-Jahrbuch* 1973–74, pp. 82–96 and 130–44. The use of the term "leitmotif" for Mozart and pre-nineteenth-century opera is technically and aesthetically inappropriate.

22. NMA X/31:2, 71.

23. Dok, 459f.

24. Dok, 374.

25. Gruber 1987, 52.

26. Richard Wagner, "The Public in Time and Space," *Prose Works,* trans. William Ashton Ellis (London, 1895–99), 6: 91; translation of "Das Publikum in Raum und Zeit," reprinted in Wagner's *Gesammelte Schriften und Dichtungen* (Leipzig, 1871–83), 10: 99.

27. Introduced in 1859 by Otto Jahn in his *W. A. Mozart* (Leipzig, 1856–59), 4: 600ff., who proposed that Schikaneder, reacting to the success of the singspiel *Kaspar der Fagottist,* turned the evil magician into a noble wise figure. Wagner owned a copy of Jahn's Mozart book.

28. Wagner, "On Opera Poetry and Composition in Particular," *Prose Works,* 6:

153; translation of "Über das Opern-Dichten und Komponieren im besonderen," reprinted in *Gesammelte Schriften,* 10: 156.

Chapter 5: "The Higher Pathetic Style of Church Music" and the Requiem

1. For example, the decree is not mentioned in the Mozart article in *GMO,* accessed March 9, 2011.

2. Dok, 346.

3. Black 2007, 130. On the Josephinian church-music reforms, see MacIntyre 1986, 26; on the *Gottesdienstordnung* of 1783 and its musical implications, see Black 2007, chap. 1.

4. Black 2007, chap. 4, sec. II, provides the first document-based discussion of Hofmann's last years as kapellmeister.

5. B-D, no. 1151; ML, 429 (translation adjusted according to the autograph). For a facsimile reproduction of the autograph, see Black 2007, 289.

6. Dok, 347; Dok-Add 2:66.

7. Since both Mozart and Albrechtsberger were court musicians appointed to the cathedral, the exertion of direct influence by the imperial court on music at St. Stephen's seems an almost foregone conclusion.

8. ML, 401.

9. Dok, 285.

10. See the critical report on the Masses K. 317 and K. 337 by Monika Holl, NMA I/1:4, 10; Black 2007, 295f., 319–32.

11. Mozart spent only a few days at the exclusive spa near Vienna where Constanze rested for much of the summer. The work was not, as frequently assumed, commissioned by the local choirmaster Anton Stoll, a friend of Mozart's, but was probably performed in 1791 at his church in Baden.

12. As convincingly argued in Black 2007, 332–36.

13. Anderson, 957.

14. Karl-Heinz Köhler edited a facsimile of the autograph score (Kassel, 1983).

15. For details, see the extended discussion in Black 2007, chap. 3, sec. IV, although Black does not propose K. 337 as a replacement for the Kozeluch Mass marked "benchè non prodotta" (but not produced).

16. Ibid., 214–18.

17. For the origin, sources, compositional history, and analytical aspects of the Requiem, see Wolff 1994.

18. Niemetschek 1808, 77.

19. Ibid.

20. See also chap. 3, pp. 89–90.

21. Tyson 1987, chap. 11. Prior to Tyson's redatings, all of Mozart's church-music fragments were considered as having originated before 1780 and mainly in Salzburg.

22. Facsimiles in NMA X/30:4 (ed. Ulrich Konrad, 2002); a fifth Kyrie, probably from the same period, is now lost (ibid., xiii).

23. Numbering system, based on approximate dates, introduced by Ulrich Konrad for NMA X:30/4.

24. Single sketch leaf, discovered in 2008 in the Bibliothèque Municipale of Nantes (France); for a description and analysis of this sketch as well as its possible intriguing connection with K. 341, see Konrad 2009. However, since the D-minor Kyrie sketch on the same leaf bears no resemblance to K. 341, Mozart either replaced the sketched Kyrie or K. 341 is entirely independent of the "Nantes" source.

25. Tyson 1987, 26f. See also NMA X: 28/3.

26. The traditional dating of this work to 1780–81 in conjunction with Mozart's visit to Munich and therefore also often nicknamed "Munich Kyrie" can no longer be upheld; cf. Tyson 1987, 27, and the musical language of the work which places it more plausibly between *Don Giovanni* and the Requiem (Black 2007, 192–98, disputes this view, but his arguments are stylistically not tenable). As no autograph score of this work has survived, its possible original fragmentary state cannot be determined.

27. Johann Christoph Adelung, *Über den deutschen Styl* (Berlin, 1785), vol. 2: sec. 396.

28. Sulzer, Johann Georg. *Allgemeine Theorie der Schönen Künste* (Leipzig, 1778–79), 3: 661.

29. Cf. Levin edition, preface.

30. Hoffmann 1814, 227f.

31. Blume 1961, 160, for example, criticizes the "uniformity" of the instrumentation in the Requiem as unlike Mozart.

32. Although Mozart did not complete the Requiem, the relevant documents indicate that the overall musical plan was entirely his and that Süßmayr largely followed the composer's general intentions, even though his contrapuntal skills did not match Mozart's.

33. See Chen 2000.

34. Used also in the *Maurerische Trauermusik*, K. 477, of 1785.

35. Stadler 1827 (see Document 22 in Wolff 1994, 149).

36. Stadler 1826 (quoted in Wolff 1994, 80).

37. Stadler 1827 (see note 35, above). The fragmentary contrapuntal study on the

melody of "Ach Gott vom Himmel sieh darein" in B minor, K. 620b (published in the appendix of the score of *Die Zauberflöte* in NMA II/5:19, 377) dates already from 1782; see Konrad 2005, 358.

38. Nissen 1828, part II, 171.
39. Niemetschek 1808, 82.
40. Not in the catalog of Mozart's library, like the Mainwaring/Mattheson (see Prologue, p. 7), but which he used for the "Song of the Armed Men" in *The Magic Flute*; see Hammerstein 1956.

Both parts of the treatise were reprinted in Vienna (1793) by the Chemische Druckerey, which later published the first performing edition of Mozart's Requiem.

Chapter 6: "Composed, Just Not Yet Written"—Music Never to Be Heard

1. Under the dates of January, March 4, and May 11, 1762. For the earliest compositions, see NMA IX/27:1 and Konrad 2005, 31 and 350.
2. The first compositions showing Wolfgang's own hand are the Minuets K.⁶ 1e–f and K.⁶ 5a of 1764 (NMA IX/27:1). Plath 1960–61 explains the differences between the hands of father and son in the early autographs.
3. For example, in the manuscripts of the pasticcio concertos K. 37 and K. 39–41 of 1767.
4. "Alles ist schon componirt, nur noch nicht niedergeschrieben": Anderson, p. 702 (not included in ML).
5. See previous note.
6. Letter of June 9, 1781 (ML, 262f.). For an authoritative study of Mozart's compositional process, see Konrad 1992.
7. Letter of October 3, 1778 (ML, 190).
8. See Schlichtegroll 1794, 1.
9. Effectively though unreliably portrayed in Peter Shaffer's play *Amadeus* (1979) and further distorted in Milos Forman's identically named film, which abetted a completely false view of the composer's personality.
10. Often part of his public concert programs (see the *Fantasie* on the Leipzig playbill, fig. 2.2), but surely a major feature of his private house recitals.
11. Letter of February 7, 1778 (ML, 128).
12. October 2, 1777 (ML, 66).
13. A view shared by Leopold Mozart, who spoke of "a miracle which God let be born in Salzburg" in a letter of July 30, 1768, to the family friend Lorenz Hagenauer.
14. B-D 4: 324.

15. "Classical," GMO.

16. Most of them came from the estate of Constanze Mozart and are housed today in the Salzburg Mozarteum.

17. The complete repertoire of fragments is published in facsimile, NMA X/30:4 (ed. Ulrich Konrad, 2002). See also Wolff 1980, Tyson 1987 (chap. 11), and Wolff 1991.

18. See the pertinent examples in the facsimile editions of *The Six "Haydn" String Quartets*, ed. Alan Tyson, British Library Facsimiles, IV (London, 1985), and at the very beginning of the autograph of the piano-violin sonata K. 454 (Stockholm: Autographus Musicus, 1982), 23.

19. Tyson 1987, 151–57; Tyson 1996.

20. Compare the case of K. 595 discussed by Tyson 1987, 156–67.

21. Wolff 1981; for the census of the fragments by Stadler and Nissen, see Ulrich Konrad's discussion in NMA X/30:4, xi–xii. and 221–22.

22. The G-minor quartet fragment K. Anh. 74 (see fig. 6.6) represents one of the very few examples of an abandoned piece. Numerical calculations in the margins of the front page and a sketch for the canon in Finale II of *Così fan tutte* (Sk 1789ß) on the verso side of the single leaf indicate that the composer decided not to bring this movement to completion.

23. Compare the case of the two piano sonata movements K. 533, as discussed earlier and in Wolff 1988.

24. The Overture to the *Magic Flute* presents a particularly striking example for this working method in a major orchestral score; see *Die Zauberflöte, K. 620.* Mozart Operas in Facsimile, 6 (Los Altos, CA, 2009).

25. Letter of December 30, 1780, Anderson, 702.

26. For a description, see Marshall 1972.

27. See Lockwood 1992.

28. *Sei Quartetti* (Artaria: Vienna, 1785).

29. Examples of the latter exist for the "Speaker Scene" of *The Magic Flute* (see p. 123) and also for instrumental pieces such as K. 414 (first movement) or K. 493 (third movement).

30. Wolff 1994, 32f.

31. On the Amen fugue, see Wolfgang Amadeus Mozart, *Requiem in d-Moll, K. 626,* completed by Robert D. Levin (Stuttgart, 1991), and Wolff 1994, 30–32.

32. Conducted mainly in conjunction with the NMA in the 1980s and early 1990s. Alan Tyson played a major role; see Tyson 1987, chap. 11.

33. The paper types of lost autographs to completed works can of course not be established, though for the most part their dates are provided by the thematic catalog. Moreover, some fragments survive only in nonautograph copies or in

printed editions, such as the Minuet in D major, K. 355, thought to have been composed in 1789.

34. For the repertoire as a whole and its chronology, see NMA X/30:4 (ed. Ulrich Konrad, 2002).

35. Including the Minuet in D major, K. 355; see Levin 2009–10.

36. In the entry for K. 575, Mozart's thematic catalog specifies "for His Majesty the King in Prussia."

37. Letter of April 16, 1791 (ML, 407).

38. Letter of April 8, 1790 (B-D, no. 1121).

39. Wolff 1980, 195–99.

40. The paper used for the manuscript is found in Mozart scores from 1789 to 1791 (NMA X/30:4, pp. 267–68). Score: NMA VIII/21, 170–73.

41. Mozart's Salzburg trio in B-flat major K. 266 belongs to this tradition. The scoring for 2 violins and bass remained the model for Haydn's many string trios, including the baryton trios (scored for two altos and bass). The only exception is the Trio for Violin, Viola, and Violoncello in B-flat major, Hob. V: 8, of 1765. See also Unverricht 1969.

42. As demonstrated systematically in Bach's three-part sinfonias, copies of which were available in Vienna (e.g., in Lichnowsky's library).

43. NMA X/30:4, p. 266; score: NMA VIII/20/1:3, 136–37.

44. Another example is in the final movement of the symphony K. 543.

45. NMA X/30:4, pp. 268–69; score: NMA VIII/20/1:3, 147.

46. NMA X/30:4, p. 273; score: NMA VIII/19:1, 190–94.

47. Robert Levin, with whom I often discuss aspects of Mozart's style, appropriately describes them as "hallucinatory" and refers to examples from K. 515/I (with the move to D-flat major, recapitulated as C-Sharp minor), to K. 546 (Adagio: the motion toward the end from F minor to C-Sharp minor to A major/minor to F major/minor and back to C minor), the four-hand fragment K. 357/I (D major to E-flat major to F major to G major and back to D), and the clarinet quintet fragment K. 516c (F major to D-flat major).

48. Wolff 1994.

49. "Natur- und Kunstwerke lernt man nicht kennen, wenn sie fertig sind; man muss sie im Entstehen aufhaschen, um sie einigermaßen zu begreifen" (August 4, 1803). *Briefwechsel zwischen Goethe und Zelter in den Jahren 1799 bis 1832,* ed. Edith Zehm; Johann Wolfgang Goethe, *Sämtliche Werke, Münchner Ausgabe,* vol. 20.1 (Munich 1991), 43.

Bibliography

———◇ ◇ ◇———

Bibliographical Abbreviations

Anderson   Anderson, Emily, ed. and trans. *The Letters of Mozart and His Family.* London, 1966.

B-D   Bauer-Deutsch = Mozart. *Briefe und Aufzeichnungen: Gesamtausgabe.* Collected and annotated by Wilhelm A. Bauer and Otto Erich Deutsch, ed. Joseph Heinz Eibl. 7 vols. NMA Supplement. Kassel, 1962–75. Vol. 8: Introduction and addenda, ed. Ulrich Konrad. NMA Supplement. Kassel, 2005.

Doc-E   Deutsch, Otto Erich. *Mozart: A Documentary Biography.* Trans. Eric Blom et al. Stanford, CA, 1965.

Dok   *Mozart: Die Dokumente seines Lebens.* Collected and annotated by Otto Erich Deutsch. NMA X/34. Kassel, 1961.

Dok-Add 1, 2 *Mozart: Die Dokumente seines Lebens: Addenda und Corrigenda.* Comp. Joseph H. Eibl (vol. 1) and Cliff Eisen (vol. 2). NMA X/31/1–2. Kassel, 1978–97.

GMO   *Grove Music Online.* oxfordmusiconline.com.

Fr   Fragment no., from *Fragmente,* ed. Ulrich Konrad. NMA X/30/4. Kassel, 2002.

K.   Köchel no., from: Ludwig, Ritter von. *Chronologisch-thematisches Verzeichnis sämtlicher Tonwerke Wolfgang Amadé Mozarts.* 6th ed., ed. Franz Giegling et al. Wiesbaden, 1964.

MGG 2   *Die Musik in Geschichte und Gegenwart. Allgemeine Enzyklopädie der Musik.* 2nd ed., ed. Ludwig Finscher. Kassel, 1994–2008.

Mitteilungen ISM *Mitteilungen der Internationalen Stiftung Mozarteum, Salzburg.*

ML   *Mozart's Letters, Mozart's Life: Selected Letters.* Ed. and trans. Robert Spaethling. New York, 2000.

NMA   *Neue Mozart-Ausgabe* = Mozart, *Neue Ausgabe sämtlicher Werke.* Kassel, 1955–2007. dme.mozarteum.at/nma.

Sk   Sketch no., from *Skizzen,* ed. Ulrich Konrad. NMA X/30/3. Kassel, 1998.

Thematic Catalog   *Mozart's Thematic Catalog: A Facsimile; British Library, Stefan Zweig ms. 63.* Ed. and transcr. Albi Rosenthal and Alan Tyson. London, 1990. Also published as *Mozart: Eigenhändiges Werkverzeichnis.* NMA X/33/1. Kassel, 1991.

Literature

Abert, Hermann. *W. A. Mozart.* Trans. Stewart Spencer; ed. Cliff Eisen. New Haven, 2007.

———. *see also* Jahn, Otto.

Angermüller, Rudolph. *Antonio Salieri: Sein Leben und seine weltlichen Werke unter besonderer Berücksichtigung seiner "großen" Opern.* 3 vols. Munich, 1971–74.

———. *Mozart auf der Reise nach Prag, Dresden, Leipzig und Berlin.* With Geneviève Geffray. Bad Honnef, 1995.

———. *Mozart 1485/86 bis 2003. Daten zu Leben, Werk und Rezeptionsgeschichte der Mozarts.* 2 vols. Tutzing, 2004.

Assmann, Jan. *Die Zauberflöte: Oper und Mysterium.* Munich, 2005.

Bär, Carl. *Mozart: Krankheit, Tod und Begräbnis.* 2nd ed. Salzburg, 1972.

Bauer, Günther G. *Mozart: Glück, Spiel und Leidenschaft.* Bad Honnef, 2003.

———. *Mozart: A Great Lover of Games.* Trans. Ray Flanagan. Bad Honnef, 2006.

———. *Mozart: Geld, Ruhm und Ehre.* Bad Honnef, 2009.

Bauman, Thomas. *W. A. Mozart: Die Entführung aus dem Serail.* Cambridge Opera Handbooks. Cambridge, 1987.

Beales, Derek. "Court, Government, and Society in Mozart's Vienna." In *Wolfgang Amadè Mozart: Essays on His Life and His Music,* ed. Stanley Sadie. Oxford, 1996: 66–117.

Bey, Henning. *Haydns und Mozarts Symphonik nach 1782: Konzeptionelle Perspektiven.* Neuried, 2005.

Biba, Otto: "Von der Bach-Tradition in Österreich." In *Johann Sebastian Bach: Beiträge zur Wirkungsgeschichte,* ed. Ingrid Fuchs. Vienna, 1992: 11–34.

———. "Mozart und die 'Alte–Musik'–Szene in Wien." In *Mozart, Experiment*

Aufklärung im Wien des ausgehenden 18. Jahrhunderts. Albertina Vienna: Exhibition Catalog. Ostfildern, 2006: 457–66.

Black, David Ian. "Mozart and the Practice of Sacred Music, 1781–91." Ph.D. diss., Harvard University, 2007.

Blanken, Christine. *Die Bach-Quellen in Wien und Alt–Österreich*. Leipziger Beiträge zur Bach-Forschung, 10.1–2. Hildesheim, 2011.

Blume, Friedrich. "Requiem but No Peace." *Musical Quarterly*, 17 (1961): 147–69.

Branscombe, Peter. *W. A. Mozart. Die Zauberflöte* (Cambridge Opera Handbooks). Cambridge, 1991.

Braunbehrens, Volkmar. *Mozart in Wien*. Munich, 1986.

———. *Mozart in Vienna, 1781–1791*. Trans. Timothy Bell. New York, 1989.

Brauneis, Walther. " '. . . wegen schuldigen 1435 f 32 xr': Neuer Archivfund zur Finanzmisere Mozarts im November 1791." *Mitteilungen der IMS*, 39 (1991): 159–63. English trans.: " '. . . owing to indebtedness of 1,435 Gulden 32 Kreuzer': A New Document on Mozart's Financial Plight in November 1791." Trans. Bruce Cooper Clarke. 1991. aproposmozart.com.

———. "Mozarts Anstellung am kaiserlichen Hof in Wien: Fakten und Fragen." In *Mozart, Experiment Aufklärung im Wien des ausgehenden 18. Jahrhunderts*. Albertina Vienna: Exhibition Catalog. Ostfildern, 2006: 559–72. English trans.: "Mozart's Appointment to the Imperial Court in Vienna: Facts and Speculations." Trans. Bruce Cooper Clark. aproposmozart.com.

———. "Exequien für Mozart: Archivfund über das Seelenamt für W. A. Mozart am 10. Dezember 1791 in der Wiener Michaelerkirche." *Singende Kirche* 37 (1991): 8–11. English trans.: "Exequies for Mozart: A New Documentary Finding Concerning the Requiem Mass Held for W. A. Mozart in St. Michael's Church in Vienna on 10 December 1791." Trans. Bruce Cooper Clark. aproposmozart.com.

Brown, Bruce, and John Rice. "Salieri's *Così fan tutte*." In *Cambridge Opera Journal* 8 (1996): 17–43.

Chen, Jen–yen. "The Tradition and Ideal of the Stile Antico in Viennese Sacred Music, 1740–1800." Ph.D. diss. Harvard University, 2000.

Croll, Gerhard, and Renate Croll. *Gluck: Sein Leben, seine Musik*. Kassel, 2010.

Dahlhaus, Carl. "Dritte Themen in Clementi's Sonaten? Zur Theorie der Sonatenform im 18. Jahrhundert." In *Analecta Musicologica* 21 (1982): 444–61.

Daverio, John. "Mozart in the Nineteenth Century." In *The Cambridge Companion to Mozart*, ed. Simon P. Keefe. Cambridge, 2003: 171–84.

Edge, Dexter. "Mozart's Reception in Vienna, 1787–1791." In *Wolfgang Amadè*

Mozart: Essays on his Life and his Music, ed. Stanley Sadie. Oxford, 1996: 66–117.

———. "Mozart's Viennese Copyists." Ph.D. diss. University of Southern California, 2001.

Elvers, Rudolf. "Die bei J. K. F. Rellstab in Berlin bis 1800 erschienenen Mozart-Drucke." *Mozart-Jahrbuch* 1957: 152–67.

Forner, Johannes. *"Fast zwei Stunden accompagniert.* Mozart und die Gewandhauskonzerte." In *Mozart in Kursachsen,* ed. Brigitte Richter und Ursula Oehme. Leipzig, 1991: 29–49.

Gruber, Gernot. *Mozart und die Nachwelt.* Munich, 1987.

Gülke, Peter. *"Triumph der neuen Tonkunst": Mozarts späte Sinfonien und ihr Umfeld.* Kassel, 1998.

Haberkamp, Gertraut. *Die Erstdrucke der Werke von Wolfgang Amadeus Mozart.* 2 vols. Tutzing, 1986.

Hammerstein, Reinhold. "Der Gesang der geharnischten Männer: Eine Studie zu Mozarts Bachbild." *Archiv für Musikwissenschaft* 13 (1956): 1–24.

Heartz, Daniel. *Mozart's Operas.* Ed., with contributing essays, by Thomas Bauman. Berkeley, CA, 1990.

Hertz, Deborah. *Jewish High Society in Old Regime Berlin.* New Haven, CT, 1988.

Irving, John. *Mozart's Piano Concertos.* Aldershot, 2003.

Jahn, Otto. *W. A. Mozart.* 4 vols. Leipzig, 1856–59.

———. *W. A. Mozart.* Rev. and ed. Hermann Abert. 2 vols. Leipzig, 1919–21; 7th ed. Leipzig, 1956 (Abert-Jahn).

———. see also Abert, Hermann.

Jonášová, Milada. "Eine Aufführung der g-moll- Sinfonie KV550 bei Baron van Swieten im Beisein Mozarts." In *Mozart-Studien,* ed. Manfred H. Schmid, vol. 20. Tutzing, 2011: 253–68.

Keefe, Simon P. "The Concertos in Stylistic and Aesthetic Context." In *The Cambridge Companion to Mozart,* ed. Simon P. Keefe. Cambridge, 2003: 78–91.

Kirkendale, Warren. *Fuge und Fugato in der Kammermusik des Rokoko und der Klassik.* Tutzing, 1966. English trans.: *Fugue and Fugato in Rococo and Classical Chamber Music.* Trans. Margaret Bent and the author. Durham, 1979.

Kobayashi, Yoshitake. "Frühe Bach-Quellen im altösterreichischen Raum." In *Johann Sebastian Bach: Beiträge zur Wirkungsgeschichte,* ed. Ingrid Fuchs. Vienna, 1992: 35–46.

Konrad, Ulrich. *Mozarts Schaffensweise: Studien zu den Werkautographen, Skizzen und Entwürfen.* Göttingen, 1992.

———. *Wolfgang Amadé Mozart: Leben, Musik, Werkbestand.* Kassel, 2005.

———. "On Ancient Languages: The Historical Idiom in the Music of Wolfgang

Amadé Mozart." *The Century of Bach and Mozart: Perspectives on Historiography, Composition, Theory, and Performance,* ed. Sean Gallagher and Thomas F. Kelly. Cambridge, MA., 2008: 253–78.

———. "A Rediscovered Autograph of Wolfgang Amadé Mozart: The 'Nantes Sketch.'" Trans. Bruce Cooper Clark. aproposmozart.com.

Konrad, Ulrich, and Martin Staehelin. " *'Allzeit ein Buch': Die Bibliothek Wolfgang Amadeus Mozarts,* Herzog August Bibliothek, Wolfenbüttel: Exhibition Catalog no. 66. Weinheim, 1991.

Landon, H. C. Robbins. *1791: Mozart's Last Year.* New York, 1988.

Levin, Robert. "Mozart's Working Methods in the Keyboard Concertos." In *The Century of Bach and Mozart: Perspectives on Historiography, Composition, Theory, und Performance,* ed. Sean Gallagher and Thomas F. Kelly. Cambridge, MA, 2008: 379–406.

———. "Wolfgang Amadé Mozarts *Menuett* für Klavier, D-Dur, KV 355." *Mozart-Jahrbuch* 2009–10: in press.

———. "My Completion of K. 427/417A." In *Wolfgang Amadeus Mozart: C-Moll-Messe KV 427: Ergänzungen und Vervollständigungen,* ed. Michael Gassmann. Kassel, 2010: 182–248.

Link, Dorothea. *The National Court Theatre in Mozart's Vienna: Sources and Documents, 1783–1792.* Oxford, 1998.

———. "Mozart in Vienna." In *The Cambridge Companion to Mozart,* ed. Simon P. Keefe. Cambridge, 2003: 22–34.

———. "Mozart's Appointment to the Viennese court." In *Words About Mozart: Essays in Honour of Stanley Sadie,* ed. Dorothea Link, with Judith Nagley. Woodbridge, Eng., 2005: 153–78.

Lockwood, Lewis. *Beethoven: Studies in the Creative Process.* Cambridge, MA, 1992.

Lorenz, Michael. "Mozart's Apartment on the Alsergrund." *Newsletter of the Mozart Society of America,* 14 (2010): 4–9.

Mainwaring, John. *G. F. Händel: Nach Johann Matthesons deutscher Ausgabe von 1761 mit andern Dokumenten.* Ed. Bernhard Paumgartner. 2nd ed. Zurich, 1987.

Marshall, Robert L. *The Compositional Process of J. S. Bach.* 2 vols. Princeton, 1972.

Niemetschek, Franz Xaver. *Leben des K.K. Kapellmeisters Wolfgang Gottlieb Mozart nach Originalquellen beschrieben.* Prague, 1798; 2nd ed., 1808. mozartsocietyofamerica.org/embp.

Nissen, Georg Nikolaus von. *Biographie W. A. Mozarts.* Leipzig, 1828.

Plath, Wolfang. "Beiträge zur Mozart–Autographie I." *Mozart–Jahrbuch* 1960–61: 82–117.

Rice, John A. *Antonio Salieri and Viennese Opera.* Chicago, 1998.

———. *Empress Marie Therese and Music at the Viennese Court, 1792–1807*. Cambridge, 2003.

———. *Mozart on the Stage*. Cambridge, 2009.

Richter, Brigitte. "Zum Zeichen wahrer ächter Freundschaft: Mozarts musikalisches Albumblatt für einen Leipziger Logenbruder." In *Mozart in Kursachsen*, ed. Brigitte Richter and Ursula Oehme. Leipzig, 1991: 145–56.

Richter, Brigitte, and Ursula Oehme, eds. *Mozart in Kursachsen*. Leipzig, 1991.

Röder, Mattias. "Music, Politics, and the Public Sphere in Eighteenth-Century Berlin." Ph.D. diss. Harvard University, 2009.

Schlichtegroll, Friedrich. Mozarts Leben. Graz, 1794. mozartsocietyofamerica.org/embp.

Schulze, Hans-Joachim. *"So ein Chor haben wir in Wien nicht*. Mozarts Begegnung mit dem Leipziger Thomanerchor und den Motetten Johann Sebastian Bachs." In *Mozart in Kursachsen*, ed. Brigitte Richter and Ursula Oehme. Leipzig, 1991: 50–62.

Sisman, Elaine. *Mozart: The "Jupiter" Symphony No. 41 in C major, K. 551*. Cambridge Music Handbooks. Cambridge, 1993.

Solomon, Maynard. *Mozart: A Life*. New York, 1995.

Tyson, Alan. *Mozart: Studies of the Autograph Scores*. Cambridge, MA, 1987.

———. "Mozart's Piano Concerto Fragments." In *Mozart's Piano Concertos: Text, Context, Interpretation*, ed. Neal Zaslaw. Ann Arbor, 1996: 67–72.

Unverricht, Herbert. *Geschichte des Streichtrios*. Tutzing, 1969.

Valentin, Erich. "Das Testament der Constanze Mozart–Nissen." *Neues Mozart-Jahrbuch* 1942: 128–60.

Waldoff, Jessica. *Recognition in Mozart's Operas*. Oxford, 2006.

Werner, Andrew J. "The Death and Illness of W. A. Mozart: An Update." *Mitteilungen der IMS* 44 (1996): 56–59.

Wolff, Christoph. "Creative Exuberance vs. Critical Choice: Thoughts on Mozart's Quartet Fragments." In *The String Quartets of Haydn, Mozart, and Beethoven*, ed. Christoph Wolff. Isham Library Papers, 3. Cambridge, MA, 1980: 191–210.

———. "'O ew'ge Nacht! wann wirst du schwinden?' Zum Verständnis der Sprecherszene im ersten Finale von Mozarts Zauberflöte." In *Analysen: Beiträge zu einer Problemgeschichte des Komponierens; Festschrift für Hans–Heinrich Eggebrecht*, ed. Werner Breig et al. Wiesbaden, 1984: 234–47.

———. "Musikalische 'Gedankenfolge' und 'Einheit des Stoffes': Zu Mozarts Klaviersonate in F–Dur. KV533+494." In *Das musikalische Kunstwerk: Festschrift Carl Dahlhaus zum 60. Geburtstag*, ed. H. Danuser et al. Laaber, 1988: 441–54.

———. "Musikalische Gedanken und thematische Substanz: Analytische Aspekte der Mozart–Fragmente." *Mozart–Jahrbuch* 1991: 922–29.

———. *Mozarts Requiem: Geschichte, Musik, Dokumente, Partitur des Fragments.* Kassel, 1991. English trans.: *Mozart's Requiem: Historical and Analytical Studies, Documents, Score.* Trans. Mary Whittall. Berkeley, CA, 1994.

———. "*à 1, 2, 3, 4 et 5 parties:* Gattungsmerkmale und Satzarten in Mozarts Streichquintetten. In *Mozarts Streichquintette,* ed. Cliff Eisen and Wolf-Dieter Seiffert. Stuttgart, 1994: 13–28.

———. "A Bach Cult in Late-Eighteenth-Century Berlin: Sara Levy's Musical Salon." *Bulletin of the American Academy of Arts & Sciences* 58 (2005): 26–31.

———. "Two Köchel Numbers, One Work." In *Music as Social and Cultural Practice: Essays in Honor of Reinhard Strohm,* ed. Melania Bucciarelli and Berta Joncus. Woodbridge, Eng., 2007: 185–95.

———. "Mozart 1782, Fanny Arnstein und viermal Bach." *Mozart-Jahrbuch* 2009–10: in press.

Wollny, Peter. *"Ein förmlicher Sebastian und Philipp Emanuel Bach-Kultus": Sara Levy und ihr musikalisches Wirken, Mit einer Dokumentensammlung zur musikalischen Familiengeschichte der Vorfahren von Felix Mendelssohn Bartholdy.* Wiesbaden, 2010.

Zaslaw, Neal, ed., with William Cowdery. *The Compleat Mozart.* New York, 1990.

Index

———◇ ◇ ◇———

Page numbers in *italics* refer to illustrations and tables.
Page numbers beginning with 199 refer to notes.